THE LIFE OF LORD FISHER OF KILVERSTONE

ADMIRAL OF THE FLEET LORD FISHER, O.M., G.C.B., etc., 1917

THE
LIFE OF LORD FISHER
OF KILVERSTONE

ADMIRAL OF THE FLEET

O.M., G.C.B., G.C.V.O., LL.D.

BY

ADMIRAL SIR R. H. BACON

K.C.B., K.C.V.O., D.S.O.

IN TWO VOLUMES   VOLUME TWO

HODDER AND STOUGHTON
LIMITED   LONDON
ST. PAUL'S HOUSE
WARWICK SQUARE
E.C.
4

First Printed . . . *October* 1929

ℓ

Made and Printed in Great Britain.
Hazell, Watson & Viney, Ltd., London and Aylesbury.

CONTENTS AND SYNOPSIS OF LORD FISHER'S CAREER

VOLUME TWO

21st October, 1904, appointed First Sea Lord in Lord Selborne's administration. On same date appointed First and Principal Naval Aide-de-Camp to King Edward.

6th December, 1904, Admiralty memorandum on the distribution of the Fleet, introducing the nucleus-crew system for ships in reserve, and withdrawing obsolete craft from foreign stations.

January 1905, committee to inquire into the reorganization of the Dockyards.

6th March, 1905, appointment of an Inspector of Target Practice.

4th December, 1905, awarded the Order of Merit ; and promoted by special Order in Council to be an additional Admiral of the Fleet, thus giving him five more years on the active list in order to carry out his policy.

10th February, 1906, launch of the *Dreadnought.*

November 1906, establishment of the Naval War College at Portsmouth.

January 1907, institution of a service of Fleet Auxiliaries—ammunition and store ships, distilling, hospital, fleet repair ships ; trawlers as mine-sweepers, etc. etc.

March 1907, creation of the Home Fleet, with *Dreadnought* as flagship, for service in the North Sea.

August 1907, new scheme of advancement of pay of naval ranks and ratings introduced.

September 1907, establishment of wireless telegraphy branch, and installation erected on Admiralty building.

9th November, 1907, speech at the Lord Mayor's Banquet.

June 1908, accompanied King Edward and Queen Alexandra to Reval on their visit to the Czar of Russia. Awarded G.C.V.O.

17th June, 1908, created honorary LL.D., Cambridge.

January 1909, strong stand over Navy Estimates.

March 1909, Cabinet inquiry into Lord Charles Beresford's allegations.

June 1909, delegates of the Imperial Press Conference entertained at a review at Spithead.

7th December, 1909, raised to the Peerage as Baron Fisher of Kilverstone.

25th January, 1910, retired from the office of First Sea Lord in order that Admiral of the Fleet Sir Arthur Wilson might succeed him and carry on his policy.

CONTENTS

PART III

LIST OF PLATES

VOLUME TWO

CHAPTER XII

MINOR REFORMS

" Nothing is stronger than custom."—OVID.

Inspector of Target Practice—Repair of ships—Development of the submarine—Reforms affecting the ships' companies—Mechanician rating—Engine-room watch-keeping—The Engine-room Artificers—Boy Artificers—Warrant officer promotion—Minor reforms—Allotment stoppages abolished—Victualling allowance continued during long leave—Naval Establishments Committee—Its work—Dockyard reform—Co-ordination of local supply departments—Estimates Committee—Estimated saving effected by the reforms.

THE following, written by a critic shortly after these reforms had been instituted, might with advantage be quoted here ; for it is well to keep in mind the opposition which Fisher continually experienced.

Then emerges slowly to the front a man of ideas. He had no social backing and no exceptional attractions of personality ; but he had the energy of a steam-engine, the pertinacity of a debt collector, and no reverence for the past or for anything but facts.

Five years ago he became the Head of the Navy, and in five years the Navy has been revolutionized. There is hardly a stone that has been left unturned. There is hardly an idea that has not been reversed. Ships, guns, gunnery, strategy, tactics, in-struction and training, diet and rewards—all have suffered a literal " sea-change." No wonder that he is not loved. No wonder that the Navy writhes like the frog under the harrow. No wonder that the naval clubs ring with the outraged sentiments of half-pay officers, and that ancient admirals grow purple at the unspeakable name, and fire broadsides at the iconoclast through the portholes of *The Times.* Fortunate for him that he has a tough integument. No shaft can pierce this armour-plated man.

II—I

He probably had feelings once ; but he has been so exposed to the weather that they have become indurated. The singular face, at once inscrutable and mobile, gives no key to any human emotion. The full eye with its curiously small pupil, the wide, full-lipped mouth drooping mercilessly at the corners, the jaw jutting out a good-humoured challenge to the world, all proclaim a man who neither gives nor asks quarter. He laughs, he cracks jokes, he talks with voluminous geniality ; but behind all these breezy externals of the seaman are his three " R's " of war—Ruthless, Relentless, Remorseless—and his three " H's " of battle—Hit first, Hit hard, Keep on Hitting.

The minor reforms that he introduced during the periods when he was Second and First Sea Lord may conveniently be grouped under three heads :

A. Those which dealt with the Navy generally.

B. Those which dealt with the Dockyards.

C. Those which affected the well-being and comfort of the men.

Those under Group A were :

I. The appointment of a Flag Officer as Inspector of Target Practice. This corresponded to the appointment in the Army of Inspector-General of the Forces. An officer, without any executive command and perfectly impartial, attended the target practices of all the Fleets in the Mediterranean and Home Waters to watch and report on the results of the practices and to advise the respective Commanders-in-Chief as to how the shooting of the ships could be improved. Fisher was most fortunate in having Sir Percy Scott available for this purpose ; there was no officer in the Navy who had so great an experience, or who had personally done so much to improve the gunnery of the Fleet. This appointment, coupled with the supply of improved sights and instructional appliances, as well as the recognition of the importance of good shooting, led to a great improvement in accuracy. So much was this the case that the year before this reform was instituted there had been in the Navy 2,000 more misses than hits, and in the year afterwards there were 2,000 more hits than misses. Not only did the advancement of the gunnery officers depend on the result of the practice of their ship, but the future employment of the Captain was made to depend, to a certain extent, on the general gunnery efficiency of his ship. Fisher had no use for *shooting* apart from *hitting*. " Hit, hit hard, and keep on hitting " was the only gunnery motto he allowed.

II. As a subsidiary point in his Redistribution Scheme for the Fleet, he introduced a regulation limiting the number of ships that were to be absent for repairs at one time from each Fleet. The previous practice had been for the whole Fleet in home waters to go at the same date into dockyard hands for repair. The result was that Germany, or any other country, knew exactly when to strike and at which moment to find us most unprepared. Fisher altered this in his Redistribution Scheme ; he allowed one battleship extra to each Fleet, so that one ship at a time could go into the dockyard and the Fleet still remain at normal strength. At the same time, to enable the ships to run for eleven months without dockyard assistance, it was strictly enjoined that all minor repairs should be taken in hand by the ship's artificers. The previous practice had, not infrequently, been to save up all repairs for the dockyards to undertake, thereby ensuring a good long time in the dockyard with the attendant advantages of rest and leave.

III. Fisher paid great personal attention to the

development of the submarine. When at Portsmouth he had foreseen the great value of these craft in war, and while at the Admiralty he fostered their development in the face of others' disbelief and of considerable opposition.

The reforms that affected the comfort of the men were much needed. He knew that in many respects life on shore had become more comfortable to the lower classes, that modern invention had brought the same increase of comfort within the possibility of ship's life, but that nothing had been done in this direction. His dictum that " the art of government lay in the intelligent anticipation of agitation " was one which he was anxious to apply to the Navy. He was broad-minded, and at this time a radical-reformer, although he had not reached the semi-socialistic views that he held during his closing years. Again, he was by no means satisfied with the prospects of advancement that were within the reach of several of the grades both of deck-hands and stokers. He loved the Navy and the men in it, and was determined to do all that he could, even at the cost of considerable increase in expenditure, to improve the conditions of the lower deck.

One of his most far-reaching innovations was that of creating the rating of mechanician, a man promoted from the ranks of the stokers to keep watch in the engine-room.

When engines were first fitted in men-of-war, the average deck officer looked on them with much the same wonder and awe that the ordinary civilian now regards his wireless receiver—a box of mysteries with which he dares not meddle except to make certain external adjustments. This reverence of machinery

persisted down to the end of last century among the
older officers. Was there not the Captain who bellowed
down the voice-pipe to go faster, and who, when the
Engineer officer said he couldn't, for they were going
as hard as they could, told him to put more oil on ?
Where the oil was to go " on " the Captain did not
know ; but he had a vague idea that oil made an
engine " go faster." The recognition of this mysterious
cult of the engine led to several superstitions. One
of them was that the only people who could be trusted
to keep engine-room watch were engineer officers and
engine-room artificers. These latter were mechanics
entered from the shore, and formed essentially the
engine-room repair staff. They picked up a certain
amount of knowledge about machinery ; but, speaking
generally, they were not specially qualified as engine
drivers. Their ranks were filled by a medley of many
trades, fitters, boilermakers, coppersmiths, etc., whose
main value to the Navy was ability to work at their
trades, and not to waste their skilled labour watching
engines revolve.

To the horror of the old-time Engineer a younger
class of deck officer arose who did not believe in the
fetish of the engine cult. He began to ask pertinent
questions. What was the knowledge that was essential
for a watch-keeping officer in the engine-room ?
What could a man do more than see that the lubrica-
tion of the bearings and journals was kept going,
more especially in these latter days of turbines which
revolved at several thousand revolutions a minute ?
Even in the old days of reciprocating engines, no one
could meddle with an engine revolving four hundred
times a minute. An old Chief Engineer officer, in the
days of trunk engines, once told us that in his opinion

the one essential in an engine-room watch-keeper was " a good nose for 'ot taller." For in those days tallow was used with the packing of the trunks, and hot tallow meant undue heating somewhere. In latter days, although tallow was no longer used, engine-room watch-keeping was a matter of common sense, adequate instruction, and a certain amount of experience. There was no mystery about it ; any man with moderate brains could perfectly well be taught, in a short time, sufficient to enable him to take charge of an engine-room at sea.

In addition to these heretical modern ideas there was the fact that the men of the stoker branch of the Navy had no great prospects to which to look forward. The deck hands had warrant and commissioned ranks to which they could rise. Chief Petty Officer was the climax of the stoker's career. Surely out of the 40,000 stokers in the Navy there were many whose brains, if developed, would enable them to attain the knowledge necessary to keep engine-room watch—at least, so Fisher argued.

He therefore set up a small Committee, on which, among others, were two very broad-minded Engineer officers, to inquire into the matter. The problem was found to be easy of solution. They proposed that certain stokers, who had passed a preliminary examination, should be put through an adequate course of instruction in mechanical work and actual watch-keeping. They were to be given warrant rank and then drafted to ships as watch-keepers. They had, further, the prospect of becoming commissioned officers. The scheme proved to be an unqualified success, and naturally was hailed with delight by the stokers of the Navy.

The engine-room artificer rating also came under review. The engine-room artificer up to 1905 had been recruited from the shore, with the rank of Chief Petty Officer. He was a skilled craftsman, but, from the point of view of the Navy, the entry of a man straight from the shore into a superior rank is an anomaly. He is ignorant of that discipline which is essential on board ship, where hundreds of men are crowded into a small space. He knows less of the internal economy and routine of naval life than a first-class boy. If he gets drunk, his substantive rank prevents his being adequately dealt with ; if to a sharp command he retorts a choleric word, he finds, to his amazement, that he stands convicted of insubordination.

There was another trouble. Most of the entries were men who had joined a trade union. It was always possible, therefore, for the same troubles to arise among the artificers in the Navy as not infrequently arise in the workshops ashore. Antagonism between the Admiralty and a trade organization was obviously a thing to be avoided. Similar difficulties have confronted all democratic nations which have sought to associate naval discipline with shore institutions. In France difficulties of this nature had led to the introduction of a number of *apprentis mécaniciens*. Fisher was not the man to blink at prospective difficulties, or to let matters slide till trouble arose. The rating of " boy artificer " was instituted, and boys entered straight from the shore and trained in artificer trades on board special depot ships. The advantage of the new scheme was immense from every point of view, when compared with that of the old method of entry. Not only were the boys entered at an age when they were entirely free from trade combination, but each boy, from his youth up, was trained with the specific object of repairing ship's machinery; they lived and grew up amongst the very class of machinery that they would have to deal with all their lives; whereas, under the old scheme, a man might have been entered who had never been associated with any larger machinery than that met with in a bicycle factory. A warrant rank for engine-room artificers was instituted under the name of Artificer Engineer, and a commissioned rank designated Chief Artificer Engineer. By this means the road was opened to any engine-room artificer to become eventually an officer.

The warrant officers of the other branches received similar treatment. Sixty men selected from among the chief gunners, chief boatswains, and chief carpenters were promoted in 1903 to Lieutenants. The number of such promotions annually was fixed, so that promotion became regularized and defined.

The following list of minor reforms, when added to those that we have already dealt with, gives some idea of the scope of the work Fisher undertook in modernizing the Navy. Some of these, of course, would have been carried out had any other First Sea Lord held office during the five years of Fisher's tenure, but this was by no means the case with the majority:

I. Drastic establishment developments.
    (*a*) 6,000 unnecessary workmen discharged.
    (*b*) Work properly divided between the Dockyards and private trade.
    (*c*) Rapid shipbuilding (so less dockyard accommodation needed in ships, basins, and docks).
    (*d*) Reorganization of administration, and Chief

Constructors and Chief Engineers of Dockyards constituted as Managers; also Director of Dockyard Work appointed to control personally dockyard business throughout, directly under the Controller of the Navy.

(e) Co-ordination of all departments in naval ports under Admirals-Superintendent, and consequent reorganization of storehouse arrangements and of harbour craft.

(f) Simplification of stocks (10,000 chairs were found to be in stock, and numerous departments had their own stocks of similar articles, resulting in a large unnecessary aggregate of the same article).

(g) Reduction of enormous reserves of unimportant stores that could at any time be replaced, with consequent saving of losses by depreciation, decay, and obsolescence. Departments using stores made responsible for the amount of stock kept.

(h) The introduction of the use of trade patterns wherever practicable, avoiding cost of special manufacture and introducing simplicity and economy in replacement; also arrangements made with contractors for special supplies in emergencies.

II. Royal Naval Reserves.

Introduction of a system of efficient training on board modern ships in commission in place of training on board hulks, or at shore batteries armed with obsolete guns. Men thereby more efficient as reserves; some always ready at naval ports; economy of expenses of training the reserves; economy from upkeep and modernizing of shore batteries and hulks.

A more efficient Reserve at less cost.

III. Royal Fleet Reserve.

The development of another reserve of active service ratings, and the retention of trained men who would otherwise have been lost on leaving the active service.

The careful building up of this active reserve by passing limited-service stokers and seamen into it after four years' service at sea. This caused long service in the Navy to be tempered by short service, and resulted in a decrease in the non-effective vote for pensions.

Entry of non-continuous service men, effecting a saving in the cost of early training.

IV. The establishment of a service of offensive mines, and vessels from which to lay them.

V. A complete reorganization of the service of auxiliary vessels for use with the fleets in war—ammunition ships, store ships, distilling ships, hospital ships, dispatch vessels, cable-laying ships, advanced base ships, armed mercantile cruisers, etc.

VI. The limitation of the number of ships from any one Fleet or Squadron under refit at any one time, and the severe restriction of repairs in dockyards which might be carried out by the ship's staff. The abolition of unnecessary periodical surveys to ships, involving stripping and practically rebuilding, resulting in great saving in the annual cost of repairs, which was assuming most serious proportions.

VII. Navigating Officers.

Improved training. Navigation School established.

VIII. Signal Schools.

A school of instruction in Signalling instituted at each of the three home ports.

IX. Naval War College established at Portsmouth.

X. The Grand Manœuvres—the practical test of trade protection, as opposed to theories on the subject.

XI. The cessation of allotment stoppages and the
payment of allowances to the men in lieu of provisions when men are on leave.

In November 1905 Fisher took steps which resulted in the removal of this long-standing grievance. When men were drafted to ships for service on foreign stations, they were allowed to allot a certain portion of their pay for the support of their families at home. It had always been the practice, in order to prevent the risk of loss to the Crown, by reason of death or desertion, for the Accountant-General to retain one or two months' allotment—the latter in the case of men drafted to the more distant stations, e.g. China or Australia. The retention of this money, which in reality belonged to the men and not to the Crown, caused great distress among the dependants of the men, and was a source of much dissatisfaction in the Fleet ; since, for two months, the families were practically penniless. A more arbitrary, unfair, and shabby practice could hardly be imagined in a Royal Service. It is no excuse to say that the system was originated when communication between the Admiralty and distant stations occupied much time. The risk involved was so slight, and the distress caused was so real, that there was no justification for the practice, and it is hardly credible that, although the desirability of abolishing the reserve had long been recognized by the Admiralty, efforts to liberate the money—the men's own money—from the clutches of the Treasury, amounting to about £70,000, had not been attended with success, because of the addition it would have caused to the Navy Estimates ! Fisher was instrumental in overcoming the difficulties placed in the way of conceding this right to the men, and their families were relieved of the necessity of choosing between borrowing and starvation.

It was also due to Fisher that sanction was obtained to the payment of a victualling allowance to the men when on long leave, his argument being that " their food was part of their wages," and should not, therefore, be withheld from them when proceeding on authorized leave of absence.

XII. Improvements in the position of the Petty Officers, and increase of pensions to Chief Petty Officers.[1]

XIII. The creation of warrant rank for the most deserving Stoker Class.

XIV. Improvements in the uniform of the men; improvements in the cooking; establishment of bakeries on board ships.[1]

XV. Promotions from warrant rank to rank of Lieutenant : 50 gunners and boatswains ; 10 carpenters ; 6 artificer engineers promoted up to 1906 : Total, 66.[1]

XVI. Ships' bands placed on a new footing and a School of Music established. This item represents £25,000 previously paid by officers out of their own pockets.

XVII. Removal of " undesirables."

The Navy relieved of a number of useless and troublesome men. A salutary lesson to others.

XVIII. Boy artificers.

Extension of training, ensuring a high grade of technical workman.

In relation to the above, a Committee was formed for the purpose of investigating the whole ques-

---

[1] Items XII, XIII, XIV, XV, and XVI represent over £200,000 given to the men of the Fleet annually in what was practically a rise in pay.

tion of the condition, organization, and administration of the various Naval Establishments on shore. This was a natural corollary to the inquisition on the Navy afloat. It had already been arranged that every vessel intended to fight should have a nucleus crew on board, and should be fully stored and armed, and in every respect ready to go to sea at a few hours' notice ; and Fisher, having satisfied himself that the ships themselves had been organized in this manner, took steps to ensure that the same state of efficiency should obtain in the supply and maintenance services for the ships—repairing, storing, and equipment services generally. The object to be attained was efficiency at all costs ; but if efficiency could be associated with economy, it would be all the more advantageous. The " Naval Establishments Inquiry Committee " was therefore set up to examine all these matters. It was made clear to all Heads of Departments, and to the officers at the several establishments, that the inquiry was not a reflection on their own administration ; but that the existing organization was due to long-established custom, and that the aim of the Committee was to view the whole of the existing methods afresh from the standpoint of the changes made afloat. Everyone concerned would therefore be invited to state his views freely and frankly, with the guarantee that no odium should attach to him for so doing. The Committee was presided over by Fisher himself.

The Committee first visited the Home Ports and Establishments, during the first two weeks of May 1905, and a thorough inspection was made of ships in course of construction, work in progress, workshops, storehouses, the systems of transportation of material, of accounting, and of control over work generally. A questionnaire was subsequently addressed to the principal officers of the several Dockyards, and as a result of the information so obtained, and of experience gained by visits to various private shipbuilding and engineering works, the Committee made a preliminary report on the 20th July, 1905. The first point touched upon in this Report was the enormous amount of capital—roughly, £22,000,000—lying idle, locked up in stocks at the various establishments. The Committee pointed out the large annual losses arising from deterioration and obsolescence in connection with these vast quantities of stores, and suggested that running contracts should be entered into, in a generous spirit, with firms of high standing, so that articles could be readily obtained as required, thus ensuring minimum stocks in the Dockyards, and yet at the same time ample supplies being available quite fresh and up to date. The underlying principle was that the contractors should carry the stocks, and not the Admiralty. For instance, a large number of chairs were found in the stores, far in excess of a year's requirements. Fisher pointedly remarked, " You don't, ashore, keep an attic stocked with chairs in case one should break down in your dining-room ! " The same excess of stocks was found in many kinds of stores. An example which was noticed by the Committee of obsolete stores being still kept in reserve was a stock of about 200 iron outrigger torpedo cases which had been obsolete for twenty years. It was ascertained that these articles were still allowed by establishment to certain classes of ships for some minor purpose, and that during the previous two years only twenty had been issued.

The system of " sealed patterns " was also attacked

by the Committee. The existing procedure was that
whenever a new article was required by the Navy, different patterns were sent in by various contractors and inspected by the officers concerned. The most suitable, altered, if necessary, to suit service requirements, was then taken as a pattern and sealed, and this sealed pattern was afterwards used for years by the inspecting officer as a guide to size, shape, and quality. An article which was originally an ordinary trade article often became obsolete ashore in course of time, so that the manufacturer had to manufacture to an out-of-date type specially for the Navy. This entailed increased cost, while a newer type in common use ashore might be both better and cheaper.

The system of management of the Dockyards was severely criticized on account of the uneconomical methods in vogue and the lack of up-to-date machinery, which involved the use of an unnecessary amount of manual labour. Many suggestions for improvements were made in regard to the supervision of work and the methods of accounting ; and attention was drawn to the waste of valuable time, and the interference with proper supervision by the responsible officers, which was occasioned by unnecessary correspondence and useless returns. As an example of indiscriminate outlay, the Committee noticed that an expenditure of £7,800 had been incurred in constructing a building in which chain cables were to be tested and stored. They expressed the view that a costly permanent building such as this was not needed for storing chain cable, which could perfectly well be stored in the open air, all that was necessary being a proper testing house. Considerable sums, they found, had been spent in structures of a more permanent character than the circumstances justified, and many of these solid structures seriously hampered the development of the Dockyards by preventing workshops and storehouses being brought nearer to the slips, dry docks, etc., where work was in progress.

At Chatham a typical case came to light showing the effect of absence of central control over local storekeeping arrangements. In order to relieve the Naval Ordnance Store Department, which was alleged to be congested, a scheme had been put forward for taking over the Army Gun Wharf, and constructing new storage for the use of the War Department at a cost to the Admiralty of some £70,000. It was evident to the Committee that much of the stock at the Naval Ordnance Depot was obsolete and useless for the existing fighting Fleet, and that, by disposing of this useless stock, the provision of further storage accommodation would be rendered quite unnecessary. But it was also discovered that, in any case, accommodation could have been found in stores that already existed in the Dockyard. This case showed the need for a competent supervision being established over store-accommodation as a whole, and for a definite instruction being issued that new store buildings should not, in future, be proposed without full inquiry into all local possibilities.

It was noticed that many condemned stores included articles that still had considerable wear in them, such as flags, chairs, furniture, fittings, etc. Naval officers on commissioning had a natural aversion to taking anything but perfectly new stores, and, in consequence, many articles were needlessly put in for survey whenever a ship paid off. The existing practice was that, if these were not considered to be worth the expense of bringing up to a practically new condition, they were condemned, although they still possessed many years of serviceable life. Here the Committee saw the way to effect a great saving, by recommending that, after once a ship had been fitted out, her stores were never to be removed *en masse* on her paying off, as had been the practice; but that any stores which were reported to be worn out should be surveyed on board and only condemned if useless for further service. At one of these visits by the Committee, Fisher looked over a dump of lamps condemned for sale, and asked the storekeeping staff what was the matter with a certain lamp. The reply was, " The glass is broken." Fisher pointed to another lamp in the heap and said, " Slide the glass out of this lamp and substitute it for the broken glass in the other." This was easily done, and the result was one perfectly serviceable lamp ! On another occasion he noticed a pile of condemned flags, and pointing out a white ensign, ordered that it should be sent to his room at the Admiralty. A week or two later the members of the Committee were surprised to see, covering half the floor-space of his room, an apparently brand-new white ensign. He explained that this was the flag selected at random from the heap of condemned stores, and that he had caused it to be sent to a well-known firm of cleaners, who for a trifling sum had returned it as practically a new flag.

It may easily be imagined that in a huge concern like the British Navy these wasteful methods entailed a large annual loss of money to the country.

The second report of the Committee was rendered on the same date as the preliminary report, and related entirely to stores at the Dockyards. It stated that in future the officers at the Dockyards who originated requisitions should be held responsible in all respects for the quantities demanded, either for specific purposes, such as new construction, or for general use, as well as for the reserve stock to be maintained ; and that special attention was to be given to stores of vital importance for the use of the Fleet in time of war. Sea-stores should be under the immediate control of the Fourth Sea Lord, leaving only the stores for Dockyard use under the Controller of the Navy.

It must be mentioned that the work of the main Committee was materially aided, in regard to the working out of details, by various Sub-Committees, the first of which was appointed in May 1905, under the presidency of Vice-Admiral Sir Baldwin Walker. Sir Baldwin Walker had to relinquish the task owing to failing health, and was succeeded by Rear-Admiral Charles Barlow, D.S.O. The opening meeting of this Sub-Committee, on the 15th May, 1905, was attended by Fisher, who outlined what had already been done by the main Committee and the general impressions they had received. He urged the Sub-Committee first to get a general view of the whole matter, and then to consider what was the most important subject to tackle. " Without care," he said, " you may be wasting time on some small thing that gives little prospect of economy. We want you to look for something where you can knock off a million. Let us get that million before you go into little details of 5s. 6d., because otherwise this Committee may go on for ten years," and with the following characteristic remarks he left the Sub-Committee to pursue its labours : " I want you to understand that whatever you want you can have ; it does not matter what it is. The whole power that is necessary is at your beck and call ; you have only to say that you want this or that, or complain of any obstacles thrown in your way, and you may depend upon it that whatever stands in the way of your progress will be removed. I do not anticipate any difficulty of that sort, but at any rate it is a good general principle to lay down, that if anybody gets in the way he is going to be run over."

The Sub-Committee set to work vigorously, and by the month of November had sent in their general report, and had also furnished separate interim reports embodying recommendations in regard to :

(1) Separation of Dockyard materials from ships' sea (equipment) stores.

(2) Naval ordnance. Revised administrative arrangements, etc., etc.

(3) Unification of stocks.

(4) Victualling stores. Reserves, storage, and inspection.

(5) Medical stores. Reserves, storage, and inspection.

(6) Obsolete and obsolescent naval stores.

(7) Reserve stocks of naval stores.

(8) Development of system of standing contracts.

(9) Reduction in number and description of articles, and substitution of commercial for sealed patterns.

(10) Association between professional officers and the Purchasing and Supply Departments with regard to the provision of technical and scientific stores.

(11) Classification of stores for peace or war purposes.

(12) Reports of a Special Committee on Contract

and Supply Arrangements. This Committee had been appointed in November 1904, under the presidency of Captain C. E. Madden (succeeded by Captain F. C. D. Sturdee) to—

(a) Review all the articles then issued to the Naval Service ; and

(b) Make suggestions for closer connection between the user, the supplying officers, and the purchasing officer.

(13) Storage accommodation for Naval Ordnance Depot at Chatham.

(14) Obsolete ordnance stocks.

These reports were made to the main Committee, who considered them carefully and passed on such recommendations as they approved for the final approval of the Board.

In December 1905 another Sub-Committee was appointed, to consider in detail the revised administrative arrangements in regard to naval ordnance proposed in the report of its predecessor, the principal subjects for consideration being :

(a) The entire dependence of the Navy upon the Army for the ordering, proof, inspection, and acceptance of naval guns, small arms, ammunition, explosives, and ordnance stores.

(b) The system of administration of the Naval Ordnance Departments at the ports, which involved divided control over the different branches of the same vital service, and caused the existence of two separate workshop departments at each port.

(c) The existing system of provision for the various branches of Naval Ordnance Services in the Navy Votes, whereby the expenses were distributed over two distinct Votes (Vote 8 and Vote 9).

This Sub-Committee was responsible for the recommendations which eventually led to the Navy setting
up its own branches for dealing with the supply of
guns, ammunition, and all ordnance stores, thereby
completing the good work which had been begun by
Fisher when Director of Naval Ordnance.[1]

With regard to the administration of the Royal
Dockyards, the main Committee recognized that naval
officers of high rank must still be in charge of the
Dockyards as Superintendents, so as to deal personally with the officers of the ships of the Fleet. Their
authority as representatives of the Admiralty must be
supreme ; but their functions should be mainly those
of general direction and supervision, leaving technical
management to the heads of departments, who should
be personally responsible to the Superintendent for the
entire conduct of the business of their departments.
The Dockyard departments were brought into line
with similar departments in private establishments,
and the superintending officers were constituted
" managers " with full authority as to management,
the extended powers thus conferred on them being,
of course, rigidly controlled by the usual financial
limitations. The latter would refer to the Admiral-
Superintendent in every matter of importance, and
the Admiral-Superintendent would issue all orders for
work to be undertaken. This administrative change
admitted also of a consolidation and simplification in
the methods of keeping accounts.

In order to bring about a much-needed co-ordination of system among all supply departments, the
Victualling, Armament, Coaling, and Store Departments, as well as the Dockyard itself, were placed under

[1] See Vol. I, page 96.

the supervision and administration of the Admiral-Superintendent.

A Director of Dockyards and Dockyard Work, responsible to the Controller of the Navy, was appointed in the place of the existing Director of Dockyards, the main duties of the new post being that of continual personal inspection of the Dockyards and Dockyard work, instead of, as hitherto, constant employment on office work at the Admiralty.

Arising out of the co-ordination of the various Naval Establishments (except the Naval Hospitals), the Commander-in-Chief, though, of course, remaining supreme in his command, was relieved of the immediate supervision of certain departments, such as the Victualling, Coaling, and Naval Ordnance, for which hitherto he had been directly responsible. Under the previous system of dual control it had been impossible to make the best use of the storage space and auxiliary services of the several establishments, and these departments were accordingly placed under the direction of the Admiral-Superintendent.

A general examination of the reserves of stores then followed and a clearance of obsolete stock was effected. Means were adopted to limit the stocks of any stores liable to become out of date. Arrangements were also made for the unification of patterns of stocks wherever possible, and for stocks of a pattern used by two or more departments to be held by the principal user only.

The whole system of ships' naval and victualling store accounts was revised and much simplified. The arrangements for victualling the Fleet in time of war were also revised, and this revision not only simplified the war arrangements, but reduced the quantities of perishable stores carried, as well as reducing the

reserves in store.

Fisher wrote in July 1906 :

The management of the Royal Dockyards has now been placed
on a much sounder footing, more akin to the organization in similar
commercial establishments, where any undue extravagance or
unnecessary executive machinery means loss of money to the
shareholders and is visited by pains and penalties on the persons
directly responsible. At the same time the possibility of ready
expansion in war-time to suit the varying requirements of a purely
naval repairing and building establishment have been maintained.

The results of the labours of the Naval Establishments Inquiry Committee were summed up by the
First Lord, Lord Tweedmouth, in his Statement ex-
planatory of the Naval Estimates for 1907–8, in these
words :

The changes in the conduct of business at the Dockyards introduced eighteen months ago have worked smoothly and well, and
I think the nation has now every reason to be satisfied that the
administration of its Dockyard work is conducted in a businesslike
and practical manner.

Associated with the reorganization of the Dockyards
was the policy of rapid shipbuilding, to which Fisher
attached great importance, since in this way a ship
was put into the fighting line fitted with practically
all the latest improvements. There was also earlier
utilization of the capital spent in new construction.
A combination of construction and a definite annual
expenditure on new ships would result in ships being
a shorter time on the building slips and in the docks
and basins and alongside jetties, etc., than when construction was spread over a longer period. Rapid
construction therefore made a fuller use of the plant
of the Dockyards and helped to save future expansion.

The removal of ships of small fighting value from

the active list had already effected considerable savings in repairs and refits, the nucleus-crew system reduced the amount of machinery, and other defects, which came to the yards for attention, and collectively the various reforms permitted of a reduction of more than 6,000 in the number of Dockyard workmen.

It is impossible to state how much money was saved by all the changes. It has been variously estimated at between four millions and twelve millions. Fisher often, when speaking of savings, referred to a conversation he had with his civilian secretary when he was Controller of the Navy. He had asked for figures showing the cost of a certain proposal. " What do you want to prove ? " asked the secretary. " What's that got to do with it ? " replied Fisher. " Everything," said the secretary. " Tell me what you want to prove, and I'll give you figures to prove it. Tell me what you don't want to prove and I'll give you figures to disprove it." This shows the difficulty of estimating the savings effected by reforms. The savings were too intricate, too far-reaching, spread perhaps over several years, and in some cases not susceptible to calculation, for the result to be exactly determined. But whether the saving was four millions or twelve millions, there is no doubt whatever that it amounted to a very substantial figure, which helped considerably to counter-balance the extra cost of the other changes which Fisher had introduced, without causing an increase in the total of the Navy Estimates.

ESTIMATES COMMITTEE

Fisher's principal financial achievement was the formation of the " Estimates Committee." This Com-

H.M.S. *DREADNOUGHT* GOING TO SEA ONE YEAR AND ONE DAY
AFTER HER KEEL HAD BEEN LAID

mittee was composed of the financial authorities of CHAP.
the Admiralty, with himself as chairman ; and associated with it, as each Vote in turn came under review,
was the Sea Lord whose duty it was to supervise that
Vote.   Fisher was most careful to explain that the
inquiry was not held for the purpose of attributing blame
to anyone, but that the object was to ascertain whether
any savings in naval expenditure could be effected.

This Committee sat daily, and rendered its first
report twenty-two days after appointment.   After a
scrutiny of the principal items, the Committee foreshadowed a possible reduction of £4,362,100 for the
next financial year, 1905–6.   The actual net decrease
shown in the Estimates for 1905–6 presented to Parliament was £3,500,000.   This result was achieved
after the cordial co-operation of the superintending
Lords and the heads of departments in the careful
examination of each Vote.   The Committee ruthlessly
discarded or reduced any expenditure which, though
possibly quite justifiable, was not considered really
essential, and could not be defended as vital to the
strength or the fighting efficiency of the Navy, and on
this cardinal point they had the authoritative opinion
of the First Sea Lord.

In the course of their inquiries the Committee found
that in many large and important items of expenditure
no direct responsibility was thrown on those who
asked for the outlay.   Consequently, officers and
officials, regardless of all questions of expense, were
apt to forward demands for everything that in their
opinion might be *advantageous* for the Service.   Provision for these demands had to be made in the Votes
prepared by the heads of departments, who were not
in a position to express any opinion on the actual

necessity for the demands sent in. The Committee emphasized the vital need for imposing direct personal responsibility for every item of expenditure shown in the Estimates.

The redistribution of the Fleet and the discarding of obsolete vessels had a far-reaching effect on the Navy Estimates. As we have seen, some Dockyards abroad were abolished altogether, and others were reduced to a *cadre*, capable of being expanded again in time of war. The personnel of the scrapped ships became available to man the new ships as completed, and a careful review of the personnel under the new conditions showed that, in lieu of the previous automatic yearly increase of men, there was actually at the moment a substantial surplus.

The Estimates for the following year, 1906–7, approved by the Balfour Government before leaving office, showed again a net decrease of £1,520,000 as compared with the Estimates of the previous year.

On the 10th January, 1906, the Estimates Committee reported that after a careful survey and subject to minor adjustments, they, in conjunction with the Sea Lords superintending the several departments, had fully satisfied themselves that no further reductions from these Estimates were feasible without sacrificing the fighting efficiency of the Fleet. In a Memorandum addressed to the Committee, Fisher pointed out that, though the 1906–7 Estimates showed a reduction of only £5,000,000 as compared with the Estimates for 1904–5, the real reduction was very much greater if certain automatic increases were taken into account, which, although in excess of present requirements, could not be cancelled owing to arrangements that had been previously entered into.

He claimed that in these two years the reduction of some 150 vessels of small fighting value, combined with the policy of rapid shipbuilding and the consequent large reductions in permanent works previously considered necessary, taken in conjunction with savings in respect of pensions and other non-effective services, represented a total saving not far short of £12,000,000 sterling, associated with which was an annual net saving of £1,292,000 (as compared with the expenditure of January 1904) in the upkeep of the Fleet. He added that this had been effected *pari passu* with the maintenance of sixteen more fighting ships of all classes in full commission at sea, and 154 more vessels in partial commission and ready for service at a few hours' notice.

The Estimates Committee strongly deprecated in their report the practice of allowing margins on Votes, as being uneconomical and having a direct tendency to lead to extravagant or unnecessary expenditure. On the other hand, they realized that if the amounts of the Votes were strictly limited to the requirements that could be definitely foreseen, a supplementary Vote might sometimes be unavoidable. They contended, however, that the fact that the Vote was reduced to the narrow limit of bare requirements must conduce to the exercise of greater care to avoid the possibility of excess, and that the alternative of a supplementary Estimate was a lesser evil than extravagant Estimates. A supplementary Estimate in respect of 1905–6 was, in fact, presented to Parliament in February 1906. This Estimate totalled £161,200 and related almost entirely to material under the shipbuilding, repairs and maintenance Vote, and to the Vote for miscellaneous effective services ; but since it was met by surpluses on other Votes amounting to £161,100, the net supplementary charge was therefore only £100. In March 1910, after Fisher's departure from the Admiralty, a supplementary Estimate of £689,100 was presented, but this was due mainly to expenditure on the four " contingent " ships for which authority was obtained in 1909.[1]

The economies in Navy expenditure in 1907–8 resulted in a saving of £1,427,091 ; but certain money (nearly one million) which had until this year been specially borrowed under the Works Loan Acts was now charged to Navy Estimates, so a saving of only £450,000 was shown, though the actual saving to the country was £1,427,091. The Estimates for 1908–9 showed a net increase of £900,000, due entirely to the automatic or uncontrollable increases to which reference has already been made, and only by the strictest economy was the increase kept down to £900,000. In the financial year 1909–10 the Estimates were further increased by £2,823,200, owing to the necessary provision for the eight " Dreadnoughts " laid down during that year. The " Committee of rigid economy " thus saved the country many millions during the years 1905 to 1910, and also established precedents, and framed regulations which effectively prevented the extravagant methods of the past being perpetuated in the future.

[1] See below, p. 89.

CHAPTER XIII

LORD CHARLES BERESFORD

He is one of those orators of whom it is said that " before they get up they do not know what they are going to say, when they are speaking they do not know what they are saying, and when they have sat down they do not know what they have said."

MR. CHURCHILL, *Parliamentary Debates.*

Lord Charles a friend of Fisher—Reasons for estrangement—No quarrel on Fisher's part—Lord Charles agrees to conditions regarding his appointment—Appointed to command the Channel Fleet—Constitution of the Channel and Home Fleets—Lord Charles commences his campaign—The precedent of Lord Hood —He asks for war plans—Further letters—Meeting at the Admiralty — Further letters — Further complaints — Fisher's views—Mr. M'Kenna becomes First Lord—The term of Lord Charles's command reduced—Writes to the Prime Minister—Inquiry determined on—Proceedings—The findings—Fisher's caustic comments—Deserted by the Cabinet—Repercussion in the *Royal Oak* affair.

UNFORTUNATELY it is necessary to deal at some length with the organized opposition of Lord Charles Beresford to Fisher and his work at the Admiralty ; since it was directly due to Lord Charles's attacks that Fisher left the Admiralty one year before he need have relinquished the post of First Sea Lord. They were indirectly the cause of nearly the whole of the opposition to his subsequent return to the Admiralty, they divided the country on the merits of his reforms ; in fact, they affected in a marked degree the greater part of his after-career. We have previously mentioned some of Lord Charles's characteristics ; but in addition must be added a charm of manner which had made him extremely popular with both the officers and men who served under him. He still was a friend of Fisher ; but he had fallen under the influence of some of the most bitter of Fisher's opponents. He was not for the moment militantly opposed to Fisher and his plans ; he was not a whole-hearted opponent, but was reluctantly pushed forward by those around him. When, however, Fisher was promoted in December 1905 to be an additional Admiral of the Fleet, which ensured him four, and possibly five, more years at the Admiralty, Lord Charles was extremely mortified. He then saw there was little chance of becoming First Sea Lord—a post he had set his heart on occupying, and one to which he most probably would have succeeded had Fisher remained longer on the Admirals' List, and retired from the Admiralty when he was promoted to Admiral of the Fleet. The main chance for Lord Charles lay in Fisher being turned out of the Admiralty, and this he did his best to bring about. In fairness to Lord Charles, it must be stated that both he and those around him considered he would make a better First Sea Lord than Fisher.

To understand the situation it is necessary to grasp the fact that Fisher had no animus whatsoever against Lord Charles until the latter part of 1908. He had known him in the Mediterranean and had sized him up. To put the matter quite plainly, he looked on him as more or less a harmless Irishman cursed with that windy speech and rebellious temperament not infrequently met with in men from that island of unrest. It has commonly been stated that Fisher quarrelled with Lord Charles ; but nothing is further from the truth. Lord Charles started the

quarrel, and persisted in his attacks ; but he did not
succeed in making Fisher seriously angry until his intensive campaign in 1908 against the Admiralty had been fairly launched.

For the moment he was innocuous. He was not taken seriously either by the Press or by the politicians ; he was, moreover, comparatively speaking, poor, and therefore unable to entertain on any large scale, and thus to spread widely his propaganda. His chance, however, came early in 1907, for in November 1906 his younger brother died in South America and left him a considerable sum of money. After that he was able to keep open house and entertain freely. It is unnecessary to enlarge on the value of hospitality when propaganda work is being undertaken.

The question of appointing Lord Charles to command the Channel Fleet came under consideration at this time. This command was about to become vacant, owing to the retirement of Sir Arthur Wilson. The time was opportune to effect a considerable change in the reorganization of the Fleets in Home Waters. The nucleus-crew manning of the ships in reserve had been put on a firm basis, and the ships so manned had been placed under Admiral Sir Francis Bridgeman. The establishment of this Home Fleet had necessitated the withdrawal of three battleships with full crews from the Channel Fleet ; but, as a counterpoise, the Commander-in-Chief of the Channel Fleet would, in case of war, have under him the whole of the Home Fleet, brought up to full complements. The Commander-in-Chief of the Channel Fleet would, therefore, then have under his orders a larger and far more efficient Fleet than ever had been the case before ; and one, moreover, that was more *instantly* efficient than had ever been possible under the old Steam Reserve organization. The actual figures stood thus :

BEFORE LORD CHARLES TOOK COMMAND

					Battleships.	Armoured Cruisers.
Channel Fleet	.	.	.	.	.	17	6
Atlantic Fleet	.	.	.	.	.	8	6
Home Fleet	.	.	.	.	.	None	None
		Total	.	.	25	12

AFTER LORD CHARLES TOOK COMMAND

Channel Fleet	.	.	.	.	.	14	6
Atlantic Fleet	.	.	.	.	.	6	4
Home Fleet	.	.	.	.	.	6	6
		Total	.	.	26	16

There appeared to be nothing in this revised arrangement to cause dissatisfaction.

Fisher, however, knew Lord Charles well ; and was also well informed of his determination to move heaven and earth to take his place at the Admiralty. He therefore, in order to avoid all misunderstandings, arranged a meeting at the Admiralty, and discussed with him the whole question of the Channel Fleet Command ; and, more particularly, the extent of his control in peace-time of the Home Fleet Divisions which would come under his command on the outbreak of war. The following agreement was drawn up :

I. Whenever desired for exercise and manœuvres the (48) destroyers under Commodore Bayly will be detached from the Home Fleet and placed under the orders of the Commander-in-Chief, Channel Fleet, but for administrative purposes they remain under the orders of C.-in-C., Home Fleet.

II. Similarly the Fifth Cruiser Squadron of six (by-and-by eight) armoured cruisers will be detached for exercise with the Channel Fleet.

III. The Atlantic Fleet and Home Fleet, being under the orders of the senior Flag Officer afloat (the Commander-in-Chief of Channel Fleet) in time of war, must necessarily be exercised together in peace, and, therefore, will exercise together at such periods as will be decided by the Admiralty on the representations of the Commander-in-Chief of the Channel Fleet. This does not in any way derogate from the position and authority of the Commanders-in-Chief of the Atlantic and Home Fleets, but is necessarily a procedure which must be adopted for war efficiency.

This document was initialled by the First Lord, the First Sea Lord, and Lord Charles Beresford ; and, agreement having been reached, on 28th January, 1907, Lord Charles was duly appointed to the command of the Channel Fleet. He did not, however, take up the appointment until about two months later.

On the 21st January Fisher described the interview, in his usual racy style, in a letter to the Civil Lord of the Admiralty, Mr. George Lambert :

I had three hours with Beresford yesterday, and all is settled, and the Admiralty don't give in one inch to his demands ; but I had as a preliminary to agree to three things :

I. Lord Charles Beresford is a greater man than Nelson.

II. No one knows anything about naval war except Lord Charles Beresford.

III. The Admiralty haven't done a single d——d thing right !

Poor old ——[1] has sent me a maudlin letter this morning and winds up with the pathetic statement that he is suffering from an utter want of confidence in himself.

On 22nd April, 1907, Lord Charles wrote to Fisher from his flagship :

I quite agree that all that can be done verbally hastens matters better than correspondence ; but you are quite wrong in thinking that I allow my Staff or anyone else to prepare anything for me to

[1] A mutual colleague.

II—3

fire off at the Admiralty, or other individuals. All my correspondence, good, bad, and indifferent, emanates in what I am
pleased to call my brain—as " Dizzy " once said.

There is not the slightest chance of any friction between me
and you ; or between me and anyone else. When the friction
begins, I am off. If a senior and a junior have a row, the junior
is wrong under any conceivable conditions ; or discipline could
not go on.

It would be impossible to state the relative position
of the Board of Admiralty and a Commander-in-
Chief more clearly ; but, in spite of holding the
views he enunciated in the letter, Lord Charles pro-
ceeded to act diametrically in opposition to them.

Within a month of his taking over the Command
he began to pick a quarrel with the Admiralty. In
the first instance he wrote to ask for war plans.

The procedure of the Admiralty for the last one
hundred years in this respect had been to issue to
every Commander-in-Chief " War Orders." These
merely dealt with certain principles to be observed
by him, which were governed by the general political
situation ; further, they detailed the list of forces
at his disposal in war-time. On these " War Orders "
the Commander-in-Chief made out his own war *plans*,
which dealt with the actual disposition of the vessels
under his command. These *plans* he was required to
send to the Admiralty for emendation or approval.
This procedure was in every respect a sensible one ;
and, moreover, was one which had been followed
by every Commander-in-Chief for many years past.
Lord Charles, however, saw a chance of embarrassing
the Admiralty, and, as already stated, wrote officially
asking for definite war *plans*. The Admiralty very
properly declined to give them ; for it was his business,
as Commander-in-Chief, to prepare his own plans,

knowing the capacities of his Captains and their ships.
It was obviously wrong to force on the man in command the opinions of others as to how he was to dis-
pose and fight the force that was allotted to him.   He
then asked to be furnished with the war plans of his
predecessors, regardless of the fact that the whole
distribution of the Fleets had been altered, and that
any plans hitherto prepared could no longer apply.
But it soon became apparent that what Lord Charles
really wanted was not the plans, but an excuse for
a controversy.   The Admiralty asked Sir Arthur
Wilson to make out war plans for Lord Charles.
Admiral Wilson subsequently described his own procedure in these words :

> The only plan I ever submitted to the Admiralty was in the
> time of strained relations in connection with the Algeciras Con-
> ference.
> Of course, when the thing was over it was much better nobody
> should see it.   When Lord Charles took over the command, Sir
> John Fisher wrote to me to say that he had asked for plans, and
> Lord Charles also wrote to me.   If I remember aright, I wrote
> to Lord Charles and said the only plan I had was the one about
> Morocco—and that could not be given out.   But I drew up a
> plan which I sent to Sir John Fisher, which was drawn up to
> represent the conditions that I thought could be put on paper
> as regards a war between ourselves and Germany, with France
> as our ally ; in fact, if I remember aright, the plans I sent in were
> conditional—I think they more or less referred to a war with
> Germany alone, and a war with France as our ally.   But I am
> perfectly certain that any plan you draw out in peace will not be
> carried out in war.

It is a very useful occupation for an Admiral to
make plans, even though they are never carried out ;
since it teaches him, in a way nothing else can, the
limitations and the possibilities of the vessels under
his command.   To have plans made out for him by

others is bad from every point of view, and if he is unable to prepare his own he is unfit to command. Lord Charles's only comment on the endeavour of the Admiralty to help him was to state that he had asked for the plans of his predecessors, not predecessor, and that he was perfectly able to make out his own plans ! The statement subsequently made by Lord Charles in his demand for an inquiry was that " when he took over the command of the Channel Fleet he found that there were no war plans, and that the Admiralty had never prepared any." This naturally seemed, to those ignorant of naval procedure and of the facts of the case, to be an effective indictment of the Admiralty, and especially of the First Sea Lord ; whereas the Admiralty procedure was time-honoured and sensible.

Another point of attack was the constitution of the Channel Fleet, especially in its relation to the Home Fleet. Lord Charles had been appointed to the Channel Fleet only after agreeing in principle to these relations ; had he not done so he would not have received the appointment ; but he had no hesitation in repudiating that agreement. It is easy to understand that an Admiral may, after actually taking command, find that the conditions of his appointment require modification ; and experience may demonstrate that improved arrangements can be devised. Lord Charles was perfectly within his right to point out how the existing state of affairs could be improved ; but any suggestions for change should not have been diametrically opposed to the general principles to which he had agreed on accepting the appointment. Moreover, Lord Charles knew that the arrangements for the Channel, Atlantic, and Home Fleets were to a great extent only temporary.

On the 14th June, 1907, he wrote to the Admiralty asking to be provided with certain specific information, basing his requests on the assumption that Germany might suddenly declare war. He remarked :

> In my opinion, if Germany was to undertake sudden hostilities with her naval forces perfectly organized in all details for a definite plan of campaign, including a landing party and a raiding party, Germany would have a considerable chance of succeeding ; or, anyway, inflicting most crushing reverses at the initial stages of hostilities, in the present totally unprepared states of the Home and Channel Fleets in regard to the preparation and organization for war.

This was henceforward to be his text. Germany might any day declare war, and unless he had always, day by day, a sufficient force sailing under his flag *immediately* to oppose the whole of the German Fleet we should meet with disaster.

The proposition was not a reasonable one. No country could prepare a sudden blow of that sort without our obtaining some warning of the intention ; more especially when invasion necessitates transports for a " landing party and raiding party." The arrangements made by the Admiralty were perfectly satisfactory for coping with any *probable* event of this nature ; it was useless to devise schemes for dealing with eventualities which were not only improbable, but which, humanly speaking, could not possibly materialize.

Lord Charles's next step was to write a letter to the First Lord, in which he stated that " the Home Fleet as at present constituted is a fraud and a danger to the State." On receipt of this letter the First Lord would have been perfectly within his rights to have ordered Lord Charles to haul down his flag, and come ashore. The Admiralty has always exacted strict loyalty from the Admirals afloat, and anything approaching criticism of Admiralty policy has invariably been treated with severe reprobation. For example, Lord Hood, when in command of the Mediterranean Fleet, wrote on the 28th April, 1795, to the Admiralty saying :

> I owe it to myself to have it upon record, particularly as I am convinced the force under my command, when united in the Mediterranean, will be very unequal to that of the enemy, and the various services committed to my charge ; but although I have not the shadow of prospect of being able to add lustre to the arms of His Majesty, I entreat to have credit for doing my utmost that they are not disgraced.

On this letter being received at the Admiralty, Lord Hood was ordered to haul down his flag and repair ashore. Lord Spencer, the First Lord, in submitting the decision of the Board of Admiralty to the King, stated in conclusion :

> But being fully persuaded that the discipline and subordination so necessary to be maintained between the Board of Admiralty and the officers entrusted by the Board with the conduct of Your Majesty's naval forces would be entirely at an end if public and official representations of this kind were allowed to pass unnoticed, he humbly and most anxiously hopes that Your Majesty may approve of the measure which he has thought it his duty to recommend to the Board on this occasion.

Lord Charles might with advantage to the Navy have been treated in a similar manner. No one comparing the two communications can reasonably doubt that that of Lord Charles was far more improper than the one written by Lord Hood ; moreover, the

services of the latter to the nation had been incomparably greater than those of the former. The First
Lord, however, decided not to take disciplinary action,
but first to have an interview with Lord Charles and
to find out exactly what it was that he did want.

The meeting took place on the 5th July, 1907.
The First Lord (Lord Tweedmouth), Sir John Fisher,
and Lord Charles were present. As was usual when
away from his staff, Lord Charles was unable to state
exactly what he did want, for he had no memory
for detail. He had his grievance—he had not enough
ships ; but he was quite unable to put his views clearly
to the First Lord, or to define his requirements.

Fisher did all he could, and went as far as it was
possible in order to satisfy Lord Charles. The following extract from the report of the interview fully
bears this out :

Sir John Fisher : " We simply want to know what you are
driving at, because we seem to give you everything you require,
and then, as I hardly like to use the word ' compromise,' or anything like that, because it is not a word that the Admiralty should
use to anyone, we say, ' Shall you be satisfied if we do with you
as we did with Sir Arthur Wilson ? ' which is the point you seem
to be going on making. There cannot be any doubt about the
battleships of the Channel Fleet being far superior to the German
Fleet. Shall you be satisfied if we make your armoured cruisers
up to six, the same as Sir Arthur Wilson had, and give you the
whole of the two divisions of destroyers at Portland under Admiral
Montgomerie, all to come under you ? We think the present
arrangement better. You say you would like these vessels per-
manently, so as to bring your squadron up to what you say were
Admiral Wilson's component parts. We do not agree, but we say,
' This is our chief executive officer afloat ; we do not agree, but
we will give him the armoured cruisers, the destroyer flotillas, and
the attendant vessels, as he presses for them.' "

Lord Charles : " I cannot see the thing straight off. I will
write to you."

Sir John Fisher : " You must have thought about it. You have been writing about it for months."

Lord Charles Beresford : " I am not sure that I have not asked for more cruisers than that in my plan."

First Lord : " I do not think the Board will agree to more than I have told you."

Lord Charles Beresford : " I see. It's a fair offer on the part of the Admiralty to meet me, and it shows you see the danger I see."

Sir John Fisher : " We think it is very undesirable for the Admiralty to remain in a state of tension with you, and the First Lord said (I think with great propriety), ' Let us have a talk with Lord Charles and see if we can arrange matters in this way and finish off the business without further irritating correspondence.' Do not let us have any more letters about it. It was hoped you would say, ' After meeting round this table this morning I can quite see that the Board of Admiralty are anxious to meet me in every way they can, as it is also my duty to meet the Board of Admiralty in every way I can ; we have fixed up the matter and here is an end of it.' "

Lord Charles Beresford : " I never come to a conclusion myself with anything without I think. On principle, being a public man, I never say a thing straight off. Have those ships you are going to give me nucleus crews ? "

Sir John Fisher : " No, they are fully manned. They are complete, the destroyers are at Portland, and they will remain at Portland under you. Simply as regards the cruisers, what we shall do is to knock two cruisers off the 5th Cruiser Squadron, and turn them over to you."

Lord Charles Beresford : " That gives me the force I am halloing for. You may depend on it, the cordiality between us exists. There is no want of cordiality on my part."

Lord Charles ended the interview with the following sentence :

I do not dictate to the Board of Admiralty. The Board has the right—it is the constituted authority, and so long as it is the constituted authority, it is responsible and no one else. It may do wrong things, but it is the responsible authority. I have never written to you, officially or privately, except in the most respectful manner.

This last remark must have been addressed to Fisher only ; for a typewritten letter to the First Lord, not even marked " private," criticizing the Home Fleet and saying that it was " a fraud on the nation and a danger to the State," could hardly be described as being " most respectful " !

It was expected that after this interview Lord Charles would cease his criticisms ; but, within a fortnight, he wrote again, and in a long letter to the Admiralty, dated the 16th July, criticized their policy in having formed the Home Fleet. It ends :

> It is for these reasons that the Home Fleet cannot, in my opinion, be regarded as an advanced striking force ready for immediate action, and if in its present state it is represented as being ready for immediate action, I venture to think that, as a figure of speech, it is not incorrect to describe it as a fraud on the public and a danger to the State.

This, it must be remembered, was written about another Fleet under an Admiral[1] not far below him in standing, and certainly little, if anything, below him in practical experience in the Navy ; who was, moreover, perfectly satisfied with the Admiralty arrangements regarding his Fleet.

The Admiralty reply put the position clearly and curtly :

> In regard to the various expressions and statements of opinion in your two letters under reply, my Lords are always ready to give consideration to representations made to them in the usual manner by officers in high command, but they cannot enter into a controversy on matters of policy with an officer acting under their authority. The disposition of the fighting units of the Fleet and the strategic policy to be followed are matters solely for the decision of the Board of Admiralty.

[1] Vice-Admiral Sir Francis Bridgeman.

Again, in connection with a report sent in by Lord Charles after some manœuvres, the Admiralty remarked :

My Lords cannot agree with some of the criticisms you express on the units of the Home Fleet which were under your orders ; [1] and they regret that you should have expressed your opinions on the value of this Fleet in your reports on the recent exercises.

This produced an impertinent retort on the 28th August :

I note that their Lordships consider that the Admiral who in war is responsible for the Fleet in Home Waters should not express his opinion as to its efficiency in times of peace.

In the meantime Lord Charles had started a fresh grievance. For many years before 1908 a very salutary regulation had existed, which required that every Captain should serve a specified time in command of a battleship in order to qualify himself for promotion to the rank of Rear-Admiral, and this was always rigidly enforced. Any officer holding an appointment either at the Admiralty, or the Dockyards, or on the Staff of an Admiral, who has not the necessary service in command of a battleship, when the time for his promotion approaches, is always relieved and sent to such a command in order that he may qualify for promotion. As a natural consequence, when Captain Sturdee, who was Chief-of-the-Staff to Lord Charles, neared the end of his time as Post-Captain he was appointed to a battleship. Lord Charles knew perfectly the regulation, and the necessity for it ; but he chose to ignore this, and to convert the incident into a personal grievance against the Admiralty.

[1] The Home Fleet was temporarily under the *orders* of Lord Charles, but so far as its discipline and organization were concerned, Sir Francis Bridgeman was responsible, and not Lord Charles.

Rear-Admiral Montgomerie, who was in command of the destroyers of the Home Fleet, was relieved of his command after one year in the appointment. There were two reasons for this change. The first was the reduction in destroyers under his immediate command, consequent on the transfer of two flotillas to the Channel Fleet as a result of the interview of the 5th July, 1907 ; and the second was that certain representations had been made by the Commander-in-Chief of the Home Fleet as regards the command. Lord Charles made this also a cause of complaint. Further, he heard from someone, who evidently was ill-informed, that the Admiralty proposed transferring Vice-Admiral Sir Reginald Custance to another command. This officer was Second-in-Command of the Channel Fleet, and supplied Lord Charles with most of the brains so necessary in Fleet matters.

At the interview of the 5th July Lord Charles had protested that cordiality existed between him and the Admiralty Board, that the Board was the constituted authority, and that he had never written to it in any but a respectful manner. Yet in November he wrote to the Admiralty saying that he had been privately informed that Admiral Custance was shortly to be transferred to another appointment, and that this officer had been of immense value to him in making out war plans. He complained that Admiral Montgomerie, who had also assisted him, had been informed that he had the option of going on half-pay or of remaining for one year only in his appointment. He referred also to the appointment of Captain Sturdee to an independent command, and then continued :

It has come to my notice that a feeling has arisen in the Service that it is prejudicial to an officer's career to be personally connected with me on Service matters. *This may not be a fact,*[1] but the impression I know exists. It is certainly borne out by the late procedure.

The removal of three such important officers from my command at or about the same time will add enormously to my exceptionally hard work. . . .

It may not have been intended,[1] but it most certainly has the appearance of a wish to handicap and hamper me in carrying out the responsibilities connected with by far the most important appointment within the Empire. . . .

The ordinary etiquette, civilities, and courteous dealings which officers of high and distinguished command have hitherto so markedly received from the Admiralty have been entirely absent in my case.

Again one must wonder why the Admiralty did not order Lord Charles forthwith to haul down his flag. With misplaced forbearance, however, they desired him to forward specific evidence of his statement regarding " the feeling in the Service being that it was prejudicial to an officer to have dealings with him." They also remarked that it was not understood on what ground the allegation of discourtesy was based, adding, " they would, however, observe that it becomes increasingly difficult for them [i.e. the Members of the Board] in their correspondence with you to avoid overstepping the usual limits of official reserve, while you continue to employ language which has no parallel within their experience as coming from a subordinate and addressed to the Board of Admiralty." The evidence asked for was not forthcoming.

Every situation in life, however grave, must have some relief in humour. So with this wretched Beresford business. When Admiral Sir Francis Bridgeman joined the Admiralty as Second Sea Lord he went to

---

[1] Italics do not exist in the original letter.

Grosvenor Street to call on Lord Charles ; and, as he had been his old Commander-in-Chief in the Mediterranean and was senior to him in the Navy, he paid the call in the forenoon. On arrival he was ushered into a room with half a dozen Admirals seated round a table at the head of which was Lord Charles. Had an aeroplane dropped a bomb, the consternation could not have been greater. The butler, thinking that Sir Francis was, like the other Admirals, a conspirator, had shown him into the room where the inner committee was plotting the downfall of Sir John Fisher and the Board of Admiralty, of which Sir Francis was a member. Fisher, who heard the story first-hand from Sir Francis, retold it with infinite humour ; how " Dash " dropped his pen on the floor and burrowed under the table to hide his identity, how the others employed various manœuvres to effect the same purpose. " Double Dash " turned his back, went to the fire and poked it. " Dash Double " hid his face in his hands under the pretence of reading hard, another discovered his shoe-lace was undone, and so on, etc. Lord Charles jumped to his feet, seized the intruder by the arm, and hustled him into another room. But for some days the revolutionary dovecot was terribly fluttered.

The following extracts from letters written by Fisher are interesting as showing how he viewed Lord Charles's insubordination :

5th January, 1908.

It's always a difficult question whether to hang or hug your enemies. But government of the Navy *viâ* modified rebellion is not good for discipline.

13th January, 1908.

" Tempus edax rerum," or, as the sailors say, " It all brushes off when it's dry." Don't tamper with the mud on your clothes when it's wet.

24th January, 1908.

Balfour asked Ottley to lunch to-day. He told Ottley Beresford was holding forth in every drawing-room in London and was doing an infinity of mischief. . . .

They are all " blue-funkers " about Beresford and overrate his power of mischief and his influence.

7th February, 1908.

——, who takes my fancy greatly, has been to see me à là Nicodemus. How that crisis will end I don't know. I suggested Cromwellian methods ; but, as he rightly observed, Cromwell wasn't cursed with colleagues.

9th February, 1908.

. . . The other print is a sort of " Brief " I prepared for Balfour, who is a cordial and good friend and is going to fight tooth and nail against any inquiry into Admiralty policy, which, of course, as he admits, implies my resignation. Now, don't you go bothering yourself to help me. *You have already sacrificed yourself far too much.* So I *entreat* you to do no more ! Beresford has behaved *very badly to me indeed* ; but, like in your own famous case with him, it is best for me to be silent and let " Time " be my avenger.

17th February, 1908.

MY DEAR FRIEND,

I know full well what you have done for me, and what you have hazarded for me and what you have forgone for me. *I know it all.* I know also that at the base of it all is the sincere and well-founded belief that it is for the public good you have acted as you have, and so that you don't care a brass farthing what anyone says, or does, to vilify you ; but now I say to you (*with knowledge of what is going on*) that Beresford, being full of money as well as malignity, will seize any opportunity of a libel action, and you can't afford it nor can I afford to help you. I don't know the wiles of libel, I only write to warn you, as I could never forgive myself if you got beat by money, and I had not tried beforehand to warn you against it.

The following letter written to Fisher in 1908 expresses well the opinion that was held by many who, though not actually in the Navy, were close

observers of naval matters :

According to my humble reading of history, the mutiny of
Beresford and —— weakens the nation incomparably more than
the *Indomitable* strengthens her. " Indomitables " want spirit of
the right sort if they are to function successfully on the day of
battle. Beresford's sulks at the manœuvres injure the Empire,
and the reference to Sir Arthur Wilson makes a bad impression
on the country. It thinks the Admiralty shirks the issue with
Beresford. The Admiralty must be supreme, but the Wilson
reference savours of arbitration between Authority, which should
be supreme, and its subordinates.

Forty-four million of us are cheering Sivier and Dorando behind
the breakwater of—not " Indomitables "—[but] 120,000 British
seamen. These seamen are riven by mutiny—sheer black mutiny.
Mutiny is condoned in high places. *You must* be obeyed, whether
you are right or wrong, and disobedience, being interpreted, spells
Ichabod to Great Britain. . . . You must be worn out with work
and worry and need a rest ; but I venture most earnestly to
express the hope that you will take a very high line with the
mutineers.

Wolseley failed from tame acquiescence in the sham of political
tonguesters. I do most earnestly trust that you will insist on
Discipline, as well as " Indomitables," whatever the Party or
Parliament may say. You are the only really big man in active
public life, and your staunchness to the nation will be highly tried.

The Admiralty had so far treated Lord Charles with
extreme forbearance, but when his attacks assumed
formidable proportions, Fisher saw that he had to
fight with his back to the wall and took his opponent
more seriously. Lord Charles continued his antagonism to the Admiralty, and Fisher became really angry
with him.

On Mr. M'Kenna relieving Lord Tweedmouth in June
1908, Fisher wrote him a letter clearly stating the
Admiralty point of view :

I think I ought to explain to you at once what the Admiralty
position *is*, *always has been*, and *must ever remain* if discipline is

to be maintained, and the authority of the Board of Admiralty over the Service preserved—and that is, that there must be no cavilling at, or criticizing of, their orders by officers on active service afloat, and more especially by those in high command ; and this is why I suggested to you, what indeed you yourself had in your mind (as to interviews with malcontents), that you could not have an amateur outside the Board of Admiralty directing naval policy in opposition to your official Board of Admiralty. If complete confidence cannot be given to the Sea Lords, they ought to be changed ; but there is an end of all things if, taking the instance you gave me, Lord Charles Beresford is to dictate to the Admiralty what particular destroyers he should have, or what should be the constitution of his Fleet : " Se soumettre ou se démettre "—that's the plain answer to give him ; or, as Mr. John Burns put it more graphically :

The quarterdeck and silence
or *Westminster and gas,*

as Beresford threatens to go into Parliament and make it hot for the Admiralty.

I think my colleagues will tell you that it is unprecedented the lengths to which Lord Charles Beresford has been permitted (I think wrongly) to flout the Admiralty ; but I have subjected my strong personal convictions to the judgment of others, and having gone so far, I think it is wisdom to wait now till the autumn, when probably matters will arrange themselves.[1]

Correspondence soon began to pass between Mr. M'Kenna and Lord Charles. On the 1st July, 1908, Mr. M'Kenna ended a long letter :

You will observe that the Fleet which would come under you in the North Sea would be amply sufficient to meet Germany alone in any strength with which she could confront us in the near future ; and I have decided to keep the Home Fleet apart, under a separate command, ready to meet any second Power.

You will further note that the Squadrons required for trade protection and local coast defence will be under a separate and independent command from the Channel Fleet.

[1] A reconstitution of the Fleets was then contemplated.

In conclusion, I will take the opportunity of laying stress upon
the imperative necessity for the cordial co-operation of the Com- mander-in-Chief of the Channel Fleet in the plans of the Admir- alty ; and I am sure you will understand the reluctance with which I mention this topic, which is, however, forced on me by my knowledge of the unhappy personal position in which you have placed yourself in relation to the First Sea Lord. It is essential for both the success of the Admiralty administration and the efficiency of the Fleet that the most cordial personal relations should exist between the Commander-in-Chief of the Channel Fleet and the whole of the Board.

Lord Charles, after receiving this letter, should have realized that the new First Lord was not a man who could be trifled with in the same manner that had been so successful with his predecessor ; but he and his advisers had passed the limits of reason. He gambled on the capitulation of the Cabinet under the threat of a national campaign.

Matters at last came to a head ; and, on further reorganization of the Fleet taking place, Lord Charles, on the 19th December, 1908, received a notice that in consequence of this reorganization in the early part of the following year, the term of his command would be reduced from three to two years.

On the 24th March, 1909, Lord Charles hauled down his flag. He was not long in returning to the charge, for on the 2nd April he wrote a long letter to the Prime Minister which, among other criticisms of the Board of Admiralty, contained the following charges against naval administration :

During the whole of my tenure of the Command of the Channel Fleet proper, that force, owing to the number of vessels constantly withdrawn from it for purposes of refit, has never, even for a day, been equal to the force which it might have to encounter in home waters. During that period the Fleets in home waters have not been organized in readiness for war, and they are not organized in readiness for war now to-day.

Had the authority of the Board of Admiralty been upheld by the Cabinet when Lord Charles first commenced his unfortunate campaign, and had the proper action been then taken of superseding him in his command, the Prime Minister would not have been confronted with a difficult situation.

Fisher aptly described the pass to which the tergiversation of the Government had brought the Navy :

13th April, 1909.

Imagine what a state of affairs, when a meeting of naval officers on the Active List, in a room in Grosvenor Street, is able to coerce a Cabinet and force the strongest Board of Admiralty to totter to its fall ! Why, the " Young Turks " are not in it ! The country must indeed be in a bad way if so governed.

The very fact that Lord Charles had been allowed to carry on his campaign against authority had caused popular opinion to be biased in his favour. It seemed to the ordinary person to be obvious that, had the Admiralty been in the right, Lord Charles would have been promptly dealt with ; the apparent disinclination of that body to do so was interpreted as evidence that the Admiralty feared to take any action that might lead to the exposure of administrative failure.

The only course now open to the Prime Minister was to inquire into Lord Charles's allegations. A strong man would undoubtedly have inquired personally into the charges. Mr. Asquith preferred to have his opinions backed by a sub-committee of the Cabinet. So, for the first time on record in the long history of the Admiralty or War Office, one of these offices was publicly arraigned and put on trial on the demand of an indisciplined subordinate. Naval discipline, and the upholding of the paramount authority of the Board of Admiralty, weighed as nothing against the fear of the political disadvantage that a Parliamentary, Press, and Society agitation might bring to the Government.

In the Navy one of the most serious disciplinary offences is that of making a frivolous complaint against a superior officer. Discipline impels immediate and implicit obedience to an order. It forbids any questioning, unless such an order should be illegal. If an order is questioned, or the action of a superior appealed against, then the onus lies on the junior to prove absolutely his contention. If he fails to do so, then he must suffer for having made a complaint that he has been unable to substantiate. Questioning orders, or criticizing the dispositions of the Admiralty by Admirals or by any other officers, has always been looked on as a flagrant breach of discipline, since it strikes a blow at the paramount authority of the Board of Admiralty.

In writing to the Prime Minister, Lord Charles therefore took a bold course ; if he failed to substantiate his charges absolutely and fully, then the maintenance of discipline in the Navy demanded that he should be at once placed on the retired list.

The Prime Minister selected the Committee of Inquiry entirely from members of the Cabinet. He originally wished to include among the number Admiral of the Fleet Sir Arthur Wilson, the most experienced of all the naval officers on the Active List and, moreover, a man whose opinion carried the greatest weight both in the Service and also with all civilians with whom he had come in contact. Truly, indeed, he was a man of all men, *sans peur et sans reproche.* In this

selection the King entirely concurred. Lord Charles,
however, objected that Admiral Wilson could not be
looked on as an entirely impartial judge. Mr. Asquith
gave way ; there was not, therefore, on the Committee one single member who had any knowledge of
the Navy or of sea-conditions. The King expressed
his regret that Admiral Wilson had not been made a
member of the Inquiry. The Prime Minister replied
that, on going into the matter, he had found that
Admiral Wilson had been Lord Charles's immediate
predecessor in Command of the Channel Fleet, and
that Lord Charles had recorded " in documents known
to Sir Arthur Wilson, various caustic criticisms on
his ideas of strategy, etc." [1] But he added that,
" although Sir Arthur Wilson was not on the Committee, we could submit all the evidence to him, call
him as a witness, and, of course, attach the greatest
weight to his opinion." [2]

An excellent piece of sophistry ; for surely if " the
greatest weight was to be attached to his opinion," he
might well have been a member of the Committee !
But to have a member of the Committee who was
thoroughly cognisant of naval details was exactly
what Lord Charles wished to avoid.

Fisher was extremely annoyed that Admiralty policy
should be made the subject of an inquiry by a Committee, merely on charges made by an Admiral guilty
of indisciplined actions. He looked on it as an
insult to the Admiralty and Navy generally, and as
cowardice on the part of the Prime Minister in fearing
to face the threat of Lord Charles's friends, that they

[1] How Sir Arthur Wilson must have smiled when he read them !—
EDITOR.

[2] *Life of King Edward VII*, by Sir Sidney Lee.

would conduct a campaign on his behalf and against
the Government throughout the country. Fisher
wished to resign ; but fortunately followed the advice
given him by the King, and remained at the Admiralty.   Had he resigned, his action would most certainly
have been interpreted by his enemies as evidence that
he feared Admiralty policy being inquired into.

Mr. M'Kenna conducted the case for the Admiralty
before the Committee.   He extracted a promise from
Fisher that the latter should keep complete silence
unless directly addressed by a member of the Committee ; as he feared that the anger of the Admiral,
at Beresford's mis-statements, might lead to the harmony of the inquiry being rudely interrupted.

Lord Charles brought with him to the Committee
his naval brains—Vice-Admiral Custance—to assist
him.

The inquiry dragged a slow course through fourteen
sittings, the lay members learning by degrees the
difference between " war plans " and " war orders " ;
between ships " attached to " and ships " under the
orders of " an Admiral.   They also for the first time
learned, to their dismay, from Admiral Wilson, who
was called as a witness, that in naval opinion it was
impossible to prevent a very great loss of merchant
vessels on our part in a war with Germany ;   and,
further, that the cost of the number of ships that
would be necessary to safeguard our merchant fleet was
far more than the value of the vessels that would be
lost in attempting such protection.   They further
learned that all plans made before a war were of little
use except as a mental exercise ; since all plans made
on surmise would never be used in actual war.   Plans
in war-time depend largely on the strategy of the

enemy, and counter-plans may vary from day to day. But the most startling thing they learned was that more than one officer occupying a confidential post in the Admiralty had supplied Lord Charles with secret information which had enabled him, through the latitude allowed to him by the Prime Minister, to turn the inquiry into a " fishing " inquiry, and to attack the Admiralty on trade protection, a matter outside the scope of Lord Charles's original charges, and of the terms of reference to the Committee.

Such a gross breach of confidence was too much for the Prime Minister, who, at the final sitting, submitted Lord Charles to a most searching and most unpleasant cross-examination on this subject.

Fisher thus described the final sitting :

12th June, 1909. 4.30 a.m.

We sat till nearly seven with —— spitting venom all the time at the First Sea Lord ; and Beresford requested a private interview with Asquith at the end of the meeting. . . . M'Kenna has most wonderfully enhanced his reputation amongst his most powerful colleagues in the Cabinet. *I'm his blessing in disguise !* Custance went back to Cornwallis and Keith, etc. That damned him ! Why not Noah ? Old Haldane shut his eyes and slept. The King has sent me a dear letter and adds, " *Don't print this.*" Isn't he sweet ? What *wonderful friends I have !* All I do is to kick their shins.

Again on the 15th June he wrote :

We have nothing to fear except the damnable deplorableness of a subordinate inside the Admiralty being called to give evidence against the First Sea Lord. Custance completely obfuscated both himself and the Committee. Beresford held forth as to his intended public address on the 30th June. The Prime Minister seemed in a blue funk of him.

Yes, we made a good day of it on Saturday (Fleet at Portsmouth). But the two most noticeable things of all were never noticed :

The swarm of destroyers, going 20 knots past the *Dreadnought*, found themselves suddenly confronted by a lot of passenger steamers and yachts which at the last moment got right in their way. The accidents might have been intense, but the young chaps kept their nerve and their speed, and scootled through the eye of the needle, just grazing them all. It was splendid to see and made my heart warm ! (N.B.—A Press Delegate—the *Toronto Globe*, I think—seized me by the arm and said, " Sir, I see the glint of battle in your eye.")

The finding of the Committee was as follows :

In the opinion of the Committee, the investigation has shown that during the time in question no danger to the country resulted from the Admiralty's arrangements for war, whether considered from the standpoint of the organization and distribution of the Fleets, the numbers of ships, or the preparation of war plans.

They feel bound to add that the arrangements, quite defensible in themselves, though not ideally perfect, were in practice seriously hampered through the absence of cordial relations between the Board of Admiralty and the Commander-in-Chief of the Channel Fleet. The Board of Admiralty do not appear to have taken Lord Charles Beresford sufficiently into their confidence as to the reasons for dispositions to which he took exception ; and Lord Charles Beresford, on the other hand, appears to have failed to appreciate *and carry out the instructions of the Board, and to recognize their paramount authority.*[1]

The Committee have been impressed with the difference in opinion among officers of high rank and professional attainments regarding important principles of naval tactics and strategy, and they look forward with much confidence to the further development of a Naval War Staff, from which the naval members of the Board and flag officers and their staffs at sea may be expected to derive common benefit.

In other words, the Committee found, in the first paragraph, that Lord Charles's allegations were unfounded ; and by the second paragraph, that his conduct towards the Board was wanting in discipline.

---

[1] Italics were not in the original.

Either of these two findings necessitated, from the point of view of discipline, that he should be placed on the retired list. But no such action was taken. The Prime Minister feared to take a strong line against so seemingly popular an Admiral.

It was, from a naval and disciplinary point of view, no part of the duty of the Admiralty to inform an Admiral afloat of their future intentions, intentions which might never materialize, and which in no way affected his present command. The insertion of this statement in the report of the Committee could only have been due to a desire to try to give Lord Charles some shadow of a grievance against the Admiralty as a set-off to his proved indisciplined behaviour.

Anyone who has read the evidence produced at the inquiry and who is at the same time cognisant of naval matters will cordially agree with the condemnation of the report contained in a letter Fisher wrote to a friend :

I was glad to get your letter, but I am most bitterly disappointed by the Committee's report. It's a most cowardly production : not in the least what it was intended to be by any of the five members on the day that Asquith cross-examined Beresford on the —— incident à la an Old Bailey attorney ! It was a dirty trick to say the Admiralty had not given their confidence to Beresford, when Beresford had abused that confidence within twenty-four hours of hoisting his flag ! [1] And again a very dirty trick to bring in the red herring about the Naval War Staff, when all five members knew about the great work done in establishing the Naval War College at Portsmouth, and the practical proof of the great advance in strategical thought in the Navy by the concentration of our Fleets instead of their previous dispersion, and

[1] He knew Lord Charles's irradicable tendency to chatter. He was not a person to whom it was advisable to communicate the intentions of the Admiralty regarding any matter that did not immediately affect his command.

the getting rid of 160 vessels that could neither fight nor run away. . . .

I am very sick about it all, considering what each member of the Committee had previously said to me.

King Edward was a King who respected all formalities regarding the Constitution ; he, of course, made no comment on the finding of the Committee. He possessed political acumen to a phenomenal degree and a wide knowledge of affairs, so that the following entry in a note-book kept by Lady Fisher is of interest. A good deal can be read between the guarded and scanty lines :

His Majesty returned from abroad 8th May, 1909. By H.M.'s command " Sir John Fisher " met him at Victoria Station, and on Sunday, May 9th, was commanded to wait on H.M. at 12.30 at Buckingham Palace. The interview was strictly private, and the only thing I was told was that H.M. said to Father that his conduct (in this disgraceful affair—K. F.) had been Dignified and Courageous. No small compliment from the King.—K. F.

This compliment was, without doubt, a great solace, but the support that it gave was private, and not public.

Thus after nearly five years of unparalleled labour for the country, Fisher found himself deserted by the Prime Minister and Cabinet ; who, without one word of commendation for the great work he had accomplished, left him with his authority as First Sea Lord undermined in the Navy and the quarry of the jackals of the Press.

POSTSCRIPT

Lord Charles Beresford did everything in his power, and mobilized his political and Society friends to use their influence, to obtain for him his promotion to Admiral of the Fleet ; but Fisher, as well as each succeeding First Sea Lord, was obdurate, and refused to include in the ancient roll of that coveted rank the name of a man who had been convicted by a Committee of the Cabinet of indiscipline towards the Admiralty ; he was, however, suitably rewarded by being given a peerage.

The matter, unfortunately, cannot be considered to have ended here. The discipline of the Navy was badly injured by the condonation of insubordination by the Cabinet. Unquestioning obedience no longer was looked on as essential. Criticism of seniors was introduced ; and the effect of the finding of the Cabinet Committee and their subsequent inaction was noticeable in the recent *Royal Oak* affair. Had such a case arisen prior to 1908 the offenders would have been shortly and sharply dealt with, and the publicity given to a most unfortunate naval episode might well have been avoided.

Discipline, such as the Navy requires, should not be meddled with, however expedient politicians may consider some temporary tampering may be for the party to which they may belong.

CHAPTER XIV

1904—1910

GENERAL WORK AS FIRST SEA LORD

He who surpasses, or subdues mankind,
Must look down on the hate of those below.
                                                    BYRON.

The Russian war scare—Sinking of trawlers—Fisher's routine
—Redistribution of duties at the Admiralty—Principal A.D.C.
—Nearly retires—The Kaiser's view of Fisher—Copenhagening
the German Fleet—Approached by von Tirpitz—The " Tweed-
mouth " episode—His interview with M. Stolypin—His letter
to M. Isvolsky—Increase in size of gun—The invasion scare—
The 1909–10 programme—Mr. Churchill's meddling—Mr.
M'Kenna's stand—Fisher's methods criticized—His critics—Sir
George Clarke—Mr. Stead on Fisher's critics—Adumbrates retir-
ing—Sir Arthur Wilson selected as his successor—How arranged
—His retirement—Mr. M'Kenna's tribute—The effects of his
work on his character—The Bacon letter.

IMMEDIATELY after Fisher joined the Admiralty
in October 1904 he was struck down by a bad
attack of influenza, with a high temperature.
No sooner had he been safely tucked up in bed than
the Russian Baltic Fleet, which was on its way out
to the Far East to take part in the Japanese War,
fired on some of our trawlers in the North Sea, mis-
taking them for Japanese torpedo craft, and several
of the fishermen lost their lives.

The reasons for the mistake were patent to any
naval officer. Vessels when looked at in the beam of
a searchlight at night are difficult to recognize.
Cruisers look like destroyers and *vice versa*. There
was no doubt that the Russian ill-trained sailors and

their almost equally green officers really did mistake the trawlers for torpedo boats when they opened fire. To the civilian mind, however, it seemed impossible that a trawler should have been mistaken for a torpedo boat ; moreover, popular feeling was on the side of the Japanese in this war, or, to be more accurate, feeling was against the Russians ; so for a short time matters looked serious, and there was a distinct chance of our becoming drawn into the war. Sir Charles Drury, who was the Second Sea Lord, and therefore doing duty for Fisher, gave the following account of what took place at that time.

He was in his flat in London one Sunday evening when a *Daily Mail* reporter arrived and asked for an interview. He told Sir Charles that he had just come from Hull, where he had seen trawlers arrive who reported that some of their fishing fleet had been sunk by the Russian warships on the Dogger Bank. The reporter said that he had already visited various Cabinet Ministers' offices and houses, and also the Admiralty, but could find nobody in authority, and finally he had come to see Sir Charles.

Sir Charles got into touch with the Cabinet, and soon after found the Ministry were taking such action as would certainly lead to war with Russia. Finding himself unable to influence matters, he went to Fisher and told him the Cabinet were sitting, and that unless he could influence them war was inevitable. Fisher got out of his bed, went to the place where the Cabinet meeting was being held, and demanded admittance. He found, as Sir Charles had told him, that if the Cabinet's proposals were adopted, war was certain. He protested, and represented his case with such strength and firmness that different steps were taken, and war was averted.

But in order to impress the Russians and satisfy public opinion, several of the Channel Squadron battleships were hurried home from Gibraltar post-haste. Fisher took this opportunity of semi-strained relations to press to the utmost his views on the uselessness and danger of keeping, on distant stations, a number of small obsolete ships that could neither fight nor run away. Using as an excuse the probability of war, he recalled quite a number of these vessels, which were paid off, never to be recommissioned. This was the first act in the redistribution of the Fleet.

He held strong views on the subject of the duties of the First Sea Lord in relation to the other Lords. He made a practice never to differ in writing from a minute written by a colleague. It was frequently necessary for the decision of another Lord to come to him for his approval before it could take effect and be acted on. In the rare cases when he happened to disagree, he invariably kept the paper back, and next day personally talked the matter over with the Lord in question. He liked his colleagues to take the initiative in all matters affecting the departments they supervised. He, however, considered that he was primarily responsible for the efficiency of the Fleet and its instant readiness for war. The old division of duties at the Admiralty did not allow enough latitude in this respect, so he arranged with Lord Selborne for a modification of the old arrangement.

On the 20th October, 1904, a new distribution was authorized, which gave the First Sea Lord responsibility and power in the following matters :

(1) Preparation for war : all large questions of naval policy and maritime warfare—to advise.

(2) The fighting efficiency of the Fleet, its organization and mobilization ; the distribution and movements of all ships in commission or in Fleet Reserve.

(3) The control of the Intelligence, Hydrographical,
Naval, and Ordnance Departments.

The new distribution of duties was at once seized
on by some critics. They considered that it gave the
First Sea Lord too much power. A grasping First
Sea Lord, it was argued, could, under these three
clauses, interfere in all the Admiralty work. This was
perfectly true ; but Fisher had no intention of meddling
with details of supply or discipline, etc., and under
the new rules he transferred much detail work to the
other Lords. His object and intention was to ensure
that the Fleet was not starved in any way, and that
nothing was inadvertently done to affect adversely its
fighting efficiency. A criticism similar to the one
put forward could, in reality, have been levelled at a
First Sea Lord under the previous distribution of
business ; for the relation of the First Sea Lord to
the other Sea Lords has always been that of *princeps
inter pares*.

Under these new rules the work at the Admiralty
ran with perfect smoothness and without the slightest
friction.

Fisher hated routine papers. It was with much
difficulty that his Secretary and his Naval Assistant
were able to corner him each evening to get his signature to necessary papers. He trusted his staff im-
plicitly, and would scribble an almost illegible " J. F."
at the foot of minutes that had been prepared for
him ; or after the word " concur," without reading,
or, rather, without appearing to read, what was
written. Any paper that required closer study was

placed on one side and dealt with by him at 5 o'clock the next morning. An awkward paper, which dealt with questions that he did not wish to be raised, would occasionally turn up, and this would be put into a drawer of his desk. There it defied the search of the office staff, whose business it was to hunt for lost papers. After a sufficient time had elapsed it would be rediscovered, and it was usually then found to have answered itself !

His hours for meals were most erratic. At times he would have no lunch at all ; on other days, any time between one and three was good enough for a hasty meal. He had a habit of working at the Admiralty on Sunday mornings. It certainly was an ideal place on that day, for there was then a deathly silence, like the darkness in the Bible " that could be felt." Lady Fisher became seriously afraid that he would have a breakdown if he continued this habit ; and one day, when sitting next to the King, she told him of her fears. He immediately took a menu, and on the back of it wrote a Royal command forbidding Fisher to go to the Admiralty on Sundays ! The Royal command, however, was frequently disobeyed.

Shortly before joining the Admiralty Fisher had pointed out to the First Lord that His Majesty's influence would be essential to carry out fully the reforms that were shortly to be launched. It was therefore desirable that Fisher should have the right of audience with the King ; and, in order to regularize this, Lord Selborne suggested that Fisher should be appointed First and Principal Naval A.D.C. The King wrote to Fisher demurring to the proposal, saying it would be better for Fisher not to have the appointment, since it might create jealousies.

On the 11th September, 1904, Fisher wrote to Lord Esher :

Apparently it had all been cut and dried between Selborne and the King (and the *appointment approved*) that I should be the King's Principal A.D.C., *vice* Stephenson, made Black Rod, which means four hundred a year and the most complimentary of all appointments, and many subsidiary advantages, more especially as it gives access to the King at any time which, as First Sea Lord, would have been most convenient. Well, the King said he wanted me to refuse it, as, on further reflection, he thought it would cause ill-feeling against me, and be put down as favouritism, and also no First Sea Lord had held it. (This was wrong : Sir Cooper Key did so.) He said he wanted me above all others, but thought it best I shouldn't be ; also he said it would enable the Government to wriggle out of giving me the extra £800 a year I asked for on leaving Portsmouth. I got £4,000 a year there, and only £2,600 at the Admiralty. As I want to entertain my brother officers as First Sea Lord, I asked for my pay, as a special case personal to me, to be made up to £3,400 a year on account of my giving up an appointment of £4,000 a year to suit them. Of course, I told the King I complied with his wishes as to the A.D.C. I feel just a bit bitter at not having it ; however, it was not for me to argue the point.

And again a fortnight later :

25th September, 1904.

Don't you go fussing, please, about my £800 a year, because if it takes all this worry to get it I would rather go without. The King told Selborne straight I would save them millions and they haggled at giving me a few hundreds, and " Behold ! this is in the House of Friends " (see the prophet Jeremiah on this topic !).

The Prime Minister, the Chancellor of the Exchequer, and the First Lord of the Admiralty, all swearing eternal friendship to me and see me d——d before they give me a shilling ; and bring me up from the plum of the Service at Portsmouth to penal servitude at the Admiralty, to suit their convenience, on half the pay and double the work ; such is life, but please don't you worry.

This grumbling over money was annoying to Fisher,

[*By kind permission of " The Daily Mirror"*

THE ANNIVERSARY OF TRAFALGAR

NELSON (*in Trafalgar Square*) :—" I was on my way down to lend them a hand myself, but if Jacky Fisher's taking on the job there's no need for me to be nervous. I'll get back on my pedestal."

Nelson looking up Sir John Fisher on his first day as First Sea Lord, Trafalgar Day, 1904.

especially as he had in his pocket an offer of a post in a private firm with a salary of £10,000 a year.

Admiral Sir Henry Stephenson, who was then Principal A.D.C., was appointed Black Rod, and Fisher succeeded him.

On the 4th October, 1904, he wrote :

> You will have heard from Knollys that I have got the A.D.C., and it all puzzles me beyond comprehension.

In January 1905 Fisher wrote :

> We have got a crisis on with the Cabinet, and we are to meet them at 3.30 to-day. I hope my two colleagues will stand firm. They are both a little wobbly, but keep this private.
> P.S.—I only just had time to dress for dinner. We had a most protracted meeting with Arnold Forster and Balfour's private secretary on the crisis.

Matters did not run very smoothly between the Admiralty and the Cabinet over Estimates and Reforms. Fisher was not satisfied with the treatment meted out to him by the Conservative Government, and on the 3rd March he sent the King a copy of a letter he proposed to send to Mr. Balfour tendering his resignation ; adding that he was going to be head of a shipbuilding firm, with £10,000 a year and practically a dictatorship. In the end he remained, and the following month the King added his name to the list of those who were to receive the Order of Merit.

The King's unvarying support was of the utmost value to the country, and an enormous help to Fisher, in carrying through all the schemes for the reorganization of the Navy.

No Life of Sir John Fisher would be complete without some mention of the influence of King Edward on his career. Fisher venerated the King, who, in turn, believed in, and had a great regard for, Fisher. The latter, in his book *Memories*, remarks :

> Without doubt I personally could not be of the very least service to him in any way, and yet in his belief in my being right in the vast and drastic reforms in the Navy, he gave me his unfaltering support right through unswervingly, though every sycophantic effort was exhausted in the endeavour to alienate him from his support of me. He quite enjoyed the numberless communications he got, and the more outrageous the calumnies the more he revelled in my reputed wickedness! I can't very well put some of them on paper, but the Minotaur wasn't in it with me.

Fisher's frank buoyant nature appealed to the King ; on informal occasions at Court he managed, in the evenings, to start a dance and enliven things up. Once at a very dull lunch party Fisher, who was sitting next to the King, said : " Pretty dull this, Sir. Hadn't I better give them a song ? " The King was delighted, so Fisher rose and gave a recitation.

In his *Memories* and *Records* Lord Fisher has given many stories of King Edward. There are three that are personal to Fisher, and deserve to be recorded. At big functions the King used often to say to Fisher, who was Principal Naval A.D.C., " Have I missed out anyone, do you think ? " for he was most careful to speak to all deserving notice. Fisher describes what happened thus :

> On one occasion a certain Admiral approached—perhaps the biggest ass I ever met. The King shook hands with him and said something I thought quite unnecessarily loving to him ; when he had gone, he turned on me like a tiger and said, " You ought to be ashamed of yourself ! " I humbly said, " What for ? " " Why," he replied, " when that man came up to me, your face was perfectly demoniacal ! Everyone saw it ! and the poor fellow couldn't kick you back ! You're First Sea Lord and he is a ruined man ! You've no business to show your hate."

And then Fisher remarks :

" The lovely thing was that a man came up I knew the King
did perfectly hate, and I'm blessed if he didn't smile on him and
cuddle him as if he was his long-lost brother : and then he
turned to me afterwards and said with joyful revenge, ' *Well ! Did
you see that ?* ' Isn't that a Great Heart ? and is it to be
wondered at that he was so popular ? "

On another occasion the King went to lunch at
Marienbad with some great people who were there
who had invited His Majesty to meet some of the
King's friends from Carlsbad, where Fisher was stay-
ing. Fisher was not asked—it was an arranged snub.
Fisher described the scene :

" The King came in and said, ' How d'ye do ? ' all round, and
then said to the host, ' Where's the Admiral ? ' My absence was
apologized for—lunch was ready and announced. The King said,
' Excuse me a moment, I must write him a letter to say how sorry
I am for the oversight ' ; so he left them stewing in their own
juice, and His Majesty's letter to me was lovely—I've kept that
one. He began by d——ing the pen and then the blotting-paper !
—there were big blots and smudges ! He came back and gave the
letter to my friend and said, " See he gets it directly you get back
to Carlsbad to-night."

On one occasion the King found fault with Fisher
for having one idea only at a time, and told him it
would be his ruin. Fisher promptly replied, " Anyhow, I am stopping with you at Balmoral, and I
never expected that when I entered the Navy penniless, friendless, and forlorn."

The last anecdote is best told in Fisher's own
language :

On another occasion I went down to Sandringham with a great
party ; I think it was for one of Blessed Queen Alexandra's birth-
days. (I hope Her Majesty will forgive me telling a lovely story

presently about herself.) As I was zero in this grand party, I slunk off to my room to write an important letter, then took off my coat, got out my keys, unlocked my portmanteau, and began unpacking. I had a boot in each hand ; I heard somebody fumbling with the door-handle ; and, thinking it was the footman whom Hawkins had allocated to me, I said, " Come in ; don't go humbugging with that door-handle ! " and in walked King Edward, with a cigar about a yard long in his mouth. He said (I with a boot in each hand), " What on earth are you doing ? " " Unpacking, Sir." " Where's your servant ? " " Haven't got one, Sir." " Where is he ? " " Never had one, Sir ; couldn't afford it." " Put those boots down and sit in that armchair." And he went and sat in the other on the other side of the fire. I thought to myself, " This is a rum state of affairs. Here's the King of England sitting in my bedroom on one side of the fire, and I'm in my shirt-sleeves sitting in an armchair on the other side ! "

" Well," said His Majesty, " why didn't you come and say ' How do you do ? ' when you arrived ? " I said, " I had a letter to write, and with so many great people you were receiving I thought I had better come to my room." Then he went on with a long conversation, until it was only about a quarter of an hour from dinner time, and I hadn't unpacked. So I said to the King, " Sir, you'll be angry if I'm late for dinner, and no doubt your Majesty has two or three gentlemen to dress you, but I have no one." And he gave me a sweet smile and went off.

This is the story about Queen Alexandra mentioned above :

My beloved friend Soveral, one of King Edward's treasured friends, asked me to lunch on Queen Alexandra's sixtieth birthday. After lunch, all the people said something nice to Queen Alexandra, and it came to my turn. I said to Her Majesty, " Have you seen that halfpenny newspaper about your Majesty's birthday ? " She said she hadn't, what was it ? I said these were the words :

> ' The Queen is sixty to-day !
> May she live till she looks it ! "

Her Majesty said, " Get me a copy of it." (Such a thing didn't exist.) About three weeks afterwards she said, " Where's that

halfpenny newspaper ? " I was staggered for a moment, but
recovered myself and said, " Sold out, Ma'am ; couldn't get a
copy ! " (I think my second lie was better than my first.)

This account of the Spanish visit is too good to be omitted :

I went with King Edward to Cartagena when he returned the King of Spain's visit. King Alfonso, whom I had previously met in England, was very cordial to me, because we had seven " Dread-noughts " ready before the Germans had one. In fact, when I told him this piece of news, as we were walking up and down the deck, with King Edward and Queen Alexandra watching us from two deck-chairs, King Alfonso was so delighted that he threw his arms round my neck, cried, " You darling ! " and kissed me. Then he put his hand in his waistcoat-pocket, took out a chocolate, and popped it into my mouth.

The banquet was a very fine sight, as King Alfonso had brought down the tapestries, pictures, and other ornaments from the Escurial. The Spanish Admirals were a grand sight. They wore the ancient uniform, and each had a great Malacca cane with a big gold top. They all came on board to call on King Edward in an old-fashioned pulling barge, and the sailors wore crimson and gold sashes.

That rowing barge and its splendid uniforms lay at the root of one occasion when King Edward was really angry with me. I had been arranging for him the details of the Great Naval Review and was summoned to Buckingham Palace to discuss them with him. I found no Equerries in attendance, no one about and the King white with anger. " So ! " he cried out to me, " I'm to go by such and such a train, am I ? And I'm to embark at such and such a time, am I ? And I'm to use your barge because it's a better barge than mine, is it ? Look here, *Am I the King, or are you ?* " The upshot of the interview was that he threw the papers on the floor with, " Have it your own way." But the secret cause of his anger was that he had made up his mind to go off in a rowing-boat like the Spanish Admirals, forgetting that there is no tide at Cartagena, whereas the tide at Cowes runs many knots, and it would have taken a rowing boat hours to do what the barge could do in a few minutes.

Fisher's period of service as First Sea Lord saw the centre of gravity of the war cloud which hung over Europe shift from France and Russia to Germany. It saw a mutually defensive *entente* created between ourselves, France, and Russia for protection from Germany. It saw the rise and expansion of the Navy of that country. Some modern historians have connected the design of the *Dreadnought* with the menace of Germany to the peace of Europe. This was not so. The mistake was to a certain extent due to the fact that the Admiralty never published reasons for the design of the *Dreadnought*, as by so doing they would have given most valuable information to Germany. As a matter of fact, when that epoch-making ship was designed in the middle of 1904, war between Great Britain and France and Russia was still a possibility. It is true that King Edward's visit to Paris, and the return visit of President Loubet to London in 1903, had started an *entente* between the two nations, but we had had French *ententes* before which had ended in nothing. Germany, indeed, had acted in a nasty manner at the time of the Kruger telegram ; but the way that she had then hung back, when unable to marshal a European League against us, went a long way to confirm the view that she would not risk losing her colonies and merchant shipping in a war with us, unless she was backed up by one or more of the Continental maritime nations.

It is as well to repeat once more that the *armament* of the *Dreadnought* was fixed solely by gunnery considerations, which were novel, and due to the great increase in battle ranges. The *speed* of the *Dreadnought* was fixed by strategical considerations (being able to overtake an enemy and bring him to action), and tactical considerations (such as having the power of choosing the range in an action). The *tonnage* of the *Dreadnought* was fixed by the above two requirements.

War in general, not war against any nation in particular, and least of all against Germany, was in mind when the design was prepared at Portsmouth in 1904.[1]

It is true that Fisher subsequently pointed out the advantage that had accrued to this country by making Germany spend £12,000,000 on deepening and widening the Kiel Canal, and by postponing any war until this had been done ; but these results were certainly not thought of at the time the *Dreadnought* was designed. During 1905 and 1906, however, attention became more and more riveted on Germany, and as our relations with France became more intimate those with Germany became more and more strained.

Fisher records that—

In 1906, at Madeira, the Germans first took an hotel ; then they wanted a Convalescent Home and, finally, they put forth the desire to establish certain vested interests. They imperiously demanded certain concessions from Portugal. The most significant of these amounted to a coaling-station, isolated and fortified. The German Ambassador at Lisbon called on the Portuguese Prime Minister at 10 o'clock one Saturday night and said that if he did not get his answer by 10 o'clock the next night he should leave. The Portuguese sent us a telegram. That night we ordered the British Fleet to move. The next morning the German Ambassador told the Portuguese Prime Minister that he had made a mistake in the cipher, and he was awfully sorry, but he wasn't going ; it was all his fault, he said, and he had been reprimanded

[1] I can personally vouch for this because Mr. Gard, Mr. Alexander Gracie, and myself—probably Fisher consulted others also—worked at the design ; and except for having turbines instead of reciprocating machinery, the *Dreadnought* sketch design in all its essential particulars was finished in the middle of 1904.—EDITOR.

by his Government. (As if any German had ever yet made a mistake with a telegram !)

Lord Esher in a letter to Fisher relates the Kaiser's view of Fisher :

In January 1906 King Edward sent me to see Mr. Beit, who had been recently received by the German Emperor at Potsdam. The Emperor said to Beit that " England wanted war : not the King—nor perhaps the Government ; but influential people like Sir John Fisher ! " He said Fisher held that, because the British Fleet was in perfect order and the German Fleet was not ready, England should provoke war. Beit said he had met Fisher at Carlsbad, and had had long talks with him, and that what he had said to him did not at all convey the impression gathered by His Imperial Majesty. The Emperor replied, " He thinks it is the hour for attack, and I am not blaming him. I quite understand his point of view ; but we too are prepared, and if it comes to war the result will depend upon the weight you carry into action —namely, a good conscience, and I have that. Fisher can no doubt land 100,000 men in Schleswig-Holstein—it would not be difficult—and the British Navy has reconnoitred the coast of Denmark with this object during the cruise of the Fleet. But Fisher forgets that it will be for me to deal with the 100,000 men when they are landed ! "

Another account given by Mr. Beit on his arrival in England agrees in substance with the above. In it the German Emperor is recorded as saying :

I admire Fisher, I say nothing against him. If I were in his place I should do all that he has done [in concentrating the British Navy against Germany], and I should do all that I know he has in his mind to do. Isvolsky, the Russian Minister of Foreign Affairs, holds the same opinion.[1]

[1] Fisher added a memorandum to this : " And yet Mr. Leo Maxse gibbets Sir John Fisher every month in the *National Review* as a traitor to his country and a panderer to Germany who ought to be hanged at his own yardarm ; and Colonel A'Court Repington, the Military Correspondent, who, as Sir George Clarke writes a fortnight ago, having fought on one side now fights on the other, is now the chosen apostle lying on Mr. Leo Maxse's bosom in this month's *National Review* ! What a queer world we live in ! "

Fisher always disagreed with the suggestion that the German Emperor, in this interview of 1906 with Beit, had referred to his idea of " Copenhagening " the German Fleet. Landing men on the Pomeranian coast was a very different matter from an attack on Kiel Harbour. He did not mention the subject of " Copenhagening " to King Edward for a year after the above letter had been written.

King Edward in 1908 visited Kiel and took with him Sir John Fisher, Sir John French, Sir Charles Hardinge, and Sir Arthur Nicolson, our Ambassador at St. Petersburg. They then went on to Reval, where the King made the Czar an Admiral in our Fleet and the Czar returned the compliment by making King Edward an Admiral in the Russian Fleet. The British Government did not relish this, and always believed that it was owing to Fisher that this came about. At all events, Fisher was very pleased, for undoubtedly it sealed our *rapprochement* with Russia. He remarked when these little courtesies were over, " It's a jolly good thing to have a King who knows how to act, as Cabinet Ministers seem to me to be always like a lot of frightened rabbits."

About this time a pernicious League, called the Imperial Maritime League, was started, which had for its main avowed intention that of hounding Fisher out of the Admiralty. The secretaries had the impudence to write to some of Fisher's personal friends asking them to join the League. Among these was Lord Esher. Needless to say, they received back a most polite, well-reasoned, but at the same time outspoken reply, which was most damning in its directness to the League and all concerned with it. In this reply there was a paragraph pointing out that

Fisher was the most dreaded man in Germany, and feared by all, from the Emperor downwards. A copy came into the Emperor's possession, and the assertion annoyed him so much that he wrote to Lord Tweedmouth, then First Lord, a letter commenting on Lord Esher in an uncomplimentary manner. Lord Tweedmouth, who was not in the best of health, handled the matter badly ; and, as is always the case in England, the opposing political party tried to make all the capital they could out of the incident. They held up their hands in simulated horror at the thought that a Minister of the Crown should correspond directly with the German Emperor, despite the fact that the correspondence, so far, had been all on one side. However, to smooth things over, Lord Tweedmouth was sacrificed, and left the Admiralty ; and Mr. M'Kenna was appointed in his stead. The annoyance of the Emperor emphasized the fact that Fisher was in reality the man whom the Germans did fear.

From the following letter it appears that Admiral von Tirpitz made a crafty attempt to get Fisher to agree to limit the size of ships and guns :

21st February, 1908.

Tirpitz asked a mutual civilian friend living in Berlin to inquire very privately of me whether I would agree to limiting size of guns and size of ships, as this is *vital* to the Germans, *who can't go* bigger than the *Dreadnought* in guns or size. I wrote back by return of post yesterday morning, " Tell him I'll see him d——d first " (them's the very words).

I wonder what Wilhelm will say to that if Tirpitz shows him the letter.

In the spring of the same year Fisher confided to the King in a personal interview his opinion that the German Fleet should be " Copenhagened," by which he meant sunk inside Kiel, or, as he picturesquely described it, treated like rogue elephants and, with tame females in the shape of our battleships on each side, hustled out of that harbour as prisoners. The King's comment was, " Fisher, you're mad." Well, so it seemed, but the matter cannot be dismissed in quite so simple a manner.

Fisher, who was always looking ahead, foresaw that when the German programme of shipbuilding, whereby they hoped to rival our Fleet, was completed, the German Government would declare war on us. He even fixed the exact date to almost within one month. September or October 1914 was his forecast. This was made almost entirely from a consideration of the date on which the alterations to the Kiel Canal would be finished, and the German harvest got in. In his opinion, the only way of stopping the advance in German naval armaments was to seize their Fleet. In fact, to repeat what had happened in 1801 when Nelson attacked the Danish Fleet at Copenhagen and broke up the Northern Confederation. The main difference between the Danish operation and that proposed by Fisher was that in 1801 we were at war with Denmark ; or, at least, she had entered a confederation inimical to us, and our Fleet had actually been fired on by Fort Kronenburg, whereas in 1908 we were at peace with Germany.

Fisher, however, had taken a wide survey of recent events. He fully recognized that the moment an occasion arose which was favourable to Germany, when she should find us either diplomatically, or, for any other reason, at a disadvantage, she would not have the slightest difficulty in discovering a pretext to declare war. The time between the declaration and the first blow might be the matter of only an hour. " Why," asked Fisher, " should we wait for Germany to have the advantage of choosing her own moment for attack ? Why not ourselves find the pretext and attack her ? " Of course, as the King said, it was a mad idea—quite against our national way of doing things. The country would have been split into two camps, one half opportunists, the other half pacifists. We are a nation with a strict code of morals whereby we regulate our foreign policy. We prefer to hold out our cheek and be smitten first ; and, in the long run, apparently it pays to do so. Fisher's ardent and practical temperament looked on such quixotism as imbecility. Hence, judged by our own standards, he was mad ; but judged by the standards of our assured enemy he was perfectly sane ; and he might even, by them, have been credited with genius, which, as the poet tells us, is near allied to madness !

He was, in fact, only echoing what Lord Bacon wrote :

Neither is the opinion of some Schoolemen to be received That a Warre cannot justly be made, but on a precedent injury or provocation. For ther is no Question, but a just Feare of an Imminent danger, though there be no Blow given, is a lawful cause of a Warre.

Fisher contented himself by grumbling that " we had neither a Pitt nor a Bismarck to give the order," and remarking, apropos of conditions in the North Sea, with the two Navies *vis-à-vis*, that " if Eve had not continually had her eye on that apple we should not now be wearing clothes."

The sequel to the " Tweedmouth " episode was rather amusing. The Kaiser minuted the report,

which Count Metternich had sent him, detailing the
English side of the incident, as follows :

> For all this it is not our Fleet that is responsible, but the abso-
> lutely crazy " Dreadnought " policy of Sir John Fisher and His
> Majesty, who believed that they could thereby place us *en demeure*.
> Now they and the deluded Britons see that they have been totally
> mistaken, and that thereby they have destroyed their old great
> past superiority, as all the States imitate them. That has made
> Britons nervous, as they have only just realized it. They will
> just have to get used to our Fleet, and from time to time we must
> assure them that it is not against them.

This shows that the Kaiser did not appreciate the
true inwardness of the *Dreadnought* design, nor did he,
at the moment, realize how, by the method of its
introduction, Fisher had manœuvred to keep our
construction well ahead of that of Germany.

The political agitation over the " Tweedmouth "
letter had rather excited public opinion in England.
Sir Edward Grey asked Count Metternich what he
thought the Kaiser would have said if King Edward
had written a private letter to von Tirpitz about the
German naval programme. The Count looked grimly
down his nose and said nothing.

Fisher was in no way taken in by Count Metternich's
protestations that the complete German naval programme was in reality the only one that had been
published ; and asked if our Naval Attaché might
visit the German yards, and so set all doubts at rest.
The Count replied that that was impossible, for other
countries would want similar privileges, and he added,
" Besides, he would see something we did not want
him to." This, naturally, made Fisher think that they
were also increasing the size of their ships, so he took
measures accordingly.

On 30th August, 1908, after quoting eulogistic re-marks by French Ministers on our Navy, Fisher wrote :

How true what you once wrote to me long ago, that one has to go to France or Germany to realize what Mahan so trenchantly writes, that 86 per cent. of the British guns are trained on Germany. But, "lest I should be exalted above measure through the abundance of these revelations, there has been vouchsafed to me a thorn in the flesh in the shape of Beresford."

N.B.—I've corrected the above words, as you will see by refer-ring to the 12th chapter of the second book of Corinthians and the 7th verse.

In the autumn he went abroad, and from there wrote to Lord Esher the following letter. He was recalled to England by the King, who feared the harm his enemies were doing him.

8th September, 1908.

It's the plain truth that I have been intending to write to you for ten days. But brilliant weather, heavenly air, and 70 degs. in the shade by the side of a rushing snow-river have continued to part me from you. But I now return to you. "The heart untravelled fondly turns to home." We have no poets nowadays like Pope, Goldsmith, and Gay, only damned mystical idiots like Browning and Tennyson that want a dictionary and a differential-calculus sort of mind to understand what they are driving at. . . .

A strange thing ! I sat several times between Stolypin, the Russian Prime Minister, and Isvolsky. I didn't begin it, but Stolypin said to me, " What do you think we want most ? " He fancied I should answer, " So many battleships, so many cruisers," etc. ; but instead I said, " Your Western Frontier is denuded of troops and your magazines are depleted—fill them up, and then talk of Fleets."

Please see enclosed from Kuropatkin's secret report. " *The foundation of Russia's safety is her Western boundary.*" Have you seen M. Rousseau (I think is his name) in *Le Temps* ? I had an extract of it and put it aside to send to you, but, alas ! it has gone. " Procrastination is the thief of good intentions," which is not so good as " Punctuality is the curse of comfort " ; but the good Frenchman (like M. Hanotaux before him) is lost in admiration of what moved Mahan to his pungent saying, that Garvin seized on with the inspiration of genius, " That 86 per cent. of the English guns were trained on Germany." . . .

I can't write any more ; the sun is shining too brightly and I must go out in it. The King, with his usual kind thought, has asked me to stay at Balmoral, where I arrive (D.V.) on 3rd October. (How good that Scotch story about the coach running D.V. on Tuesdays and Thursdays and on Saturdays *whether or no !*)

P.S.—I've got Sir Philip Watts into a new *Indomitable* that will make your mouth water when you see it, and the Germans gnash their teeth.

On his return he wrote the following letter to Mr. Arnold White, enclosing a copy of what he had written to M. Isvolsky. What a great pity it is that his far-sighted views regarding Turkey and Russia were not made the pivot of our European diplomacy !

November, 1908.

Private and secret.

You will see by the enclosed bit of paper that you were in my mind long ago. The King sent for me to stay with him and " docked " my holidays a fortnight, as H.M. said " the mice were beginning to play while the cat was away," and, My Dear Friend, the reason that I am writing on this paper is sentiment ! I went straight through from the Tyrol to Balmoral. H.M. was right, but I need not trouble you with that story. What will interest you is Kuropatkin's Pyramid, which I enclose because of its bearing on the interview I had with Stolypin, the Russian Premier, at Riga (we made a close friendship), and he asked me about the resuscitation of the Russian Navy, and my immediate reply to him (being in entire ignorance then of Kuropatkin's suppressed *Memoirs*) was, " Resuscitate your Western frontier ; the garrisons are depleted—and the store-houses are empty." He looked hard at me and said not another word. I felt I had got home ! When Isvolsky came here recently, I (being a mere nobody) was astounded at his confidence and astounding confessions to me, and Benckendorff, the Ambassador, took me to the door of my carriage. As they were so free with me I was equally free with them—*vide* my letter —but I felt I was writing to Stolypin, as Isvolsky was only a frightened rabbit. Stolypin was the man—a Gladstone in his courage. Perhaps some day you will come and see me at 6 p.m.

after 9th November, as most convenient to you, to talk of other things. I am getting sick, and meditating a sudden and unexpected departure *à la* Elijah ; but I am not going to jeopardize. I shall look out to have Elisha standing right under, so that the mantle shall not miss ! All this deadly private, but I am really getting wearied out with all the flabby " blue funkers " all round me—who parley with mutiny and don't see that the great swelling pride of the masses will come in with a roar for an irresistible Navy and territorial Army, and all the rest d——d rot ! Two wise men, the old Sultan and the Austrian Emperor, said in December 1899 that the British Fleet was the only, sole preventative at that date of a big European war.

This was Fisher's letter to M. Isvolsky :

15th October, 1908.

You were very kind to me last night in your frankness, and I feel impelled to put my humble views on paper for your favourable consideration. I think you are assured that I have been a consistent advocate of England's utmost friendship with Russia. Since I came to Admiralty as First Sea Lord just four years ago I have always maintained, from a sailor's point of view for fighting purposes, that what we wanted was a quadruple alliance, Russia, England, France, and Turkey ; and each of the four Powers would benefit. Each gains. I need not give you the reasons ; they are so obvious. I urged all this in October 1904, when it was very unpopular to do so ; but, thank Heaven, it is all coming round to the blessed confirmation.

I was equally opposed to the Japanese Alliance, and still am. The very worst thing that England ever did for herself. You can also see that this was not a popular thing for me to advocate, but again, thank Heaven, it is gradually dawning on the English mind that we were wrong. The reasons for this, also, are too obvious to need to be told to you. I am only speaking from the fighting point of view.

Now I come to this point. The biggest mistake possible just now would be for either Russia or England to alienate or weaken the Turks. If they both get nothing whatever out of the Turks, then Russia would be as much in favour with Turkey as England just now. Again, if a word were now spoken about the Dardanelles, there would be a great agitation in England. Wait some little time, and then let Russia make her own private arrangements

THE FIRST SEA LORD
By William Nicholson

with a grateful Turkey, and you may rest quite sure that England
won't then object, for the simple reason that anything that will
bind Russia, England, and Turkey together is to England's advantage and far outweighs any objections to what Russia naturally
and rightly wishes in regard to the Dardanelles.

I fear you will think it very presumptuous of me to write all
this, but I am certain that English opinion is not ripe just yet to
say anything about the Dardanelles, and it would alienate the
Turks and allow other people to come into the discussion, whereas,
later on, it can be done between Russia and Turkey.

On 26th June, 1904, your General Kuropatkin wrote " that the
foundation of Russia's safety is her western boundary." It's
the same menace that Russia has to fear in the Anatolian Railway,
and the absolute certainty that the Heir to the Austrian throne
will work fully and absolutely with the German Emperor.

The Quadruple Alliance of Russia, England, France, and Turkey
is an obvious necessity for all four Powers. I only write as a
sailor from the fighting point of view and as an onlooker, and I
hope you will forgive my presumption in writing to you ; but I
happen to know the Grand Vizier (Kiamil Pasha), and years ago
we talked all this over when I was Admiral in the Mediterranean and
he was the Vali of Smyrna, dreaded by the Sultan but worshipped
by his countrymen. Please consider this strictly private and only
written with a desire to be of service, and please don't trouble to
answer.

Ever yours truly.

During the " Morocco " crisis, when Germany
" rattled the sabre " and created a war scare which
fizzled out at the Morocco Conference, Fisher and Sir
Arthur Wilson, who had commanded our Fleet, arranged
a plan of campaign which has never been divulged, and
probably never will be. But not improbably it was
a descent on Kiel Harbour. However, this is only
guess-work. Fisher and Wilson both were determined
not to reveal their plan to anyone. Fisher wrote :

17th January, 1909.

I rather want to keep clear of Defence Committee till Morocco
is settled, as I don't want to disclose my plan of campaign to

II—6

anyone, not even C. B. [Charles Beresford] himself. I haven't even told Ottley, and don't mean to. The only man who knows is Wilson, and he is as close as wax. The whole success will depend on *suddenness and unexpectedness*, and the moment I tell anyone there is an end to both.

The Army is too big for a little war and too little for a big war.

At every point the Germans found themselves check-mated by Fisher. The *Dreadnought* and the " Dread-nought " cruisers had been introduced with a sufficient start to defy their number being overtaken, and by Fisher's skilful strategy, in spite of incurring the most vehement opposition, the distribution of the Fleet had been gradually altered so that one morning the Germans awoke to the fact that 86 per cent. of the guns of the British Navy were trained in their direc-tion.

The German Emperor's optimism about being able to overtake us in battleship strength was to receive yet another rude shock. In 1909 it was decided to arm our large ships with a 13·5-inch gun instead of the 12-inch, which hitherto had been the main arma-ment of the " Dreadnoughts." This again has been held out as evidence of megalomania on Fisher's part. It was nothing of the sort, for the main reason that induced us to install the larger gun was the necessity of getting *increased accuracy of hitting*. This was, surely, a laudable object ; but, as usual, the reason for this change was not appreciated, or even known, by those who condemned it most loudly.

Everyone knows that if a rifle bullet and a 12-inch shell are fired with the same velocity, the 12-inch shot will go much farther than the bullet. The same applies throughout all sizes of shot ; the larger the diameter the farther that shot will travel for the same original velocity. Now, the 12-inch gun of the "St. Vincent" class of "Dreadnoughts" was a poor gun so far as accuracy was concerned. Each successive shell, as it fell at a range of 10,000 yards, instead of falling in an area of, say, one acre, fell in an area of two or three acres. This was because the velocity at which the shell was ejected from the gun was too high ; this caused unsteadiness in the projectile at the muzzle, it wobbled, and the shooting became inaccurate. It was possible with the 13·5-inch gun to reduce this muzzle velocity, as it was called, reduce the wobble, and so get accurate repetition at every discharge ; and (owing to the fact that the larger shell kept up its velocity better than the lighter one) still to ensure that the 13·5-inch projectile would have the same velocity as the 12-inch at battle ranges. Thus the disturbing elements due to high muzzle velocity were eliminated ; and no loss of velocity was incurred at the important place, namely, the enemy's ship. It was therefore not megalomania, but common sense, that led to the introduction of the larger gun. Incidentally, the larger shell held a bigger bursting charge, and for this reason greater damage would be inflicted on the enemy's ship. This was a secondary and not the main reason for the introduction of the larger gun. The new armament entailed an increase only of about 1,300 tons in the ship.

At this time also the torpedo was increased in size from 18 inches to 21 inches in diameter. This also was absolutely essential. The mechanical details of the Whitehead torpedo were developing by leaps and bounds, battle ranges were increasing year by year, and the range of the torpedo had to increase to follow suit. No King Canute in any single country can dare to attempt to arrest progress in armaments. Only international agreement can do this, and that, Heaven knows! is difficult enough to bring about. For any man deliberately to adopt the second best is to act traitorously, and it would have been sheer lunacy in 1908 for Fisher to falter, when he felt convinced that it was practically certain that war would be forced on us in 1914.

The chief matter which engaged the attention of the Committee of Imperial Defence, especially during the latter part of this period, was the question of invasion. Field-Marshal Lord Roberts, during the last few years of his very active life, threw the whole of his remaining energy into this subject. He started rifle ranges and generally awoke, once again, some vestige of martial feeling in the villages and towns. This was all to the good. He based most of his propaganda on the probability of our country being invaded by the Germans; this again was innocuous until the question of an increase in the Army at the expense of the Navy was proposed. This was a matter in which Fisher was obliged to intervene. The invasion prophets based their creed on the assumption of " a bolt from the blue," in other words, a *sudden* landing of a force large enough to do material harm to the country. Lord Roberts, aided by Colonel Repington, held forth at the Committee of Imperial Defence; newspapers were mobilized, and all the machinery of a campaign started. The whole scare was an absurdity; and is one of the very best examples of the want of clear thinking on naval subjects on the part of those without practical sea-knowledge. " What can be easier," shouted the " bolt - from - the - blue " campaigners, " than to put sixty thousand men on to ships, rush them across the North Sea, either in a fog or when the Fleet is away at manœuvres, and throw them ashore ? In forty-eight hours, before the War Office could bring a sufficiency of troops to bear, incalculable damage will have been done," etc.

The answer of the Admiralty was a simple, plain, straightforward denial of the possibility of putting 60,000 men on to ships without our having ample warning. The armada required to carry troops to this number, and their impedimenta, was so great that, even after months of secret preparation, several days would be necessary to effect the actual embarkation, during which time this large number of ships would have to be withdrawn from their commercial work, which fact could not fail to be noticed. Men-of-war, even on emergency, are bad troop carriers. The whole proposition, from a practical seafaring point of view, was an absurdity. Nevertheless, the campaign received support ; the naval opponents were dubbed the " Blue-water School," and the Press adherents of the latter styled the soldiers the " Blue-funk School." Thus the matter dragged on, and even after the scare had been for the time killed and buried, it was subsequently resurrected after Fisher had left the Admiralty.

The most important naval question that came forward for discussion in 1909 was the number of capital ships that should be laid down in the following year.

The " Cawdor " programme, approved by the Unionist Government, had allowed for four capital ships being laid down annually, and in compliance with this programme three battleships and three " Dreadnought " cruisers had been launched in 1907.

It will be simpler to deal with launching dates than
with the somewhat uncertain dates of so-called " laying down."

The Liberal Government, in 1906, had questioned
the necessity for starting three battleships that year ;
and the Admiralty were unable, on actual figures, to
defend the demand for so many. The position then
was, that in 1909 there would be in commission four
British " Dreadnought " battleships and three cruisers,
while Germany would have only one battleship. The
Cabinet therefore decided that it would suffice if two
battleships were laid down that year, and no cruisers.

After the resignation of Sir H. Campbell-Bannerman,
Mr. Asquith became Prime Minister, Mr. Lloyd George
Chancellor of the Exchequer, and Mr. Churchill was
admitted into the Cabinet. The two last and Mr. Lulu
Harcourt banded together to carry out social reforms
and to reduce armaments ; for, being novices in international politics, they had persuaded themselves that
the German Emperor's assurances regarding his Fleet
were sincere.

When the programme for 1908 came under discussion, a still further cut in the " Cawdor " programme
was proposed ; and again the Admiralty, *on figures,*
could not object. The forecast showed that in 1910
we should have seven battleships and four cruisers
completed, while Germany could have only three
battleships and one cruiser. It was quite useless to
try to fight the Cabinet in the face of such figures ;
but, nevertheless, the Sea Lords sent a written remon-
strance to the First Lord.[1] The memorandum, dated
3rd December, 1907, had been signed by the four
Sea Lords. The following extract clearly shows that

Lord Tweedmouth.

even at that time they were anxious about the possi-
bility of accelerated German shipbuilding, and later their anxiety was proved to be fully justified :

We therefore consider it of the utmost importance that power be taken to lay down two more armoured ships in 1909–10, making eight in all, as unless there is an unexpected modification in Germany's anticipated shipbuilding programme, resulting in her not completing seventeen ships by the spring of 1912, it will be necessary to provide eight new British ships to be completed by this date, the last two being laid down at the end of March 1910.

In the autumn of 1908, however, the Admiralty became thoroughly alarmed. Evidence was forthcoming from several sources that, in the face of our limited building programmes, Germany was meditating a great effort to equal our " Dreadnought " Fleet. It was quite clear that, unless our building was accelerated, in four years' time we should have exactly the same number of battleships that Germany could put into commission.

From a detailed comparison of the German Estimates with the returns of actual expenditure, Mr. M'Kenna, then First Lord of the Admiralty, arrived at the conclusion that either Germany was laying down more ships than those given in the yearly programme or she was greatly accelerating the rate of construction of the ships authorized. Information was also obtained that Messrs. Krupp, although bound by an international agreement among steel manufacturers to buy nickel only through the Nickel Syndicate, had placed orders for some three thousand tons of nickel through another channel. This showed conclusively that they wished this extra purchase to be kept secret ; and, further, that they were contemplating very extensive increase in gun and armour manufacture ; for, at that time, the chief use of nickel was in connection with those two naval armament materials. Information was also obtained from the Naval Attachés of more than one foreign country that more ships were actually being laid down than Germany officially acknowledged.

In a memorandum presented by the First Sea Lord to the First Lord early in 1909, the situation as viewed at the time is clearly set forth. It stated :

> We concur in the *statement* of the First Lord that there is a *possibility* that Germany by the spring of 1912 will have completed twenty-one " Dreadnoughts " (including large " Dreadnought " cruisers) ; and that there is a *practical certainty* that she will have seventeen by that date ; whereas, presuming we lay down six during the coming year, we shall have only eighteen. [It is interesting, in this connection, to note that *in 1913* Germany had in commission exactly the number forecasted, namely, seventeen.]

The memorandum also went on to state :

> The question might be asked why warning was not given at an earlier date, but the information about the ante-dating of the laying down and completion of the German ships of the 1909–10 programme, and the further evidence pointing to a continuous acceleration of shipbuilding in subsequent years, was not known until quite recently.

The battle for this large programme was then fought out in the Cabinet, and here Mr. M'Kenna at first stood practically alone. Mr. Churchill opposed him vehemently, disputing the figures and treating the Admiralty arguments as mere figments of an alarmist brain. The Chancellor of the Exchequer, naturally, was opposed to the additional expenditure, while the Secretary of State for War was anxious to obtain funds for his new Territorial Scheme and joined

the opposition. No member of the Cabinet was convinced of the necessity for the ships. It was Mr.
Churchill, however, who took the leading part in
opposing the Admiralty proposal, and he gave no
thought to the certainty that, if his views were wrong
and the figures quoted by the Admiralty were right,
as in fact they were, the Empire would be placed in a
position of grave peril.

The actual end of the battle was most dramatic.
Fisher had been informed by Mr. M'Kenna that he
believed his resignation was inevitable, and in confirmation of this forecast Mr. Churchill and his adherents
gained the day at what was understood to be the final
discussion in the Cabinet. The fight seemed over when
a new and powerful ally appeared on the scene. On
being told of Mr. M'Kenna's resignation, Sir Edward
Grey realized at once that the matter must be of
more urgent import than the Cabinet had recognized.
He examined again closely the Admiralty statements,
and having done so, requested a reconsideration of the
case. The Prime Minister accordingly called another
meeting of the Cabinet, and as he, in turn, had now
been convinced by Sir Edward Grey, the Admiralty
programme, with some immaterial provisos, was
accepted in its entirety. The provisos were introduced in deference to the Ministers whose hostility
to the Admiralty programme had been publicly
declared, and gave rise to the slogan, " We want eight,
and we won't wait," which for some months resounded
in the House of Commons.

Had Mr. M'Kenna's resignation taken effect the
whole Board of Admiralty would most certainly have
declined to serve on a new Board.

Let us consider what *might* have happened if the

decision had been adhered to and four ships only had
been laid down then and in the two succeeding years.
In the summer of 1914, when war was declared, we
should have had only sixteen " Dreadnoughts " to the
German fourteen. When the *Audacious* was sunk on
the 27th October, we should have been reduced to
fifteen against the German fifteen. By the 1st January,
1915, new ships would have come into commission,
but with the *Monarch* and *Conqueror* seriously damaged,
there would have been only fifteen " Dreadnoughts "
available to meet the German sixteen. Who would
have been held responsible ? Certainly not Mr.
Churchill, for the political kaleidoscope had moved
too often in the interval. The whole incident shows
the danger of non-expert members of the Cabinet
ignoring the representations and advice of those who
possess special knowledge.

When Mr. Churchill subsequently became First
Lord of the Admiralty nothing more was heard of
cutting down the naval programmes. It was a long
time, however, before Fisher forgave him, although
their correspondence did not cease entirely. On the
28th February he wrote :

> . . . I confess I never expected you to turn against the Navy
> after all you have said in public and private (*et tu, Brute !*). I
> am sure you won't expect me to enter into any discussion with
> you, as there can be only one exponent of the Admiralty case—
> the First Lord.
>
> As to want of foresight on the part of the Admiralty, the Sea
> Lords expressed their grave anxiety in a memorandum presented
> to the First Lord [Tweedmouth] in December 1907. The Cabinet
> ignored that anxiety and cut down the Estimates. You want to
> do the same again ! We can take no risks this year—last year we
> did. We felt then there would be time to pull up—the margin
> now is exhausted. I reciprocate your grief at our separation. I
> retain the memory of many pleasant duels !

And again on 4th March[1] :

It's kind of you to send me . . . It's too sad and most deplorable. Let us write the word " finis." The Apostle is right ! The tongue is the very devil ! (N.B.—Yours is slung amidships and wags at both ends.)

Yours till the Angels smile on us.

P.S.— . . . I think it would be quite lovely to call the four extra " Dreadnoughts "—

No. 1.   Winston.

  ,, 2.   Churchill.

  ,, 3.   Lloyd.

  ,, 4.   George.

How they would fight ! Uncircumventable ! Read this out to the Cabinet !

It only remains to add that Fisher's loyalty and gratitude to Mr. M'Kenna for his noble stand on this memorable occasion caused him to defer acceptance of Mr. Churchill's offer in October 1914 to come back to the Admiralty, as First Sea Lord, until he had ascertained that Mr. M'Kenna did not object to him serving with Mr. Churchill ; and this, it should be remembered, in spite of the fact that the dearest wish of Fisher's life for the previous ten years had been to serve as First Sea Lord during a war.

The question has often been asked whether Fisher used the best means to bring about his reforms, whether he was not too drastic, whether the velvet glove might not have guided the measures through their difficult stages more quickly and with less friction, whether he paid sufficient attention to the criticisms of genuine doubters; and numerous other points of this sort have been raised. It is always

---

[1] These two strong personalities had each an irresistible attraction for the other. Three times a clash of views caused seemingly irreconcilable separation, but three times the magnetism of mutual regard again brought the two together.

difficult to say what might or might not have happened if, in any circumstances, a course had been
adopted different from the one that was pursued. In
this case there are several matters that have to be
taken into consideration.

We must remember that, both as Director of Naval
Ordnance and as Controller, Fisher had piloted reforms
through the Admiralty and past outside opposition.
Even in so straightforward a matter as the Admiralty
taking over their own ordnance from the War Office—
when important officials of both departments stated
that such a course was absolutely necessary to prevent
disaster in war-time—even under these conditions he
had met with solid opposition and obstruction, and
in the end it took sixteen years to complete the entire
change.

In introducing water-tube boilers into the Navy he
had again met with obstruction and opposition, this
time from the House of Commons. A change which
the veriest tyro in naval tactics must have seen to be
of overreaching importance to the Fleet was opposed
by no fewer than sixty members of the Government
party, who forced on the Admiralty a lamentable
waste of both time and money. Fisher, therefore, was
under no misapprehension as to what was entailed in
trying to introduce reforms into the Navy. *Athanasius
contra mundum* was with him no mere figure of speech;
mundum was but a slight exaggeration. He felt that
unless the whole of the reforms came like a thunder-
clap together, and not piecemeal, there would be no
chance of his getting one tithe of them through before
his time at the Admiralty came to an end. His view,
expressed with his usual picturesqueness, was that by
introducing the lot together their very diversity would

lead to divergence of opinion among the critics and " they would kick each other's shins instead of mine."

Another point that was firmly fixed in his mind was that the reforms had to be accepted as they were presented, and without any alteration. When once chipping was allowed, it would never stop. His two battle-cries were, " The efficiency of the Navy and its instant readiness for war," and " The scheme, the whole scheme, and nothing but the scheme."

He had taken the greatest care in working out the details with the help of Committees, so that he knew that his schemes were workable ; and that, after passing through the fiery furnace of Committees, the isolated views of critics, who presumably had not the same data to work on as an Admiralty Committee, were not of any very great value. He could therefore take a stand on what had been worked out, and refuse to countenance any modifications.

Looking back over the past years and reviewing briefly the extent of the opposition by which Fisher was faced at the very commencement of his term at the Admiralty, and taking into account the great growth of that opposition under the ægis of Lord Charles Beresford and his henchmen, there is little doubt that he was right, and that by no means other than those he adopted could the reforms have been introduced.

It is true that Fisher in some ways aggravated the opposition ; this will be dealt with later ; for the moment we are only concerned with Fisher in 1904 when he started his great campaign which laid the foundations of the reorganization of the Navy, which, in its turn, largely contributed to our winning the war.

Dealing now with the criticisms which we have said were levelled at Fisher and his reforms, it must be observed that these were of several different kinds. There was good honest criticism from genuine doubters, or from those who thought they saw better methods of obtaining the same objects. There was criticism of the " made-to-order kind " from journalists ; and, finally, there was criticism from those who had not the welfare of the Navy at heart, but who made the reforms an excuse for launching a personal vendetta and an opportunity for gratifying petty grievances and pent-up spite. There were several naval officers who disliked Fisher, and were jealous of his success. It will have been noticed, even in the few letters that have been cited, that Fisher referred constantly to the jealousy that his own rapid advancement and preferential appointments were bound to create among his contemporaries and immediate seniors. They could not urge that Fisher's advancement was un-deserved, but they fell back on indefinite charges that he had risen by repressing those who had assisted him, and who, it was inferred, were equally deserving. This accusation was made despite the obvious fact that he towered over all those around him, his genius and strong individuality placing him in a higher class than any of his contemporaries.

The senior officers who had held high posts at the Admiralty naturally regarded any reforms with sus-picion. They had themselves had the chance of introducing similar schemes ; but either they had not thought of them or had not considered them to be advisable. They looked upon their introduction now almost as a reflection on themselves. Lord Walter Kerr, the previous First Sea Lord, was a notable exception. He took no part in any agitation ; for he was of far too generous a nature to indulge in criticisms of his successor, even though he might not agree with all of his proposals.

Fisher also met with opposition from a totally different quarter. Lord Sydenham describes his own participation in this opposition in his book of reminiscences. He explained how he (then Sir George Clarke) was greatly opposed to the construction of the *Dreadnought*, though, apparently, he had no knowledge of the developments in naval gunnery which primarily had impelled this design ; at all events, he makes no reference to them in his book. In his opinion, the *Dreadnought* design, conceived at a time when our naval preponderance in battleships was overwhelming, was a dangerous mistake, and he did everything in his power to cause approval for the new ship to be reconsidered.[1] He pleaded with Sir Henry Campbell-Bannerman to appoint a Committee to reconsider the whole question of building policy ; and the Prime Minister was apparently inclined to do so ; but the Admiralty proved obdurate. He remarks in his book : " As I pointed out, it should be an axiom of our policy never to lead in ship construction, but always to follow with something better." This type of argument was not difficult to meet, for inevitably, if you " followed with something better " you must for a time at all events be leading ! Sir George Clarke advocated that we should let other countries get ahead of us, and then surpass them *if we could*. But suppose we could not overtake the lead thus gratuitously given ?

On p. 209, Vol. I, the duties of the Secretariat of the Defence Committee have been set out, and it will be

---

[1] *My Life's Work*, by Lord Sydenham, page 205.

seen that interference in technical departmental business was quite outside their sphere. It was a fear
that the Secretariat might usurp these functions that
had caused many people to be doubtful of the success
of that Department when first its creation was suggested. Moreover, the criticisms made by Sir George
Clarke were not submitted in the form of official
memoranda, inviting replies from the Admiralty and
so affording that Department an opportunity to rebut
his arguments ; but they were supplied privately to
the Prime Minister, and were not even intended to be
seen by the Admiralty. Sir George Clarke also carried
on a correspondence with various Admirals, and col-
lated their opinions in order to support his arguments.
In his reminiscences he notes a letter written by
Admiral Prince Louis of Battenberg on 16th March,
1905, in which he says :

> I do cordially agree with all you say, especially the fever which
> has seized hold of J.F., . . . also the senseless way in which he
> insults and alienates our senior men. . . . However, he shall have
> my views in season and out of season, from high and low altitudes,
> now that he has asked for them.

This letter would seem to be most damning to
Fisher and his schemes, and if the views expressed
were conveyed to the Prime Minister, they must
undoubtedly have influenced him against Fisher. The
uselessness of support collected in this way is shown
by a letter written by Prince Louis to Fisher only
three months afterwards, after he had had the opportunity of studying in detail and grasping the whole
scope of the reform schemes. He ends this letter :

> Let your detractors do their worst ; no one pays any attention
> to them.

TWO PHOTOGRAPHS OF KING EDWARD VII AND SIR JOHN FISHER ON BOARD
H.M.S. *DREADNOUGHT* ON HER FIRST CRUISE

II. 96

Again, in December of the same year he writes :

I need hardly repeat to you that I am ready to serve you in any capacity you may decide. The " Statement " [1] is admirable. I shall certainly encourage my boy George to qualify in engineering. He has great tastes that way.

This correspondence shows the danger of drawing any conclusions from a single letter such as quoted in Lord Sydenham's book.

This secret campaign was fortunately disclosed, owing to one of the communications to the Prime Minister accidentally being forwarded to the Admiralty. Lord Sydenham in the same book writes naïvely :

Sir Henry Campbell-Bannerman gave serious consideration to my representations intended only for his private information ; but he inadvertently sent some of them to the Admiralty over my name. When he realized what this might mean, he expressed regret in the kindest terms ; but I gathered that there was danger ahead and that my position had become insecure.

Was ever so impossible a situation created for a new department, which, above all things, had to work in complete confidence with the Admiralty, than that created by the Secretary of the Committee of Imperial Defence ? Imagine the feelings of the Admiralty when they found that, secretly and without their knowledge, this trusted official had been corresponding with malcontent Admirals and communicating their views to the Prime Minister !

Sir George Clarke was appointed Governor of Bombay, Captain Charles Ottley, Royal Navy, succeeded him, and the Secretariat of the Defence Committee

---

[1] Lord Cawdor's statement to Parliament.

settled down again, and confined itself to its proper functions. Opposition carried on privately in this and similar ways was most troublesome to Fisher in his struggles for reform, and it needed a tenacious character, an even temper, and a sense of humour to deal with this class of opponent.

There was also much obstruction on the part of a section of the Press, though Fisher had ardent supporters as well as keen critics. Fair criticism is a good tonic, but some of the more virulent of his detractors went far beyond the bounds of fair or reasonable comment.

Mr. Stead writes of this in his usual trenchant style :

The most monstrous accusations were hurled against him by men who were not worthy to black his boots. At the time when he was risking everything by his dogged determination to keep up the supremacy of the Navy, he was denounced as a traitor in the pay of Germany, who had gone to Whitehall in order to betray us to our rival. Those of us who knew the motive of these attacks could afford to smile. As for Fisher, he heeded them as little as if they were but the icy spray which hurtles through the air when a destroyer is dashing at full speed through the waves. After all, detractors and calumniators have their uses. As the Devil has been said to be the most efficient advertising agent of the *Bon Dieu*, so envious libellers and unscrupulous traducers are serviceable in creating a background of shadow, against which the radiant central figure of the hero stands out in clearer relief than would have been possible but for the zeal with which they had plied their blacking-brushes.

" Never fight a chimney-sweep ; some of the soot will stick," was one of Fisher's favourite sayings ; but it is equally true that some soot will stick from contact with a chimney-sweep even if there is no fight. So it was with Fisher ; some of the soot that was thrown did stick. The world is ever prone to believe

the worst. Untruth is usually so much more sen-
sational than the truth, and a lie that passes
from mouth to mouth is hard to overtake and
contradict.

This period had its lighter moments. Fisher was
assailed by one set of critics who said our Fleet was
already too large, and at the same time another set
was urging that the Fleet was dangerously weak.   He
accordingly had two statements prepared, one showing conclusively that it was too small, and the other
equally conclusively that it was too large, and these
were used, as required, to combat the arguments of
the rival schools.

Another class of criticism which was as venomous
as it was futile was that which was initiated in the
House of Commons. It should always be borne in
mind that the naval officers in the House of Commons
can never be among the most experienced of our
Naval Service.   If they were so, they would be actively
employed at sea instead of taking up shore-going
work.   Moreover, the affairs of the Navy change
so quickly that even a few years of absence place a
man quite out of touch with modern developments.
The fact of possessing a title of naval rank, grown rusty
with age, frequently endows the opinions of the
holder in Parliament and the Press with a prestige
far above its true worth. We have seen how well-
meaning but ignorant members muddled the water-
tube boiler question. Admiralty reforms met with
similar treatment. In the House of Commons the
opinions of an out-of-date Naval Lieutenant or Commander are apt to carry a weight at least equal to that
of any single member of the Board of Admiralty.

Fisher frequently received quotations that were

complimentary to him from his admirers. Here is one :

3rd June, 1909.

I am not going to say one single word, no matter what the provocation, as it would only " advertise the advertiser." Silence is deadly, I think, however great the calumny.

I had some lines sent me yesterday which I thought very nice. Written in A.D. 1598 by Sir Henry Wotton :

> You meaner beauties of the night,
> That poorly satisfy our eyes
> More by your number than your light,
> You common people of the skies,
> What are you when the moon shall rise ?

He also received others of a different kind ; like the following, when he was returning to the Admiralty :

> Now, maidens, put your red aprons away,
> The Bull of Seville is coming this way.

Or this from a lady :

> There he sits among the flowers,
> Counting only sunny hours,
> Heeding neither rain nor mist,
> The brazen-faced old Optimist.

He got a good deal of sympathy from his friends in his uphill fights. To one he wrote :

5 a.m. Sunday = The early bird.

My dear Friend,

I wake up with the thought of your kindly visit yesterday and so appreciate your sympathy. Sympathy is the greatest force in the world; the Bible says so. Those idiots of parsons mistranslate it and call it " love " ! and don't realize that when St. Paul called it " charity," when he explained all its attributes, he meant *Sympathy.*—Sermon ended.

Before leaving for his cure abroad in August 1909, he wrote to Mr. Arnold White :

I am about starting on leave, and must send you a few parting lines of gratitude before I start, as I don't want you to imagine I am unmindful of all your buffetings on my behalf! Beresford is still Beresfording and Custance still Custancing! All the Dukes and Duchesses have been shepherded into the Beresfordian fold and mutiny is being further organized in the higher ranks of the Service. The lower are staunch and un-knife-and-fork-able! However, the right always wins. I think I shall stop where I am till I am kicked out. A gross lie has been propagated that I sent the signal incident to *The Times*.[1] I never knew anything whatever about it till I saw it in *The Times!* I think you have been kindly judicious in abstaining from any notice of it at all. I wrote to Parsons, the inventor of the turbine, to congratulate him on the unprecedented feat of the *Indomitable* going straight from the builder's yard and making an Atlantic record. For invariably there are preliminary canters.

He was beginning to cogitate over retirement, and wrote Mr. Arnold White :

10th October, 1909. 4.40 *a.m. My First Thoughts. BURN THIS.*
You are the " *Bovril of letters* " ! (copyright in the United States of America !). I have just seen the *Referee* of the week before last. In *2* lines the *2,600* questions of the Beresford inquiry, and Beresford judged out of his own mouth! The whole Ox is there. *Bless you !*
I only got back the night before last, and am getting tons of kindly advice. I'm invited to perform hari-kiri. I prefer the Christian rite of crucifixion. The French didn't kill Nelson when they shot him in the back ; they immortalized him ! For the sake of the greatest of all things—*Discipline*—I must remain at present and be supported. Heaven be thanked, I have more ginger than even twenty years ago, and *Athanasius contra mundum* is my elixir of life ! I am not going to " lag superfluous on the

---

[1] This refers to Lord Charles Beresford's signal, which Sir Percy Scott refused to obey, as he maintained it was dangerous, and would have caused a second *Victoria* disaster. Fisher had nothing to do with this.

stage." I'm not such a d——d fool! I am going when I am asked to stop. That's Machiavellian! (read *The Prince* by that wonderful man). Burn this letter the moment you have read it, and say not a word of its contents, or I'll never speak to you again, for you would ruin my plans.

Up till the end of November 1909 it was uncertain whether he would or would not retire from the Admiralty on his sixty-ninth birthday. He had been five years at the Admiralty, but, without doubt, he could have remained on for another year if he had desired. What finally caused him to leave was his wish to leave the post of First Sea Lord in safe hands. Sir Arthur Wilson was the only Admiral who was really fit to succeed him; but this distinguished officer was only two years younger than Fisher. If Fisher remained for another year, Wilson could only have held the appointment for one year, and it is improbable that he would have been appointed for so short a time. Fisher therefore decided to leave in the following January.

He had a few years previously saved Admiral Sir Arthur Wilson from retiring. He considered that it was most desirable to retain the Admiral on the Active List, and it was therefore decided to promote him to Admiral of the Fleet—a rank to which Admirals are advanced entirely by selection. Sir Arthur had refused the promotion on the plea that " he did not see why he should be selected over the heads of other Admirals." Fisher pointed out to the King the great value of this officer to the Navy, and asked him to insist on Sir Arthur accepting the promotion. When, therefore, Sir Arthur was received by the King on giving up his appointment as Commander-in-Chief of the Fleet in Home Waters, His Majesty handed to him his commission as Admiral of the Fleet. It was therefore impossible any longer for Sir Arthur to refuse.

Sir Arthur's previous refusal of promotion was typical of the man. He was, without exception, the least egotistical of human beings, but at the same time a man of extraordinary tenacity and of indomitable pluck (he had earned a V.C. for fighting " Fuzzywuzzies " with the hilt of his broken sword when the square, in the fighting near Suakin, was temporarily broken). He had no regard for himself or for his own comfort ; he looked on his body as merely a shell to carry out the dictates of his mind. He did not seek rewards or orders, and later he refused a Peerage when it was offered to him. He was undoubtedly the finest Admiral of his day in command of a Fleet, and he had been for five years in command of our largest Fleets. He was scrupulously just and extraordinarily level-headed. He had no communications whatever with the Press ; but, unfortunately, was not himself an adept at argument, and, therefore, he was always at a disadvantage when dealing with politicians.

It was necessary, for the maintenance of discipline in the Navy, that the Admiralty should be kept free from Lord Charles Beresford's adherents ; it also was most desirable that Fisher's successor should have the confidence of the Navy, and at the same time be one who would not attempt to initiate any reactionary policy, and whose free action would not be cramped by prejudice. Sir Arthur Wilson had all these qualifications, and Fisher's account of how the matter was arranged is interesting. In conversation with a friend afterwards he said :

I will tell you how Wilson got it. M'Kenna has acted like a white man throughout. It is not known that for twenty-four

hours he was out of the Cabinet ; but he got his terms, and Beresford was put on the beach and the " Dreadnoughts " were sanc-
tioned.[1] M'Kenna and I have worked happily, and he is the best
First Lord we have had for many years. M'Kenna asked me if
Wilson could be induced to succeed me. I said there was only
one man in the country who could do it, and that was the King.
M'Kenna went off to the King armed with a brief as to why Wilson
was necessary. The King then sent for Wilson to Sandringham,
and the King told me himself the curious nature of the interview.
Sir Arthur Wilson reluctantly consented, and he then said to the
King, " Only once, Sir, have I asked a favour of anyone since I
entered the Navy, and that was of Sir John Fisher. When he
was about to lay down the appointment of Controller of the Navy,
Fisher had already arranged for his successor, but he cancelled
the arrangement and secured the appointment for me. I assure
you, Sir, that I was absolutely the worst Controller the Navy has
ever had, and if I am to succeed Fisher again I may probably
become the worst First Sea Lord in the annals of the Navy."

Thus the matter was arranged. Fisher had been
very wise to secure a suitable successor.

On 13th January, 1910, Fisher wrote :

Strictly Private.

Have no fear about Wilson ; he assured M'Kenna the other day
he was fully satisfied as to Admiralty policy in regard to " Dreadnoughts," and that we had acted most wisely in keeping back
when German building permitted it, so as thereby to get *far more
powerful ships,* and what was proposed for next year fully met his
views, and that utter rot was talked as to our want of destroyers.
Burn this letter also, and don't quote. But I write just to set your
mind at rest. *Do you know that the ships we have just laid down
are as beyond the " Dreadnought " as the " Dreadnought " was beyond
all before her ?*

And they will say again, " D——n that blackguard," " Again a
new era of ' Dreadnoughts.' " But imagine the German " Wake
up " when these new ships by-and-by burst on them.

70,000 *horse-power ! ! ! and guns that will gut them ! !*   Oh my !
that I was born too soon !

[1] The " eight Dreadnoughts " of the 1909–10 programme.

Beresford gave out the other day that he was *promised* to be First Lord of the Admiralty " to keep Wilson right " ! ! !, and he was sure of Portsmouth [1] and a change of Government.

A dear friend came to see me yesterday and said the work done in the last five years was so vast in every position of the Navy, and all done so at once and together, that the mind failed to grasp it all ! *It's really true.* But I have not done it. It was the splendid band who worked with me. " I have culled a garland of flowers ; mine only the string that binds them " (Montaigne) ; but all the same, as my friend said, " Never was baser ingratitude shown to anyone " than to me by *both* political parties ! But I don't mind. After all, the *mens conscia recti* counts.

But the lovely thing of all, my dear friend, is the fact that what I did in the years before of my life far transcends what has been done in the last five years,[2] but no one knows it ! Too much fighting for writing. But I never meant to write all this. Even Mahan wrote a polite letter of compliment.

P.S.—I forgot to say to you in my letter this morning that I had thought myself very much alone ; but my eyes have been opened by such a mass of telegrams and letters from all ranks and classes in the Navy,[3] and, of course, one thinks of Elijah when he once felt lonely and saw all those chariots of fire around him when his eyes were opened.

Those who knew Fisher best felt his retirement as a personal loss. Mr. Stead wrote :

" I don't know how you feel about it," said a friend the day after Fisher's retirement, " but I feel pretty bad. It is almost as if Nelson had stepped down from his monument in Trafalgar Square." That is not an exaggeration. We all feel more or less like that, from the King upon his throne down to the scurviest of the curs who snapped at the great man's heels. For Fisher was a great man—one of our greatest men. His greatness was attested alike by the devotion that he commanded from all the greatest, and the fierce rancour of animosity which he aroused in the worst, of his contemporaries.

[1] He was standing as member for Portsmouth.
[2] An example of the class of exaggeration that Lord Fisher indulged in in his later years.
[3] On retiring from being First Sea Lord.

" Oh, Jacky !—well, Jacky is splendid—simply splendid ! "
There you have it. That is the way in which he impressed
everybody who was anybody who ever had to do with him.

This is but one of many tributes paid to Fisher on
his retirement.

In the House of Commons the First Lord, in introducing the 1910–11 Estimates, stated :

In January 1910 the Board of Admiralty were deprived, to their
deep regret, of the invaluable assistance of Admiral of the Fleet
Lord Fisher of Kilverstone, G.C.B., O.M., G.C.V.O., who had asked
to be relieved from his post on reaching the age of sixty-nine.
Lord Fisher, in addition to most distinguished service as a sea-
officer, has had a career of unexampled success in high administrative office at the Admiralty, first as Director of Naval Ordnance,
afterwards as Third Sea Lord and Controller, then as Second Sea
Lord, and finally as First Sea Lord. The measures which are
associated with his name and have been adopted by several successive Governments will prove of far-reaching and lasting benefit
to the Naval Service and the country.

But of all, the most eloquent is the following personal one from his First Lord, Mr. M'Kenna :

I will let you know at once when I hear from Wilson. I wrote
to him with a heavy heart, and I have been unhappy these two days
at the thought of your leaving. You have been so good to me,
so understanding of my difficulties, so skilful in teaching me, so
brave in your support of my political anxieties, so affectionate in
your personal relations, that I have neither heart nor wish to go
on without you.

It is doubtful if a retiring First Sea Lord, or
indeed a retiring technical colleague in any of the
public services, ever received from his political chief
such an eloquent tribute of affection and esteem.

POSTSCRIPT

ADMIRAL OF THE FLEET LORD FISHER

Lord Fisher in 1910, when he left the Admiralty, had changed a good deal from the Sir John Fisher who went to the Admiralty in 1904. His five years' service at Whitehall had aged him in certain respects. Physically, he still was ten years younger than his age ; but he was not, of course, able to stand the same arduous work that he had been able to dispatch when he had thrown himself heart and soul into the initiation of his reforms. His mind was as clear as ever ; his memory seemed unimpaired, but his judgment was not so sound, nor so detached, as it had been in his palmiest days.

The strain he had been through had been tremendous. For a considerable part of the time that he had been First Sea Lord, namely, from Lord Selborne's departure to Mr. M'Kenna's advent, he had had to fight single-handed an array of adverse forces. He had started with a complaisant Cabinet and a well-disposed Prime Minister. The Press, on the whole, had, to commence with, received his reforms well. Before he left office he had to deal with a Cabinet whom Lord Charles Beresford had frightened into covert hostility, and a Press which, among its number, still counted many stalwarts, but also included virulent opponents. The opposition he had encountered had, in fact, been more than any ordinary man could have surmounted.

How much of this was due to Fisher and his methods it is very difficult to say. A certain amount of the opposition that he had met with might have been dispelled, had he only carried on the same methods of pacification which marked the early part of his administration. In the old days he had his opponents all marked down, and he would go to great lengths to win them over to his views. He would approach an objector and say, " My dear fellow, I know exactly what you think about the scheme ; I know you will say so and so, and so and so ; now I will show you the other side " ; he would then proceed to demolish the objections. In this way he never allowed a doubter to state his objections, and so to commit himself ; the opponent was therefore in the happy position of having nothing to retract, which made his acquiescence all the easier. But the combination of age, opposition, and success had made him less careful to placate, and more inclined to override. To use a Biblical simile, he " took the wheels off his chariot so that it drave heavily," and thus opposition mounted up against him.

His consciousness that all his reforms had first passed through the fiery furnace of committees, dis- cussions, and debates helped to make him intolerant of other people's objections. He quite forgot that they had not had the benefit of the same committees to assist them in coming to their conclusions. The mere fact of his conviction that his view was the right one did not help them to see the case from his point of view, nor to alter the angle from which they examined the subject. In addition, the evidence that Fisher had accumulated of the factious spirit and interested motives that lay at the root of much of

the opposition with which he had been met, inclined
him to impute, in his own mind, and not infrequently
in conversation, similar motives to men who were
mere honest doubters : the result was that, instead of
smoothing and explaining, he grew to be at times
dogmatic and rather unreasonable.

He had also imbibed the doctrine of expediency
from his contact with politicians, and some of his
actions, although strictly within the law, savoured a
little of sharp practice. Naval officers are, on the
whole, rather simple folk with old-fashioned views of
right and wrong, so that they regard with disfavour
any signs of over-astuteness in the regulation of the
affairs of the Navy.

The above were the weaknesses of approaching old
age in a man who had packed ten years' work and
expended ten years' energy in the previous five. But
Fisher was still Fisher. The old fire burned as fiercely
as ever, the old strength of character still remained.
The welfare of the Navy and its instant readiness for
war was still the aim that he placed above all others.
His position as First Sea Lord cut him off to a great
extent from intimate communication with the officers
of the Fleet, and he felt this isolation greatly. Often
for long periods he received no congratulations and
encouragement from those afloat. In fact, one officer
has left on record that on New Year's Eve, 1908,
when he wished Fisher a " happy New Year," Fisher,
almost with tears in his eyes, said, " Do you know,
Dumas,[1] you are about the only officer in the Navy
who wishes me that ? "[2] Happily, the next morning,
with the New Year, came several letters which were
indeed balm to his soul.

[1] Captain Philip Dumas.   [2] See also page 105, P.S. to letter.

It must be confessed that a good deal of that isolation came from an unfortunate habit Fisher had con-
tracted of causing private letters he had received to
be printed for restricted circulation without the permission of the writers, and without giving them the
chance of editing them.   He himself was so indiscreet
a letter writer that he never appreciated the inconvenience that an unguarded remark in a letter might
cause to others.   At least thirty per cent. of the
interesting letters he wrote, and which have been preserved, bear the inscription " Burn this."   It is most
extraordinary how rarely this injunction was carried
out.   In one letter we find him stating that he has
heard that the most unscrupulous of his detractors
had collected a number of his indiscreet letters, and
proposed to publish them, in order to entangle him
in libel actions.   " But I don't care," was his comment.
" At all events, I meant every word that I wrote."

This weakness of publishing letters from other
people in one case did him considerable harm as well
as entailing much inconvenience on the writer.   This
particular letter was one written in the early part of
1906 by an officer, Captain Bacon,[1] who had lately
joined a ship in the Mediterranean, having previously
been Fisher's Naval Assistant at the Admiralty.
This he had printed for private circulation, and a copy
fell into the hands of unscrupulous agitators, who
invented the accusation that Captain Bacon had been
appointed by him to command a battleship in the
Mediterranean for the purpose of spying on Lord
Charles Beresford.   No greater lie was ever invented.
But the mud spattered by the accusation has stuck
so firmly that it is necessary to state fully and exactly

———
[1] The author of these volumes.

what led to the letter in question being written. Unfortunately, as the name of King Edward VII was mentioned in the letter, it was impossible to publish it fully in the Press at the time, and so explain and controvert the untrue aspersions on the characters of the two officers concerned.

At the time Sir John left the Portsmouth Command to take up the appointment of First Sea Lord, Captain Bacon had been four years in command of the submarine boats then in commission and building ; he was anxious to be appointed to a seagoing command, so as to qualify early for promotion and subsequent command ; but, having been associated with Fisher in the preparation of the skeleton of his reforms, he consented, after considerable demur, at the earnest request of the Admiral, to go to the Admiralty as his assistant ; but stipulated that it should be for one year only.

Towards the end of 1905 Captain Sackville Carden was obliged, for private reasons, to relinquish the command of the *Irresistible*. Captain Bacon, having completed his year at the Admiralty, asked Sir John to have him appointed to that ship, as he wished, among other reasons, to serve under Lord Charles Beresford, who had the reputation of being an excellent Commander-in-Chief. Sir John demurred to the proposal, not wishing to lose his help and also, perhaps, being somewhat afraid that his late assistant might fall a victim to Lord Charles's charming personality, and possibly be led to view the reforms too much from his angle of view. Captain Bacon, however, persisted, and he consented ; but the parting was not a particularly cordial one.

While the Captain was in the Mediterranean Fisher

occasionally wrote to him, chiefly about his appointment to the *Dreadnought*. The First Lord had promised the command of that ship to Captain Hugh Tyrwhitt ; Fisher, however, was determined that Captain Bacon should have it. Captain Tyrwhitt eventually asked for the Commodoreship of the East Indies Station, and the matter was settled. Captain Bacon wrote occasionally criticizing some of Sir John's proposals ; but the only mention of Lord Charles in these letters was to eulogize him as a Commander-in-Chief, for the Captain had soon developed a genuine appreciation of Lord Charles's charming personality, which aroused real affection in those who served under him.

About March 1906 the *Renown*, which had been to India with the Prince of Wales, returned through the Mediterranean ; and, at Corfu, met the Royal yacht with King Edward and King George of Greece on board. The Mediterranean Battle Fleet was ordered there also.

The Prince of Wales, who always had the welfare of the Navy most thoroughly at heart, was much disturbed by the many criticisms of Sir John Fisher's reforms he had heard from senior officers while in the East, and when Captain Bacon called to pay his respects, the Prince, during the few minutes that were at his disposal, tackled him severely on the subject. The Captain asked for a longer interview on a subsequent day in order to explain more fully the scope and reasons that underlay the various reforms. This interview was graciously granted, and took place after church on Sunday, a couple of hours before the Fleet was due to sail.

Previous to this interview Captain Bacon had been

honoured by an invitation to dine on board the
Royal yacht. After dinner, King Edward sent for
him and expressed his concern at the criticisms he had
heard of the reforms from both Lord Charles Beresford and Admiral Lambton, and mentioned that the
Prince also was much disturbed. Captain Bacon
explained that the requirements of the Navy as viewed
from Whitehall were much wider and more compre-
hensive than those visualized by officers in the more
restricted areas of the foreign stations, and that competent committees had examined and approved of
each proposal. The King then asked if, as Sir John
Fisher's late assistant, he did not keep him informed of the feeling of the Fleet ; to which he
replied that Sir John Fisher knew perfectly the objections of all the senior officers who disagreed with the
proposals, and that, as an officer serving afloat, he
had avoided writing about the Fleet he was serving
in except in the most general terms. The King
pointed out that it was his duty, as late confidential
Naval Assistant, to keep Fisher *au courant* with the
general opinion of the Fleet.

After the interview with the Prince on the following
day, Captain Bacon sat down and wrote a long letter to
Sir John, detailing what had happened, commencing
with the statement, " Lord Charles and Admiral
Lambton have been getting at the King." This was,
of course, a crude and colloquial way of stating the
case, allowable from one who had been private secretary writing to his former Chief ; but when the statement was excerpted from the body of the letter and
put into public print, it was skilfully used to convey
the impression that he had reported on Lord Charles
and Admiral Lambton in an underhand way. Of

II—8

course, while at the Admiralty Sir John Fisher had often discussed with his assistant the objections of Lord Charles and Admiral Lambton, since both of these, quite properly, had written criticisms of the earlier reforms to Sir John setting out clearly all their objections. There was nothing that Sir John and the Captain had not discussed together. There was nothing, therefore, in the letter which would have needed any alteration before publication (had the opportunity been afforded to him), except the opening sentence, which should have been altered to, " The King has spoken to me of the objections to the schemes that have been placed before him by Lord Charles and Admiral Lambton."

Fisher, of course, had no right to circulate copies of the letter privately to his friends without the writer's permission ; but that was Fisher all over : he had an obsession for printing any details that interested him and issuing them broadcast. Quick to act in small matters without much thought, he never appreciated that he was acting in any but an ordinary manner. His reading of the letter was that it was a plain, matter-of-fact report of an interview with the King, which it was necessary that he (Fisher) should know of ; he never saw the interpretation that detractors might read into the opening sentence and the use they might make of it.

It is on this incident that the widespread belief was based that Fisher used underhand methods in carrying out his reforms. For years a stigma has remained on his character (the soot he so often referred to) in the minds of thousands who knew him not and even with many who were his ardent admirers. It is for this reason that the incident has been treated at a length

which, otherwise, would be out of all proportion to its
intrinsic importance.

Two failings which Fisher developed during his
service as First Sea Lord and which, in all probability,
told most against him and alienated some of his previous admirers, were an increased tendency to exaggerate and an increased loquaciousness, which, combined together, caused him to speak his mind on
many occasions regardless of the effect his views
might have on others. This tendency to exaggerate
increased as time went on, and gave an unfortunate
turn to some of his more violent expressions. His old
saying that " he would break anyone for the good of
the Navy," became that " he would break anyone
who opposed him." The two were, to Fisher, synonymous, but bore different interpretations to those who
might casually hear him talk ; since the latter conveyed the impression that he was a relentless autocrat.
His unguarded sayings were often a cause of embar-
rassment to the First Lord, Mr. M'Kenna.

Again, he did not hesitate, at times, to say that
So-and-so was " no gentleman." He, of course, did not
mean this to be taken literally, but merely that the
man had done something of which he did not approve.
This and other such exaggerated sayings did him
much harm.

These faults of approaching old age were, however,
entirely superficial, and should count as little when
weighed in the balance against his sterling services to
the Navy and the nation.

PART III

CHAPTER XV

THE INTERREGNUM, PART I: 1910—1911

Letters—Visit to America—The barber's story—His impressions of America—Prophesies that Mr. Woodrow Wilson will be the next President—Press campaign against him continues —Further letters—Thinks of writing his Life—His views on our policy regarding Turkey—Lord Charles Beresford's book —His views on explanations—Recalled to England—The Engineer problem again—Mr. M'Kenna goes to the Home Office and Mr. Churchill to the Admiralty.

"SO Jacky is growing roses, is he ? Well, all I've got to say is that those roses will damned well have to grow." Thus spake an officer who knew Fisher well, and had served with him afloat.

After leaving the Admiralty, Lord Fisher divided his time between his son's place in Norfolk, Kilverstone Hall, and travelling abroad. He also visited the United States to be present at the wedding of his son, who married, most happily, Miss Jane Morgan, daughter of Mr. Randal Morgan, of Chesnut Hill, Philadelphia. He was brought back in 1912 to preside over a Royal Commission on oil and oil resources, after which he again returned to a life of more or less ease, until once more he was recalled to pull the Admiralty out of the mess into which it had drifted in the early months of the war.

These four years are best dealt with by excerpts from the scores of letters he wrote during that period, for they show his views at the moment. He rarely dealt with incident ; his brain was for ever cogitating

on the Navy and the problems connected with it,
and, not unnaturally, his mind often reverted to his
five years of labour and the scurvy treatment he had
received at the hands of the politicians and a section
of the Press.

On the 10th February, 1910, he wrote to Mr. Arnold
White, who had sent him an article he was writing
on the Navy :

Controversialists are opposed to you, but those main lines you
go on are above controversy, which is why I admire your plan.
Sir William White and others of his kidney damn by inferences
which your big points blow away.

I can truthfully say I never sought the Press, but I recognized
it as the one and only engine that could effect the vast revolution
from shipbuilding to bread-baking—from kettles to turbines—
from fossils to Nelsons—as *without the Press it could not all have
been done.* It may not be politic to say this, but it is true. I
never gave *déjeuners* to the Press like Beresford and Co. at Claridge's
or in my flagship—even you yourself, perhaps twice you have
lunched with me ; I don't think anyone else ever has—perhaps
Thursfield [1] once ! Those are eloquent facts !

13th February, 1910.

I am so glad to hear from you this morning that you are not
precipitate with your letter ; for, since I wrote to you, I have
heard of Sir William White's envenomed purpose (as " Ciris " in
the *Spectator*) to have anyone's blood who backs me, and I understood Strachey supports him ! What a huge and colossal mistake
these men do make ! It's not the *personality*, it's the MESSAGE
that tells. No use attacking the voice-tube. It's the message
that carries. The two very greatest men in the world said that,
John the Baptist and St. Paul ! The Baptist, " I am a voice."
Paul said, " My bodily presence is weak and my speech con-
temptible " ; *the message—" For his letters say they are weighty
and powerful."*

I think a good text for my Midshipman's *Vade Mecum*, which

───

[1] Sir John Thursfield, one of the earliest and best known of naval
correspondents to the Press.

PHOTOGRAPH TAKEN AND SENT TO SIR JOHN FISHER BY THE EMPRESS MARIE OF RUSSIA, OF A GROUP ON BOARD RUSSIAN ROYAL YACHT *STANDARD*, 1909

1. Lord Hamilton of Dalzell.
2. The Chevalier de Martino.
3. Sir Arthur Nicolson.
4. M. Stolypin, Russian Prime Minister.

5. The Czarina.
6. M. Isvolsky, Russian Minister of Foreign Affairs.
7. Sir John Fisher.

8. Sir Charles Hardinge.
9. Baron Fredericks.
10. Grand Duchess Olga.
11. The Czar.

12. Princess Victoria.
13. The Grand Duke Michael.
14. Count Benckendorff, Russian Ambassador.

II. 120

I hope some day to bring out, will be some allusion to this.
I think, the origin !

The four things that make a life :

     I. A great inspiration.
     II. A great cause.
     III. A great battle.
     IV. A great victory.

Give me those four things, and then we shall preach our Gospel of Rest and build an Altar of Repose.

Lord Fisher was at this time disturbed at the prospect of what the General Election might bring to the Navy, and writes :

KILVERSTONE.
18*th February*, 1910.

Things look ugly. The one to be sorry for is Balfour if Asquith turned out at once. However, I'm a pure outsider ! There will be desperate efforts to supplant Wilson [1] by Custance,[2] so I hear from many quarters ; but M'Kenna will be the real loss to the Navy. The sacred fire of efficiency burns brightly in him, and he's a born fighter and a good hater, which I love (as Dr. Johnson did) with all my heart.

You really must come here when the weather is nicer—it's lovely ! I've never known till now what joy there is in nature. Even beautiful woman fades in the comparison ! I've just seen the wild swans flying over the lake. " The world forgetting, by the world forgot," is appropriate to me now.

The death of King Edward in May was the greatest blow Lord Fisher had had since the loss of his brother Philip in the *Atalanta*. The King had been one of his firmest supporters, and without his backing Lord Fisher could never have carried through his reforms ; moreover, he had a genuine affection for the King as a man and a profound respect for his abilities as a politician and a man of affairs.

[1] Admiral of the Fleet Sir Arthur Wilson, First Sea Lord.
[2] Admiral Sir R. Custance.

On the 7th June he wrote :

I can't shake off my sense of loss in the King's death. Though personally it makes no difference, of course. Yet I feel somehow a sense of isolation—which I can't get over—and no longer seem to care a d——n for anything. . . .

As you told me, it was miraculous I left the Admiralty when I did. It was the nick of time. A. K. Wilson is doing splendidly and is unassailable. I had much pressure to emerge the other day, but I won't ; nor have I the heart now.

25th June, 1911.

I still get pestered from all quarters to return, *but I won't.* I won't get between the limelight and A. K. Wilson ! When he goes, I am ready.

In response to the letter which threw doubts on the strength of the Navy being maintained in the new Estimates, he wrote :

7th October, 1910.

I have no fear about the Navy Estimates, and it has been splendid Balfour meeting M'Kenna at Balmoral. All the same, " *Keep on knocking."* That unjust judge neither feared God nor regarded man, but the poor widow's importunity " bested " him ! I am having numberless invitations, but *J'y suis, j'y reste.* Even Lloyd George effusively asked me to visit him ! How eloquent that bit of Lecky's *Map of Life* when Newman, the Cardinal, had finished his job : " He put down his tools and enjoyed himself with his God " ! *He* chose the right God. *Others* make roses, or racehorses, or rabbits their god ; but the point is the same. " Undue prolongation of an active life is a grave misfortune."

All his life Lord Fisher loved an apt phrase.

11th October, 1910.

I've *just* got the *Seamen's Letters* ! I opened page 303 by chance. (No, not chance, Heaven-sent !)

" Chaps that fought like the Devil sit down and cry like a wench."

What a magnificent epitaph ! There's a bit of Stevenson I know by heart, Nelson at Copenhagen, do read page 130 and pages 135 and 136 of *Virginibus Puerisque*, fine-paper edition, Chatto & Windus, 1905. " And, mark you, undemonstrative men would have spoiled the situation. The finest action is the better for a piece of purple ! "

Yes, emotion can sway the world. The heart, not the brain, gets victory !

In 1910 he visited America for his son's wedding. He was treated with great consideration ; special arrangements were made for passing his belongings through the Customs, and many other details were arranged for his comfort. On the way over in the steamer an American gentleman congratulated him on the fact that his son's fiancée had come over to England and vanquished his son, instead of (as is usually the case) his son going to America to capture her. This pleased Lord Fisher greatly.

He seems also to have made great friends with the barber on board the *Baltic*. He always did make friends in all spheres of life ! The barber told him a story which Lord Fisher relates as follows :

It appears that he had been barber in the train from Chicago to New York, that never stops, " even for a death," so he told me ; when the train suddenly stopped at a small village and a lady got out. Mr. Thompson, the President of the Railway, was in the train, and asked why. The conductor showed him an order [to stop there] signed by a great man of the railway. When Mr. Thompson got to New York he asked this great man, " What excuse ? " and added, " I wouldn't have done it for my wife." The answer he got back was, " No more would I " !

Lord Fisher, in his *Memories*, completed the story in this way :

The sequel to this story is, that I told this tale at an international cosmopolitan lunch party at Lucerne, and said, " The curious thing is, I knew the man." Then Mr. Chauncey Depew wiped me out by saying, " And I know the woman ! "

He was fortunate in meeting, and making friends with, Mr. Schwab, of the Bethlehem Steel Works, who was afterwards to help so largely in supplying us with submarine boats during the war. Lord Fisher's impressions of his visit are given sketchily in the following letter. It is a great pity that he did not record them more fully.

December, 1910.

The Election being over—a thing of apathy, and no one seeming to care a d——n—you may have time to read a letter.

I enjoyed America immensely, but am overjoyed to be back.

" The heart untravelled fondly turns to home,
And drags at each remove a lengthening chain."

But I shan't be surprised if I go over there to die! I had a wonderful welcome, and they seem to know me more than in my own land. (But the Scripture mentions that!) The magnitude of Men, Things, and Ideas impressed me tremendously. I think I saw all the great men and had fascinating *tête-à-tête*. Everything is big. St. Peter's at Rome will go inside the waiting-room of the new Pennsylvania Railway Station, and they return you your money if the train is late; and one street in Philadelphia is twelve miles long, three times wider than Regent Street, and houses both sides all the way! But their school apparatus is the wonder! Nationalities of all types pour into the country, Germans, Hebrews, Irish, Slavs, now in thousands and thousands, and yet in the second generation they are all pure Americans. It reminds me of the Chicago Sausage! No matter what species of pig goes in at one end, they are the same identically tasty sausage that comes out of the other end of the apparatus. No trace of the flavour of the original Porcus! Their language all English, their literature English, their traditions English as forced into them by the school machine, and, quite unknown to themselves, their aspirations are English! All sorts of unpronounceable names without a vowel came and *bragged* to me that their mothers, grandmothers, uncles, sisters, aunts, cousins were English. We shall be d——d fools if we don't exploit this great fact for the peace of the world, and the dominance of our race! A great English-speaking federation, absolute independence of the units, but a solid whole against the universe.   When I went from Pennsylvania into New Jersey my motor-car was stopped at the frontier to get a new label hung on it ; and I could have had a divorce if I wanted, just as easy as a new label !

They told me their population is now 100 millions ; and yet only 25 persons to the square mile, Germany 250, I think, and England 550, about.   They are going to be 250 millions.

Seventy multi-millionaires gave me a private lunch, and they asked me to " raise the Middle West " (as they called it), but *festina lente*, and much judgment is wanted.   I'm going to begin with Lord Morley and Rosebery.   I think it will come about— Germany and Japan are coalescing to exploit China and threaten the United States.   No one mentions it any more than Gambetta mentioned " Revenge," but it is running like wildfire through the American mind !   Hence the plunge about fortifying the Panama Canal dead in the face of our treaty against it.   They know England is on their side.   And Taft is sowing the seed for an English *entente*, and the next President, Woodrow Wilson,[1] Governor of New Jersey, whom I had a *tête-à-tête* with, is dead on.   (Burn this.) I told them it was a d——d fine old hen that hatched the American Eagle, and they madly cheered ; and that George Washington was one of the *greatest Englishmen*, because he made England prosperous, by teaching us how to manage our Colonies.

The following extract is illuminating, as it shows how both Mr. M'Kenna and Admiral Sir Arthur Wilson had to fight against the " Little Navy " section of the Cabinet, those who had bound themselves to limit armaments and devote the money to social reform.   Looking back at those fateful years, anyone must stand aghast to see how near we stood to being unprepared when 1914 came.   All honour to the stalwarts who defeated the Cabinet intrigues.

KILVERSTONE HALL.
5th August, 1910.

To LORD ESHER.

M'Kenna has just been here on his second visit (so he liked the first, I suppose ; I mention this as an inducement for you to come).

[1] It was nearly two years after this letter before Mr. Wilson was nominated as a candidate for the Presidency.

He has shown me various secret papers. *He is a real fighter*, and the Navy Haters will pass over his dead body ! If our late Blessed Master was alive I should know what to do, but I feel my hands tied now. Perhaps a kindly Providence put us both on the beach at the same moment ! Who knows !

"*The lights begin to twinkle on the rocks.*" I've told —— and others that the two-keel-to-one policy is of inestimable value because it eliminates the United States, *which ought never to be mentioned ; criminal folly to do so*. Also it gives such an ample margin as to allow for discount.

The insidious game is to have an inquiry into ships' designs, which means delay and no money.

After a particularly bad bout of vilification in the Press he wrote :

18*th October*, 1910.

I am content to be vilified if the country wins by it.

26*th January*, 1911.

I've just heard you've kindly sent me a book to Kilverstone, which will reach me in due course, and many thanks for it. With much reluctance I paid a second visit last week to England ; however, it was a very good thing that I went, as I was able to " direct the whirlwind and control the storm." But it does sicken me to cross the trail of these pimps, and intriguers, and unabashed liars. Still, as M'Kenna truly says, I'm bound to do my best for the Navy, and so I went, and saw, and conquered ! (So I think.) I will send you a longer letter later on ; just now I'm very occupied, but I wanted to thank you for the book.

28*th January*, 1911.

I really sat down to write to you to thank you sincerely and deeply for not having gone under in the past, which I should have done but for those like you, and especially that great man [King Edward] who left us on the 6th May last, whose memory never leaves me.

31*st January*, 1911.

You never said anything more to the point when stating that some fool, zealot, or traitor gives us away to foreigners. A zealot

lately did this in [the case of] the *Lion*. The Germans were absolutely unconscious of the magnificence of our new 13½-inch gun
or of the 70,000 h.p. . . . . A friend staying here with a foreign
wife told me her German nephew employed in Krupp's Works
had said the *Lion* was a revelation to them, and at that time they
possessed no bigger gun than the 12-inch. But our —— of a
zealot gives us away, so we lost all the advantages of what had
been, so far, a wonderful secret. I only hope our submarine secrets
may not get out. The Germans and others have several more to
go to the bottom before they reach our present position.

P.S.—The one absorbing anxiety is, shall we go ahead as we
ought to in the development of submarines and internal-combustion propulsion ? *These are the two burning naval questions of
the day ;* all the rest *rot.*

Again Mr. M'Kenna stood firm under trial, for we
read :

14th February, 1911.

They took M'Kenna up to a pinnacle of the temple ; but all
they got out of him was " Vade retro Satanas," and behold, there's
hardly a ripple, except among the Duchesses.[1]

9th March, 1911.

I am getting on beautifully with my British-American union.
. . . It doesn't much matter which of the three, Woodrow Wilson,
Governor Hudson, or Champ Clark [will be President], but we
mustn't hustle Providence. Rebecca was a d——d fool. Jacob
would have had it all the same without her hustling him.

Yet still more vile attacks caused him to write to
Mr. Arnold White :

23rd February, 1911.

I wish you would not trouble yourself to fight for me as you
do ! It's no good. *" They hate me the more ! "* (like his brethren
did Joseph) because the d——d dreams come true ! *Resurgam !*
I am buried for a year. Wait and see. But in the tomb I am
not wasting time. But certainly it is curious how persistently

---

[1] " The Duchesses " being his generic term for the Society ladies
who followed Lord Charles Beresford, and held drawing-room meetings
to glorify him and his views.

and unceasingly my enemies pursue me ; and Esher, the day I left England, gave me a lurid illustration of this malignant and even ferocious spite ; and yet I have been a whole year away in the wilds of Norfolk. Nine days supposed to be enough to be forgotten. *I can't make it out !* I believe the secret is, I have such splendid friends. If you see the paradox !

A great personage said sneeringly to a man I had dug out because of his brains, " Oh, you're a great friend of Lord Fisher's." He answered, " Yes, sir, I am proud of it ; and when both of us are forgotten, his memory will live."

You see, a d——d thing like that bites. BURN THIS.

6th *April*, 1911.

I am getting on very nicely with my *Reminiscences*. There is a great temptation to publish " here and now " (as the Salvationists say). *How it would make a lot of despicable villains sit up !* As I told you, I want no panegyrist to make me out a plaster saint nor a boudoir pimp like —— to represent me with forked tail and horns.

The " invasion scare " apparently was once more to the fore, for he wrote :

5th *April*, 1911.

It would be simply silly of me to return to England to knock the bottom out of an empty bomb that can't explode. No ! The danger is an organized attack to get M'Kenna knocked out. Extremes have met. Socialists and Tories, from widely different motives, want to get him out of it ! but they won't.

They made sure they had him on the Archer Shee [1] case, but he is stronger than ever because of it. You can't do a man a greater service than to attack him unsuccessfully. I'll be back all right in 1912. My proper date is 21st October, 1912, but I've compromised ——. (I hate that d——d word compromised ! ! !) Some of the notes I find myself making are so delicious that I am sorely tempted to follow your advice :

" There's a chiel amongst us taking notes,
    And, faith, he'll print them " ;

but how about libel actions ! ! ! !

---

[1] A charge was made against a naval cadet and the lad was withdrawn from the Navy. The charge was afterwards proved to be untrue, and due compensation awarded to him. Lord Charles Beresford made this an opportunity for a strong attack on Mr. M'Kenna.

25th April, 1911.

No doubt you've been here [Florence] often. It does one invigorate to breathe the air of Michael Angelo, and see his " Dawn " in the Medici Chapel, and feel the sacred force of Savonarola, and muse where Machiavelli wrote and Galileo pondered ! What pigmies we are now !

6th June, 1911.

As to accepting your most seducing invitation, I have sworn, and I am steadfastly purposed not to come between the limelight and my successor [Sir A. K. Wilson], and my plan has more than justified itself ; so I am determined to stay abroad quite clear away till he goes next year, and then I shall emerge, I hope, with renewed effect.

Reculer pour mieux sauter.

Resurgam.

But I am not idle now ; *I am working like a mole.* Mind, all this I write to you is deadly secret ; but I know I can trust you and your sweet sister—so I think aloud to you both ! I have been vehemently urged to return home from all sorts of influential quarters, and especially for the Committee of Imperial Defence, because of wild fears that the fundamental policy of the British Empire, that it solely rests on the British Navy, is at stake. *But I had no fear.* All the wire-pulling in the world won't alter the *vital British policy that the coasts of the enemy are the frontiers of England !* and that great fundamental truth has been swallowed like an oyster by all the Dominion Prime Ministers ! (Keep this to yourself and burn this letter !) These d——d fools who talk about Invasion and about our commerce being destroyed and the Declaration of London being an awful catastrophe and (fifty-one silly Admirals sign a paper !) are of inestimable value—though asses—because they keep the pot boiling ! I wouldn't have them contradicted for the world ! They keep up the Navy Estimates ! The Navy Estimates would be done away with but *for them ! Bless their foolish hearts ! I* love them ! Though they don't love me ! Don't you worry about either the British Empire or the British Navy ! (They are synonymous terms !) We are the Lost Ten Tribes of Israel ! We can't go under !

Lord Salisbury gave up the key of Germany in the North Sea when he gave Heligoland to Bismarck's threatenings ; Gladstone gave up the key of Germany in the Mediterranean when he gave

up Corfu, which locks up Trieste and the Adriatic! Another
Prime Minister gave up Minorca, the key of France; another
Prime Minister gave up Ceuta and Tangier, that lock the Mediterranean. Another gave up Curaçoa, which locks up the Panama
Canal. Another Prime Minister (the biggest d——d fool of the
lot !) gave up Java. And so I might go on; and yet, in spite of
the idiots who govern us, we never were so absolutely paramount
as now! Why? Because our Navy at this moment could take
on all the Navies of the world! "Let 'em all come"!

Yours till hell freezes.

(*Signed*) FISHER—The world forgetting—by the
world forgot !

BAD NAUHEIM.
25th June, 1911.

You will see in the *Standard* of 29th May the London Correspondent of the *Irish Times* lets out about "Lord Fisher and war
arrangements"; but as the *Standard*, in the very same issue,
makes the announcement in big type, "We [Great Britain] are in
the satisfactory position of having *twice as many 'Dreadnoughts'*
in commission *as Germany and a number greater by one unit than the
whole of the rest of the world put together !*", I don't think there is
the very faintest fear of war. How wonderfully Providence guides
England ! Just when there is a quite natural tendency to ease
down our naval endeavours comes AGADIR !

" Time and the Ocean and some Guiding Star
In High Cabal have made us what we are ! "

" The Greatest Power on ' Airth,' " as Mr. Champ Clark would
say ! (You ought to meet Champ Clark.) He is likely to succeed Taft as President, *but I put my money on Woodrow Wilson.*[1]
He is Bismarck and Moltke rolled into one. . . . I need not say
that I remain in the closest bonds with the Admiralty. I never
did a wiser thing than coming abroad and remaining abroad and
working like a mole.

I shall not return till July 1912.[2]

Most damnable efforts against me continue in full swing; nevertheless, like Gideon, "Faint yet pursuing" is my motto. . . .

[1] It was not till a year after this that Mr. Wilson was nominated
as a candidate for the Presidency.

[2] He was forced to depart from this resolve.

And yet because in 1909 at the Guildhall, when our naval supremacy had been arranged for in the Navy Estimates of the year, I said to my countrymen, " Sleep quiet in your beds," I was vehemently vilified with malignant truculence, and only yesterday I got a letter from an Aristocrat of Aristocrats, saying that he had heard it stated by A Man of Eminence, the day before, that I was in the pay of Germany ! It is curious that I can't get over the great personal blank I feel in the death of our late Blessed Friend, King Edward ! There was something in the charm of his heart that still chains one to his memory—some magnetic touch.

15th July, 1911.

I haven't heard anything lately of the ——. I suppose they are still flourishing. . . . *What a lot of work for the day of judgment* ! ! ! !

The following letter to Lord Esher is extremely interesting, as it shows what a marvellous foresight Fisher possessed. Had Turkey been on our side in the Great War, a conclusion might have been reached eighteen months earlier than was the case.

LUCERNE.
20th September, 1911.

Through dancing with a sweet American (and, indeed, they are truly delightful, especially if you have the same partner all the evening), I hear, *viâ* a Bremen multi-millionaire, that though the most optimistic official assurances of peace emanate from Berlin, yet there is the most extreme nervousness amongst German business men because of the revelations to them of the French power, both financially and fightingly, so unexpected by them. I suppose if a Pitt or a Palmerston had now been guiding our destinies we should have war. They would say that any peace would be a bad peace, because of the latent damnable feeling in Germany against England. It won't be France any more, it will be England that will be the red rag to the German Bull. And as we *never* were so strong as at present, then Pitt and Co. would say the present is the time to fight. Personally, I am confident of peace. I happen to know in a curious way (but quite certainly) that the Germans are in a blue funk of the British Navy, and are quite assured that 942 German merchant steamers will be " gobbled up " in the first forty-eight hours of war, and also the d——d uncertainty of *when* and *where* 100,000 troops embarked in transports and kept "in the air" might land!

N.B.—There's a lovely spot only ninety miles from Berlin; anyhow, they would demobilize about 1,000,000 German soldiers; but I am getting "off the line" now!

I really sat down to write and tell you of a two days' visit paid to me here by the new American Ambassador to Berlin. *He is a faithful friend.* He is *very, very* pro-English. (He has such a lovely daughter whom I have been dancing with, a perfect GEM! If she don't turn Wilhelm's head, I'll eat my hat!) My friend was American Ambassador at Constantinople when I was Commander-in-Chief of the Mediterranean Fleet. You know it was a ticklish time then; at the worst of the Boer War the British Navy kept the peace. That old Sultan (Abdul Hamid) told me so, and gave me a five-hundred-guinea diamond star, bless him! and he called Lord Salisbury a d——d fool for having left him in the lurch and for having said that "England had put her money on the wrong horse" in backing Turkey, the Turks being the *one* people in the whole world to be England's fast and (if put to it) *only* friend! Well, my dear friend, Leishman saw this *then* in 1899, and sees it now, and hence we were locked up for hours in a secret room here. It all bears immensely on the present Franco-German crisis! That "*greater than Bismarck,*" who is now German Ambassador at Constantinople (Marschall von Bieberstein), and who is the real director of German policy (Waechter is only his *factotum!* as I will prove to you presently!), and so has been led to bluff at Agadir—but those choice words of Lloyd George [1] upset the German apple-cart in a way it was never upset before! (I suppose they were "written-out" words, and Cabinet words, and they were d——d fine words!) Before I go on with the next bit of my

[1] In a speech at the Mansion House on 21st July, 1911, Mr. Lloyd George, then Chancellor of the Exchequer, said: "I conceive that nothing would justify a disturbance of international good-will except questions of the gravest national moment. But if a situation were to be forced upon us in which peace could only be preserved by the surrender of the great and beneficent position Britain has won by centuries of heroism and achievement—by allowing Britain to be treated, where her interests are vitally affected, as if she were of no account in the cabinet of nations—then I say emphatically that peace at that price would be a humiliation intolerable for a great country like ours to endure."

letter I must explain to you that Leishman is a very great friend and admirer of Marschall von Bieberstein and also of Kiderlen-Waechter, the present German Foreign Minister. . . .

Well, dear friend, it's a good thing that Leishman loves England. *He says our Turkish Policy is the laughing-stock of Diplomacy!* Every schoolboy knows that we have a Mahomedan existence and the Turks love us, but all we do is to kick them. As Leishman truly says, the Germans were in the dust by the deposition of Abdul Hamid and England was " All " to the New Turks, but slowly Marschall has worked his way up again, and the Germans again possess the Turks instead of England. The Turkish Army, the very finest fighting Army in the world, was ours for the asking, and " Peace—perfect Peace " in India, Egypt, and Persia, but we've chucked it all away because we have had d——d fools as our Ambassadors ! And how can it be otherwise unless you put in men from outside, as, for instance, Bryce at Washington ? Our strength is Mahomedan, but we are too d——d Christian to see it, and fool about Armenian atrocities and Bulgarian horrors ! Tories and Radicals are both the same. Isn't it wonderful how we get along ! Look at Delagoa Bay, that might have been ours; indeed, *was* ours, only we fooled it away ! Look at Lord Granville and the Cameroons ! Well ! I haven't given Leishman away ! The real German *bonne-bouche* was the complete belt across Africa, but this only if the right of pre-emption as regards the Belgian Congo could have been acquired. I simply tremble at the consequences if the British Red Coats are to be planted on the Vosges Frontier. [Meaning the use of our Army as part of the French Army on the Continent.]

1st October, 1911.

You tell me that Lieut. —— attacks me. A few weeks ago, in a letter to the *Daily Mail*, he said, " Oh, for five minutes of Fisher ! " (or words to that effect). It's the *old, old* story : " To-day Hosanna, to-morrow crucify." I keep on being pestered to return home. *I won't.* Whatever may be his peculiarities, the limelight must be kept on A. K. Wilson. If I came home it would be shifted on to me, and also his status in the Committee of Imperial Defence is immensely magnified by my abstention from its sitting. No; as I have often told you, it don't matter what d——d fools rule us, England remains *top dog* ! Never in our whole history have we been so powerful or so feared as at the present moment.

Phillips [1] writes me that Beresford is bringing out a book this month published by King. (Who is King ? I have never heard the name.) The book is called *The Betrayal*, and, of course, I am the betrayer. I fancy it is hoped I shall be compelled to bring a libel action. There will be disappointment. I was assured of £20,000 damages over one gross libel, but I declined. I told them of Archbishop Whately's advice, " Never fight a chimney-sweep ! You may knock him senseless, but some of the soot comes off on you."

The one great rule of life is, " *Never explain.*"

I. Your friends don't want an explanation. They believe in you.

II. The friends who want an explanation ain't friends.

III. Your enemies won't believe any explanation.

I never in all my life have ever yet explained, and don't mean to. The Day of Judgment will clear up things all right, and it ain't so far off. Perhaps the Battle of Armageddon is coming along now !

Fisher never gave up the belief that we should have taken the initiative, so far as the declaration of war was concerned. He wrote :

Last week [dancing] I had my arm round the waist of the wife of the biggest millionaire in Bremen, and she confided to me that her husband had written to say all the German mercantile world were in a " blue fright " (as she called it) of England making war. Yes, I suppose if we had Pitt or Palmerston with us they would have forced France into war ; because they were firm believers in fighting at your own time and recognized, perhaps, the greatest of Nelson's sayings, that " you don't want a simple victory over your enemy ; you want to annihilate him " ; and this he did at the Nile, Copenhagen, and at Trafalgar. *God bless him !*

LUCERNE.
10th October, 1911.

. . . I yesterday had a long letter from M'Kenna begging me to return and " put the gloves on again," and in view of his arguments I am going to do so when A. K. Wilson vanishes early next year ! It is, however, distasteful to me. I have had a lovely time here.

[1] Mr. F. J. Phillips, one of his secretaries when First Sea Lord.

REIGATE PRIORY, SURREY.
20th October.

. . . I am here three days with Winston and many of the Cabinet.
I got a very urgent letter to come here, and I think my advice
has been fully and completely digested ; but don't say a word,
please, to a soul ! I am returning direct to Lucerne on Wednesday ;
after Tuesday at Kilverstone."

LUCERNE.
9th November.

These are very ticklish times indeed ! I have got to be extremely careful. I must not get between Winston and A. K. W.
in any way—it would not only be very grave, but fatal to any
smooth working. So I begged Wilson not to write to me. With
extreme reluctance I went to Reigate as I did ; but M'Kenna
urged me on the grounds of the good of the Navy ; and, from what
Winston has since said to a friend of mine, I think I did right
in going.

He received information that there was an organized
conspiracy among a certain clique of officers to kill
the new scheme of education by boycotting all the
midshipmen who took up engineering.

Letter to Mr. Leyland, 7th November, 1911.

Sir X. Y. is pestiferous ! he is playing up to —— and to the
snobs, who all think it is ungentlemanly to be an engineer and
are doing their utmost to ruin the Navy by calling those of the
New Scheme Midshipmen " Greasers " who evince any partiality
for engineering knowledge. X. Y. was twice passed over as a
Rear-Admiral for employment because he was a soft ass. In a
misguided moment I persuaded Lord George Hamilton to employ
him ; he now bites the hand that fed him. . . . I obeyed an
urgent summons and spent Saturday, Sunday, and Monday in a
country house at Reigate with Winston and other Cabinet Ministers. I had no sleep for four nights ; when I was not talking I
was writing. My brain was buzzing like a hive of bees. They all
fell on my neck and kissed me. Time will show if they are
liars. . . . I never met a politician yet who was not an " *oppor-
tunist*," except M'Kenna, and he twice threw up and walked out
of the Cabinet for the good of the Navy ; but they had got even

with him at last !   This is why I was reluctant to meet his enemies (D——n them).   But I made a point of spending 3½ hours with M'Kenna while Winston was waiting for me.

Mr. M'Kenna, the finest First Lord of the Admiralty we have seen in modern times, was superseded by Mr. Winston Churchill, who at once began to bring in a scheme for a Naval War Staff.   His ideas were not agreed to by Lord Fisher or by Admiral of the Fleet Sir Arthur Wilson.   These two Admirals had far more general experience of the Navy than any other officers, and both were strongly against the creation of a Chief of the Staff other than the First Sea Lord.   This arbitrary act of overriding the experience and advice of the two greatest Admirals of modern years brought retribution to Mr. Churchill later on in the early years of the war.

CHAPTER XVI

INTERREGNUM, PART II: 1911—1914

Men must be taught as if you taught them not,
And things unknown proposed as things forgot.
                                                    POPE.

The War Staff—Lord Fisher's belief in Sir Arthur Wilson—His
labour to arrange for Sir John Jellicoe being Commander-in-
Chief in 1914—His interviews with Mr. Churchill—The new
Board—His visit to Bologna—Trafalgar Square and the Admirals
—Feeling in Germany—Annoyance at the War Office schemes
—Death of Mr. Stead—His anger with Mr. Churchill over the
appointment of Admirals—Determines never to speak or write
to him again—Enticed back by being made Chairman of an Oil
Commission—Visited at Naples by the Prime Minister and Mr.
Churchill—Influenced in his decision by a sermon—Fame—
His fight for Cromarty—Desire for rest.

WHEN Mr. Churchill came to the Admiralty,
knowing nothing at all about the Navy, and
not appreciating that the Navy, both in
peace and war, is fundamentally a different machine
from the Army, he was determined to introduce a
War Staff at the Admiralty modelled on the one at
the War Office.   Lord Fisher afterwards wrote :

I loved Sir Arthur Wilson's reported reply to the maniacs who
think the Navy is the same as the Army.   If it is not true, it is
ben trovato.   He said the Naval War Staff at the Admiralty [under
the old system] consisted of himself, assisted by every soul inside
the Admiralty, and, he added, " including the charwomen—they
emptied the waste-paper baskets full of the plans of the amateur
strategists, Cabinet and otherwise."
No such rubbish has ever been talked as about the Naval War
Staff. . . . A Naval War Staff at the Admiralty is a very excellent

organization for cutting out and arranging foreign newspaper clippings.

The outcome of this expanded Naval War Staff beyond its real requirements, such as I have indicated, and which were provided for when I was First Sea Lord, was that a Chief of the Staff, in imitation of him at the War Office, was planked into the Admiralty and indirectly supplanted the First Sea Lord. I won't enlarge on this further. It's many years before another war can possibly take place, and it's now a waste of educated labour to discuss it further. All I would ask is for anyone to take up the last issue of the Navy List and see the endless pages of naval officers at the Admiralty or holding shore appointments. There has never been anything like these numbers in all our sea-history ! It's deplorable !

The Naval College which I established at Portsmouth is absolutely a different affair. There it can be arranged that all the officers go to sea daily, and work as if with the Fleet, with flotillas of destroyers which are there available in quantities. These destroyers would represent all the items of the Fleet ; and the formations of war and the meetings of hostile Fleets could be practised, and so constitute the Naval War College, a real gem in war efficiency.

At the time when Mr. Churchill's scheme was being forced on the Admiralty, Lord Fisher also wrote :

7th November, 1911.

I had left a secret memorandum gradually developing the War Council at the Admiralty (which I started before I left) with a War Staff, the War College at Portsmouth being the germ of it all. Winston has swallowed it whole.[1] The argument for a War Staff is that you *may* have a d——d fool as First Sea Lord, and so you put him in commission, as it were. But if there is a Barham as First Sea Lord, he'll run the war and no one else.

I never told anyone my real plan of War, no more would A. K. W. ;[2] but A. K. W., not being a Machiavelli, wouldn't tell the Cabinet anything. I, on the other hand, told them so much that they thought me perfect. I gave them 600 pages of print of

[1] As already pointed out, Lord Fisher was always much averse to Mr. Churchill's scheme of having a Chief of the Staff who was not First Sea Lord. This was no part of the scheme here referred to.

[2] Admiral of the Fleet Sir Arthur Wilson.

war plans. *A. K. Wilson is a very great man.* Beresford and Co. are trying to discredit him. Both in strategy and tactics he rolled up every Admiral ever pitted against him, and his fighting views are absolutely impregnable. Repington wrote letters to Cabinet Ministers maligning Wilson and questioning the readiness of the Fleet. The German Emperor knew its readiness, so did the whole of the mercantile community of Germany. Their fear was that England would force Germany to fight! I have all this *absolutely first hand!*

The following letter contains a wonderful prophecy of the actual date that war in Europe would break out. Lord Fisher named October because the German harvest would be gathered by that date. Three years before the outbreak of the war he was only two months out in his forecast.

November 1911.

My two private visits to Winston were fruitful. I tell *you* (*and you only*)! the whole secret of the changes! *To get Jellicoe Commander-in-Chief of the Home Fleet prior to October* 1914, which is the date of the Battle of Armageddon. He will succeed Callaghan automatically in two years from the 19th December, 1911. So will have all well in hand by the before-mentioned date! " Nunc Dimittis." *Everything revolved round Jellicoe!* If ever you breathe a word I *can never forgive you!* *No one* sees it and I don't want them to. Winston presses me to pay him another visit. I have refused. I have spent six days and nights with him, and he is saturated. He will do well. He is *brave.* He dropped A. K. W. like Wilhelm dropped Bismarck. The cases were identical. You will understand! You instinctively hit the nail on the head. Young Admirals at sea are an imperative necessity. Physical endurance is vital. *Voilà!* Callaghan and Jellicoe! and all must be junior to the last named.

It's curious being a mole! I don't want to get trapped and skinned, so don't give me away!

The remark about Sir Arthur Wilson which follows is of great interest, as it affords the only clue to what was the joint scheme arranged between Lord Fisher and Sir Arthur. " And in five seconds he would have pounced" can only mean a pounce on something— perhaps Heligoland or Kiel. As the plan was destroyed by Sir Arthur after the crisis was over, no one will ever know what was arranged.

Is it in the faintest degree conceivable that A. K. Wilson was unready ? I am perhaps the only person in the world who ever knew his war plans (he told the Defence Committee so !). *And in five seconds he would have pounced !* But he had the sagacity to see that the Germans would have been simply mad to fight, so he slept quiet in his bed while Repington was inspecting the Home Fleet ! And Cabinet Ministers receiving letters from a soldier as to how the Fleet ought to fight ! Of course, we are the lost Ten Tribes of Israel. There is no other explanation why the British Empire don't sink.

He then turns to an amusing anecdote :

An American looking down the crater of Vesuvius in eruption said, " It looks like Hell." An Englishman heard him and said *sotto voce, " How these Americans do travel ! "*

LUCERNE.
10th November, 1911.

MY DEAR ARNOLD WHITE,
    I think I ought to let you know I've been in England since 27th October to 31st October. I went with extreme reluctance, but Winston Churchill sent me a pressing letter, and M'Kenna, with splendid self-effacement, so urged the good of the Navy that I went, and had a Saturday to Monday in the country with Winston and some of his Cabinet colleagues, and I only hope I did good ; but I do not trust any politician. They are, all of them, " opportunists." Winston Churchill has since told a friend of mine that he intends to " lean " on me. We shall see !
    There's a d——d pernicious report being spread that A. K. Wilson had no war plan and that the English Fleet was not ready. To throw rotten eggs at the man who undoubtedly will be our Admiralissimo for the next five years certain is simply damnable. He has " rolled up " every Admiral and every combination of Admirals ever pitted against him for about nine years on end

(and Beresford and his satellites most of all), both in strategy and
tactics, and his dispositions of the Fleet were all studied and perfect.   As I believe I am the only one ever to be trusted with his
plans, I can speak.   But you see how secret this is, and you must
never breathe a word.   But that —— Repington hates A. K. W.
for having steam-rollered him with his famous memorandum on
" Invasion," and wrote a lot of d——d nonsense in private letters
to Cabinet Ministers ; hence this pernicious lie.   I need not say
to you that A. K. W. has not been polite.   It's not his way.   He
can't suffer fools gladly.

In November 1911 a new Board of Admiralty was
appointed.   Mr. M'Kenna went to the Home Office
and Mr. Churchill to the Admiralty.   Needless to say,
after this no more was heard from the latter of naval
reductions.   Fisher busied himself over the constitution of the new Board.

2nd December, 1911.

*I have had an immense triumph over [the constitution of] the Board
of Admiralty.*   No one suspected any of the new men.   I would
have gone further and got rid of the one that has been kept.   I
always warned M'Kenna he was stupid in his selections ; but he
thought himself so paramount as to be able to neglect his colleagues.   In the end they wrecked him, and dear old Wilson,
though splendid and unsurpassed, was not a Machiavelli, and these
lawyers in the Cabinet just " walked round " him, *similia similibus
curantur.*   When a cunning rogue talks at you, you must talk
back at him.   Dear old Wilson only smiled.   That ain't enough
in this wicked world.   Winston Churchill has again, two days
ago, pressed me to pay him another private visit.   I don't think
it's judicious.   I am letting it stand over.   The greater your
friends [1] the more careful you ought to be of their susceptibilities.

Apparently Lady Fisher's love for the antique did
not appeal to Fisher, for he wrote to his son from
Bologna on the 20th December, 1911 :

We are here in the most awful hole I ever was in.   Mother
insisted on coming to this hotel because Charles V was born here

[1] This referred to Mr. M'Kenna.

or lived here 600 years ago (I should have thought it much older by the smells), and the wine we had at dinner reminded me of old Vavasseur's. I objected, and the proprietor explained it had been several hundred years in bottle. In fact, the whole place is Rip Van Winkle, and nothing will induce me ever to give in again to Mother's craze for ancient history. (Thank goodness we are going to an hotel at Naples that has only just been built.) I had an amusing time buying refreshments to-day, as I asked for a church instead of cheese. I thought *chiesa* was the Italian for " cheese " ; anyhow, it is in German, and they might have known what I meant.

Fisher was rather hard on the Italians, considering *formaggio* is their usual word for " cheese."

The idea of our Army forming an obscure detachment of a continental army was always to Fisher like a red rag to a bull.

December, 1911.

I shouldn't have written again so soon except for just now seeing in a Paris paper that Sir John French, accompanied by four officers, has landed at Calais *en route* for the French Headquarters and expatiating on the evident intentions of joint military actions. Do you remember the classic interview we had with the late King in his cabin ? If this is on the *tapis* again, then we have another deep regret for the loss of that sagacious intuition !

King Edward may not have been clever, but he never failed in his judgment on whose opinion to rely.

I enclose you a letter from ——, received a little time ago ; he is a very eminent civil engineer. There is a " dead set " being made to get the midshipmen under the new scheme to rebel against engineering ! —— and Co. are persistently at it through their friends in the Fleet, and calling those midshipmen who go in for engineering " Greasers." The inevitable result of the present young officers in the Navy disparaging and slighting this chief necessary qualification of engineering in these engineering days will be to force the throwing open of entry as officers in the Navy to all *classes of the population,* and adopting State education and support till the pay is sufficient to support.

24th December, 1911.

. . . I have had a hectic time with four hurricanes crossing the Channel, and balancing on the tight-rope with one end held by Winston and the other by M'Kenna, but they both held tight and I am all right. Without doubt M'Kenna is a patriot to have encouraged ME to help Winston as he has done ! I have not heard what the War Staff is doing. It does not trouble me. My sole object was to procure Jellicoe to be Commander-in-Chief of the Home Fleet on 19th December 1913, and that is being done by his being appointed Second-in-Command, and he will automatically be Commander-in-Chief in two years from that date. All the recent changes revolved round Jellicoe, and NO ONE sees it !

NAPLES.
3rd January, 1912.

. . . I fully agree with you about the Navy want of first-class intellects. Concentration and Discipline combine to cramp the sea-officer. . . . Great views don't get grasped. Winston urges me to come back, but he forgets the greatest of all the great Napoleonic sayings, " J'ordonne ou je me tais." Besides, you see, I was the First Violin. However, Winston is splendidly receptive. I can't possibly write what has happened, but he is a *brave man*. And as sixteen Admirals have been scrapped, I am more popular than ever ! ! !

A lovely woman two days ago sent me this riddle : " Why are you like Holland ?—Because you lie low and are damned all round." But there it is. Jellicoe will be Admiralissimo when Armageddon comes along, and *everything that was done revolves round that, and no one has seen it*. He has all the attributes of Nelson, and his age.

25th February.

I see another General is to be deported into Trafalgar Square ! [Lord Napier from opposite the Athenæum to make way for King Edward's statue.] Why don't they pull down the Duke of York's, who sold commissions to haberdashers *viâ* Mrs. Clarke (*qui facit per alium facit per se*). When Nelson looks round London, he only sees one naval officer, Sir John Franklin, and he died from ice, not war ! Where are Hawke of Quiberon, Rodney, Cornwallis, Howe, Benbow, and all of Nelson's Captains ? Was this country made by sailors or soldiers ? If monuments are any guide, then the sea had no victories for us.

Labouchere said to me the other day at Florence, "Where would you be if you had not been attacked with spiteful malignancy?" I suppose there is something in that.

I have been working like a mole at the adoption by the Imperial Conference of a "*world-wide English-speaking Government monopoly of wireless.*" I think it will come off! Don't breathe a word about it, please! Wireless is the pith and marrow of war! *You can't cut the air!* You *can* cut telegraph wires, and the hourly developments of wireless are *prodigious.*

Yours till "charcoal sprouts."

NAPLES.
7th March, 1912.

I have had strangely intimate opportunities of learning the very inside of German feeling towards England. *It is bitterly intense and widespread.* Without any doubt whatever, the Germans thought they were going to squeeze France out of Morocco. You can take that as a fact, no matter what lies are told by the German Foreign Minister, and Clemenceau's unpublished speech will have proved it. But he said enough. And how treacherous to England was ——! What a dirty business! Anyhow, as a *German Admiral of big repute* wrote confidentially and privately a few days since, "German public opinion is roused in a way I had not before thought possible." And as far as I can make out, the very worst possible thing was Haldane's visit—a British Cabinet Minister crawling up the back stairs of the German Foreign Office in carpet slippers; and, judging from all that is told me, it has made the Germans worse than ever, and for a variety of quite opposite reasons, all produces the same result. Any more Heligolands would mean certain war; it is very peculiar how we have left our impregnable position we occupied before Haldane's visit to take up a most humiliating, weak and dangerous one.

4th April, 1912.

You sent me *Punch* of 27th March, and the spirit moves me to draw your attention to the pith and marrow of Winston Churchill's speech, which "Toby M.P." has extracted in the following incomparable sentence—*golden*: "We must always be ready to meet *at our average moment* anything that any possible enemy might hurl at us at his *selected moment.*" . . .

I hope you consider Winston's speech on the Navy Estimates

A GROUP ON BOARD RUSSIAN ROYAL YACHT *STANDARD*, 1909
Sir John Fisher   Grand Duchess Olga   The Czar

a fine performance—it was splendidly built up, I think. I have
seldom been more gratified than in reading in an American newspaper (we revel in Americans here), " That every brick in the
edifice of Winston's speech was baked six to eight years ago."

Abuse and the cold neglect of the Cabinet had caused
Lord Fisher to welcome praise. He became particularly susceptible to this class of honest flattery, and
made up many differences of opinion he subsequently
had with Mr. Churchill when soothed by soft sayings.

2nd April, 1912.

. . . As you say, Winston has done splendidly. He and I last
November discussed every brick of his speech at Devonport Dockyard while visiting the 33-knot *Lion* " Dreadnought " by night
alone together, and don't accuse me of too much egotism, but he
stopped dramatically on the Dockyard stones and said to me,
" You're a great man ! " . . . We are lagging behind in out-
Dreadnoughting the *Dreadnought.* A plunge, of course—a huge
plunge—but so was the *Dreadnought.* So was the turbine, so was
the water-tube boiler, and, last of all, so was the 13½-inch gun which
now holds the field, and the whole Board of Admiralty (bar
Jellicoe) and all the experts dead against it [1]—but we plunged !
So it is now : we want more speed—less armour—a 15-inch gun
—more sub-division—oil only—and chauffeurs instead of engineers
and stokers, and a " Dreadnought " that will go round the world
without requiring to replenish fuel ! The *Nonpareil !* Winston
says he will call her the *Fisher. I owe more than I can say to
M'Kenna.* I owe nearly as much to Winston for scrapping a dozen
Admirals on 5th December last so as to get Jellicoe Second-in-
Command of the Home Fleet. If war comes before 1914, then
Jellicoe will be Nelson at the Battle of St. Vincent ; if it comes
in 1915, then he'll be Nelson at Trafalgar ! . . .

Again, I've had quite affectionate letters from three important
Admirals. Why should I come home and filch their credit ? All
this is to explain to you why I keep abroad, as you ask me what
are my future plans. . . .

[1] This was not so. His expert advisers at the Admiralty were the
original pushers in the matter ; but he gave it his whole-hearted
support.

II—10

The banner unfurled on the 21st October, 1904, by the d——d scoundrel [Fisher himself] who on that day became First Sea Lord had inscribed on it:

" The fighting efficiency of the Fleet
and
Its instant readiness for War,"

and, as Winston bravely said, " that is now the case and no credit to himself," but he ought to have gone further back than M'Kenna for the credit. *It was Balfour.* He saw me through. No one else would allow a hundred and sixty ships to be scrapped, etc. But you've had enough!

25th April, 1912.

. . . I fully agree with you that the schemes of the General Staff of the British Army are grotesque. Their projects last August, had we gone to war, were wild in the extreme. You will remember a famous interview we two had with King Edward, in his cabin on board the Royal yacht—how he stamped on the idea (that then enthused the War Office mind) of England once more engaged in a great Continental war! " Marlboroughs cheap to-day " was the kettle of fish advised by the militarists!

I walked the sands of Scheveningen with General Gross von Schwartzhoff in June 1899. The German Emperor said he (Schwartzhoff) was a greater than Moltke. He was the Military German Delegate at The Hague Conference; he was designated as Chief of the General Staff at Berlin, but he was burnt to death in China instead. I had done him a very good turn indeed, so he opened his heart to me. There was no German Navy then; we were doing Fashoda; and he expatiated on the rôle of the British Army—how the absolute supremacy of the British Navy gave it such inordinate power far beyond its numerical strength, because two hundred thousand men embarked in transports, and God only knowing where they might be put ashore, was a weapon of enormous influence, and capable of deadly blows—occupying, perhaps, Antwerp, Flushing, etc. (but, of course, he only was thinking of the Cotentin Peninsula [1]), or landing ninety miles from Berlin in that fourteen miles of sandy beach (in Pomerania)— impossible of defence against a battle fleet sweeping with devastating shells the flat country for miles like mower scythes— no fortifications able to withstand projectiles of 1,450 lb.

[1] I.e. our landing in France near the Channel Islands.

Yes, you are *so* right ! The average man is incapable of a *wide* survey. He looks through a pinhole and only sees just a little bit much magnified. Napoleon and Cromwell ! where are they ?

Mr. W. T. Stead was drowned when the *Titanic* struck an ice-floe. Lord Fisher lost a very great friend. He wrote to Mr. Arnold White :

28th April, 1912.

Though you differed from Stead, you were both very little different from each other, both of you " Dreadnoughts " as against the evil, and for the good, fearing no power on earth and wanting no man's favour ! It's lovely to read that 2,500 friends attended his memorial service at the Westminster Chapel ! It says, "No more could get in " ! *Why !* that's more than attended any memorial service I know of at Westminster Abbey. Old Stead was talking to a friend of mine in the smoking-room when the ship struck ! He told me he would die in his boots ! and so he did ! I loved Queen Alexandra for sending her Equerry, General Brocklehurst, to represent her at the memorial service. It's a puny spirit that don't recognize greatness in any social stratum, however low down ! I have cause to keep his memory dear. He resisted most insidious blandishments even only to be silent— but he fought for me tooth and nail ! As, indeed, you are again like him in so doing ! When they told him at Berlin that England needn't be frightened, he replied, " Certainly not. For every ship you lay down, we lay down two." So he really was the originator of " two keels to one " !

. . . The Prime Minister invited me to the Defence Committee last Thursday, but I am doing a little of " Achilles sulking in the tent," as he and Winston, to serve their political ends, have been doing a bit of truckling lately, and I have " let fly," which won't make me any more popular among the parasites ! It is really damnable how men can be brave in December and funkers in April ! Perhaps I ought to have been on the spot !

I've two days ago by King's Messenger got home eight sheets on the subject you have so much at heart, of German annexation of Belgium and Holland ! It won't happen while the British Navy is kept in its present position and overwhelming supremacy, which France knows is the only thing to keep the German Army out of Paris. Our soldiers are grotesque in their absurd ideas of war, but, happily, they are powerless. It is Antwerp we shall seize, and not go fooling on the Vosges Frontier, and the Germans will smell Hell when they find us at Cuxhaven !

The great advantage of absence is *Littera scripta manet* ; the effect of a personal discussion passes off, while the written word remains.

In April 1912 Mr. Churchill appointed three Admirals to important commands. He wrote to Lord Fisher explaining his reasons for these appointments, who on April 22nd replied :

. . . I fear this must be my last communication with you in any matter at all. I am sorry for it, but I consider you have betrayed the Navy in these three appointments, and what the pressure could have been to induce you to betray your trust is beyond my comprehension.[1]

He then criticized these appointments in detail, and continued :

It is the deepest disappointment to me that you have not been able to see your way to resist pressure. Anyhow, all I can do is to avoid any further communication with the Admiralty. The mischief is done.

Vestigia nulla retrorsum.

　　.　　　.　　　.　　　.　　　.　　　.　　　.

There are splendid officers of superior rank in the Navy, but, alas ! in a naval disaster there is no time to send for a Roberts to retrieve the incompetency of a Buller. You have arranged a Colenso. I am going to transfer my body and my money to the United States. I can't remedy what has been done, and it's no d——d use squealing. A naval Colenso is irreparable, irremediable, eternal.

Adieu.

Yours,

(*signed*) FISHER.

Admiral Sir Berkeley Milne was one of the officers referred to. He had had an excellent record in the

---

[1] This is the second breach between the two.

Navy in all its ranks, and was perfectly qualified to command the Mediterranean Fleet. But this was not enough for Fisher ; he demanded that two other requirements should be satisfied : first, that an Admiral appointed to the command of a fleet in peace-time should be the one best suited to command that fleet in war ; and secondly, that every Commander-in-Chief afloat should, in October 1914, be junior to Sir John Jellicoe.

Rightly or wrongly, he considered that there were other Admirals more fit to command in the Mediterranean in war-time ; also Sir Berkeley Milne was senior to Sir John Jellicoe.

The peculiar interest attaching to this appointment is due to the subsequent escape of the *Goeben* and *Breslau,* to which Mr. Churchill, in his volume *The Aftermath,* assigns the main reason for Turkey's entering the war against the Allies. The fear felt by Turkey of the Russian ships in the Black Sea was such that that country would not have dared to face the Russians without the protection afforded by the two German ships. After full inquiry, the Admiralty approved the dispositions of Sir Berkeley Milne during this episode. No blame of any sort can therefore attach to him. But, as is the case in every naval *contretemps,* there remains the doubt whether a younger officer less orthodox professionally, might not have devised and put into execution other dispositions which might have produced better results. It is useless now to speculate what these might have been ; but it is impossible to forget that an alternative appointment, as urged by Lord Fisher, who had a great experience and unerring instinct in such matters, was disregarded by Mr. Churchill.

NAPLES.
29th April, 1912.

. . . You say to me, "Come home!" You remind me of *"personal influence."* I KNOW IT. Three days ago I was invited to name one of three week-ends in June to meet two very great men at a country house. No one else. The day before yesterday Winston Churchill asks me. Hardly a week passes without such similar pressure from most influential quarters—*"Why don't I come home and smack and pulverize?"* Of course, they one and all exaggerate—that in ten minutes I could *"Sweep the board,"* and so on! I know exactly what I can do. I've been fighting fifty years! *But I don't want a personal victory!*

. . . I'm going to take my body and what little money I have . . . to the United States in the near future. It would be no use my coming home. *The mischief is done!* [1] . . . From patriotic motives I have given Winston of my very best in the replies going to him this day from Brindisi by King's Messenger as regards designs and policy and fighting measures.

Lord Fisher was far too useful to the First Lord to be left to carry out his intention of remaining abroad and estranged from home. He was known to be an enthusiast regarding the introduction of oil and its many possibilities into the Navy; he was therefore enticed to England by the offer of being made Chairman of an Oil Commission.

NAPLES.
19th May, 1912.

I had a letter from W. C. this morning, and he and the Prime Minister have decided to come direct here to Naples to spend a few days, and a telegram has just come saying they arrive on 23rd May. . . . I suppose [the reasons are] the coming Supplementary Estimates, and also types of new ships about which I am deadly antagonistic with every living soul at the Admiralty, and one of the consequences [of which] has been that a great Admiralty official has got the boot ! ! ! So Winston is right when he writes to me this morning that in all vital points I have had my way! He adds: "The future of the Navy rests in the hands of men in whom your confidence is as strong as mine, . . . and no change of Government would carry with it any change of policy in this respect."

[1] This refers to the above-mentioned appointment.

21st May, 1912.

My address will be Hôtel National, Lucerne, where I go on 27th May. I was going the day after to-morrow, but Asquith and Winston Churchill asked me *secretly* to be here at Naples for four days to see them (*en route* to Malta), and to keep my time *absolutely free*. I have no idea what for! And they have given out that they are going direct to Malta from Genoa; but it will surely leak out if the Admiralty yacht is here for four days.

To his son :

18*th May*, 1912.

Winston has this moment telegraphed to see me in the Admiralty yacht. . . . It is really wonderful his coming here to see me after the awful letters I have written to him! I suppose I ought to take it as a compliment!

Lord Esher, Sir John Jellicoe, and Captain Hankey, the Secretary of the Committee of Imperial Defence, have all three written to me begging me to keep on my former terms with W. C. as being of the utmost importance. . . .

To his daughter-in-law :

LUCERNE.
23*rd May*, 1912.

. . . I threaten to come and stay with you *end* of July or perhaps beginning of August ; *but all is yet uncertain*, as unless I have my own way absolutely—I told them this, but as the Prime Minister is "dead on" for having me back, I expect all will be right! They invented a long story which was put in all the papers that the Admiralty yacht was driven into Naples by the bad weather! It's quite curious how everyone is always so afraid that it should be thought that they have seen me! I saw in yesterday's *Standard*, which I picked up by accident, that some Member of Parliament writes that it is well known that I am running the Navy and the Admiralty all the time ! ! !

This is another extract from one of the many letters to his daughter-in-law, whom he invariably addressed as " My sweet Jane " :

LUCERNE.
9*th June*, 1912. *Sunday*.

There's a splendid doctor here whom the Comtesse de Flandres recommended highly to me, and I had him when I had a bit of a chill, and he thoroughly enjoyed examining me all over several times—and he preached me a sermon ! He told me everything was splendidly sound and especially my heart, and if only now I would do no more work I might live for many, many happy years. But if I went to hard work again, then no one could tell ! I think there's a great deal in what he said. All the same, I quite expect I shall be hauled out next Friday; but I shall be serenely happy if I am not !

He then breaks off to talk about her father being painted by Herkomer, which he had arranged and in which he was greatly interested.

What a triumph that your dear Father is being painted by Herkomer ! I am more delighted than I can tell you ! and I loved your telegram ! It will be the picture of the year in next year's Royal Academy. Frances [1] ought to be done also. I think he could make a splendid picture of her—do tell your Father. Herkomer is such a real genius. I'm going to write to Herkomer and tell him he has got to surpass my picture when he does your Father !

That he had no great desire to meet the Prime Minister or Mr. Churchill is shown by the following extract from a letter to Mr. Arnold White :

. . . Asquith and Winston Churchill ask me secretly to be here at Naples for four days to see them *en route* to Malta, and to keep my time *absolutely free*. I have no idea what for ! . . . Anyhow, I've twice refused to go in the Admiralty yacht. If Mahomet comes to the mountain, why, the mountain can't well help it. . . .

To his son :

17th June, 1912.

I'm worn out with writing. Eight sheets to Sir Francis Hopwood yesterday—nine to Winston Churchill to-day in answer to a long and pressing letter from him received this morning. You can go on writing here, as there is no chance of my leaving here. It really makes me blush what they say of me as being the one

---

[1] Her stepmother.

and there is no one else. However, I've got to be sure of my
ground. I'm just tired out with writing, so can't say a word
more. I'm extremely reluctant to give up my freedom ; but the
clergyman here preached a most eloquent extempore sermon
yesterday morning. I've never seen him before in my life, and
he fixed his eyes steadfastly on me and said, " No man still possessing all his powers and full of vitality has any right to say, ' I
am now going to rest, as I have had a hard life,' for he owes a duty
to his country and fellow-men." It was an arrow shot at a
venture like the one that killed Ahab.

Had the circumstances been reversed, and Lord
Fisher and Mr. Churchill changed places, we should
have had little doubt that the clergyman had been
primed by Lord Fisher to persuade a member of his
congregation. It is exactly the class of foresight, pre-
conception, and action which was characteristic of
Lord Fisher.

The following extract shows the class of pressure
that was put on him, and the subtle flattery and
appeal which dragged him from his rest once more to
put his giant shoulders to the wheel :

The natural, inherent, unavoidable difficulties are such that
require the drive and enthusiasm of a big man. . . .

No one else can do it. . . .

Perhaps no one else but you can do it at all.

It means that you will have to give your life and strength, and
I don't know what there is to give you in exchange or return.

When you have solved the riddle, you will find a very hushed,
attentive audience. But the riddle will *not* be solved unless *you*
are willing, for the Glory of God, to expend yourself upon its toil.
I recognize it is little enough I can offer you. But your Gifts,
your Force, your Hopes, belong to the Navy, with or without
return, and as your most sincere admirer and as the Head of the
Admiralty, I claim them now for the Navy, knowing well you will
not grudge them. You need a plough to draw, your propellers
are racing in the air !

Yours in warm regard,

W. C.

Here is a pæan of triumph over the success of one of his reforms. The statement that no one else supported him is, of course, an exaggeration. He had many supporters, but also many opponents. In his later years he was always wont to dwell on the opposition rather than on the support he had received :

12th June, 1912.

. . . This instant news has come to me that there are 540 eligible and selected candidates for 60 vacancies for boy artificers in the Navy at the approaching examination ! When I introduced this scheme eight years ago every man's hand was against me, and the whole weight of Trades Unionism inside the House of Commons and out of it was organized against me . . . We were dominated by the Engineers ! We had to accept engine-room artificers who had been brought up on making bicycles ! *Now,* these boys are employed on the marine engine ! and they have knocked out the old lot completely. Our very best engine-room artificers are these boys ! Not one of my colleagues or anyone else supported me ! *Do you wonder that I don't care a d——n for what anyone says ?*

21st June, 1912.

At last fame has come to me ! ! ! As I was going to interview Sir E. Grey, Lord Haldane, Lloyd George, M'Kenna, Sir Arthur Nicolson, and Sir Robert Chalmers, I thought I would go to Solomon *en route* and get a swagger "buttonhole." When I asked what I had to pay, I was told, "My Lord, we could not think of charging your Lordship anything." The nearest approach to this before was when I saw my photograph on a pound of starch. . . .

I've had a hectic time ; no sleep for three nights now.

Lloyd George, Lord Redesdale, and Sir Robert Chalmers, and Winston are coming to Kilverstone on 20th July. I am taking down to-day a ton of champagne, port, sherry, whisky, and claret. I've got all I wanted, but I am most depressed at relinquishing my freedom.

KILVERSTONE HALL.
30th June, 1912.

The recruiting HAS begun. The 8 will follow :

We want 8.
We won't wait.

No other course but that now in progress would have done it.
I don't mind personal obloquy, but it's a bit hard to undergo
friends' doubts of me ; but the clouds will roll by. I've got all
my " working bees " round me here of the Royal Commission [on
oil and the internal-combustion engine]. We shall "stagger
humanity."

KILVERSTONE.
July 1912.

I want a month's holiday. I have been working like a galley-
slave since the 19th June, the day I left Lucerne. I often wish
myself back. *Fancy!* A dance every blessed night there
now ! ! ! and here I am getting up at 4 a.m. to drudge and slave.
I should be just going to bed then if I were at Lucerne. We're
just going up to see one of the London boys who is ill with rheuma-
tism. Mother thinks it only growing pains ! Just imagine some
of these children twelve years old who have never seen a green
field in all their lives before ! It's awful. They are all so clean
and well dressed and well mannered. One little girl of fourteen
at Mrs. Carter's is a perfect little lady, and so very nice-looking.
We have spent all our money on cricket bats and wickets and
skipping ropes, etc.[1]

2nd August, 1912.

At the Defence Committee yesterday . . . we had a regular
set-to with Lloyd George (supported by Harcourt and Morley
chiefly) against the provision of Defence for Cromarty as a shelter
anchorage for the Fleet, and the Prime Minister adjourned the
discussion to the Cabinet as the temperature got hot ! As you
know, I have always been " dead-on " for Cromarty and hated
Rosyth, which is an unsafe anchorage—the whole Fleet in jeopardy
the other day ; and there's that beastly bridge which, if blown up,
makes the egress risky without examination. . . . Also Cromarty
is strategically better than Rosyth. . . . Also Lloyd George had a
row about the airships—Seely's Sub-Committee. We *must* have
airships.

29th December, 1912.

. . . I'm getting sick of England and want to get back to Naples
and the sun and the *dolce far niente* ! What fools we all are to work
like we do ! Till we drop !

[1] Children sent down by the Country Holiday Association.

The Commission over which Lord Fisher was called on to preside to investigate the oil resources of the world and their relation to this country and the Royal Navy was, to a great extent, a secret inquiry ; that is, a promise was given to all the witnesses examined that their evidence would be treated as confidential and never published. This, of course, was necessary in order that the large oil interests might agree to disclose their resources. The main result of the Commission, as far as this country was concerned, was the agreement entered into by the Government with the Persian Oil Company. The following statement kindly supplied by Lord Greenway gives practically all that can at the present time be made public :

In no direction was Lord Fisher's wonderful foresight and great breadth of vision more strikingly demonstrated than in his early appreciation of the great part which oil fuel was destined to play in future naval warfare. So long ago as in 1886 he was known in the Navy and in official circles as the " Oil Maniac " (a title of which he was in later years justly proud), and when he took office as First Sea Lord in 1904 he set about taking every possible step to ensure the securing of supplies from countries which either belonged to or were politically allied to the British Empire. One of his first steps in that direction was to enter into a contract with the Burmah Oil Company (then practically the only producer of oil in the British Empire, with the exception of the Shale Oil Companies in Scotland) for the relatively small quantity of fuel oil which that company was then in a position to produce. Another was to urge the Colonial Office to do its utmost to encourage the development of the oil resources in the Island of Trinidad. A third was to induce the Burmah Oil Company to come to the assistance of Mr. W. Knox D'Arcy in the development of his concession in Persia, which has since been proved to contain some of the most prolific oilfields ever yet discovered. In these efforts to develop new sources of supply which would be more readily available to the requirements of this country than those previously existing, and which would, at the same time, be under absolute

British control, he was very strongly supported by Lord Selborne (First Lord, 1900–5), Mr. Pretyman (Civil Lord, 1900–3, Financial Secretary to Admiralty, 1903–6), and Mr. Gordon Miller (Director of Contracts), all of whom had become strong disciples of his in the necessity for adopting fuel oil for naval purposes ; but the main inspiration undoubtedly came from Lord Fisher himself, and not the least of the merits by which his name will be handed down to history is that of being the " pioneer of oil fuel for the Navy."

When, in 1911, Mr. Winston Churchill assumed the post of First Lord of the Admiralty, the advantages of oil fuel for naval purposes and the necessity for ensuring, as far as possible, ample sources of supply which would be independent of foreign control, had been so clearly demonstrated that there was no longer any question as to the policy to be adopted if we were to retain our rank as a naval Power. Mr. Churchill took up the cause of oil fuel with his usual vigorous enthusiasm, and in 1912 caused a " Royal Commission on Oil Fuel and Oil Engines for the Navy " to be appointed, the chairmanship of which he invited Lord Fisher to accept. Little is known as to what transpired at this Commission, as its Report was not published, but one outcome was that the potentialities of the Persian oilfields as great producers of oil were revealed, and eventually, in July 1914, after an examination of the fields by an expert Committee (under the leadership of Admiral Slade), which was sent out by Mr. Churchill, the British Government entered into a long contract with the Anglo-Persian Oil Company, by which it secured for the Navy a large proportion of its peace-time requirements of oil fuel and the whole call on its production at times of war. At the same time an agreement was concluded whereby the Government, by investing £2,000,000 to be expended on further developments (the programme for which has since been far exceeded), secured a controlling interest in the company.

Mr. Churchill, when giving, in the first volume of his book *The World Crisis*, an estimate of the financial result of this investment, showed that the then return was £40,000,000. To-day [1928] at the much enhanced value of the shares held by the Government, a further £20,000,000 can be added to these figures—a colossal gain on an investment which was embarked upon, in the face of great opposition, merely as a measure of national defence ! The only measure of defence [with the exception of the purchase of the Suez Canal shares] ever entered upon by the British Government which, instead of costing tax-payers a large sum of money, has given them an enormous profit !

The credit of carrying through these extraordinarily favourable contracts is, of course, entirely due to Mr. Churchill, and, more particularly, to the able and forceful manner in which he dealt with the consequent Money Bill in the House of Commons in the teeth of the strongest possible opposition. From the point of view of the Navy it was a great feat of statesmanship for which the country should always be grateful.

The story of Fisher's connection with oil would not be complete without some reference to the circumstances under which, in the year 1905, the valuable D'Arcy Persian oil concession was within an ace of being lost to this country. The concession was granted to Mr. D'Arcy by the Persian Government in 1901. By 1905 his expenditure on the concession, without finding oil deposits in a position to be commercially available, was so large that he was unable individually to bear the strain on his purse any longer, and he therefore set about trying to obtain financial assistance. This he was offered on very advantageous terms by a foreign group, but having great faith in the enormous potentialities of the concession, and being a strong believer in the importance of oil for national purposes, he was very reluctant to let it pass out of British hands, and made strong appeals to the British Government for the assistance he needed, since at the time it would have been quite impossible for him to get it from the British public. This, particularly in view of the then unproved state of the concession, could not, equally of course, be provided by the Government ; but Lord Fisher, in his anxiety to ensure independent sources of supply of oil fuel for the nation, took up Mr. D'Arcy's cause very warmly and eventually preserved the British control of these oilfields by inducing the Burmah Oil Company to come to his rescue.

Later, while the Oil Fuel Commission was sitting, he [Fisher] confided to a friend that, so far as could be judged by the evidence which had been brought before him, the Persian oilfields were likely to prove to be the richest in the world and to afford the solution of the difficulty with which the country was faced in not having any oilfields of consequence within its own territories. He characteristically added, " We must do our d——st to get control of the Anglo-Persian Company, and to keep it for all time, as an absolutely ' all-British ' Company." One wonders if the " Oil

Maniac," when making this remark, was merely playing the rôle of a seer, or whether he was not actually *facile princeps* in the negotiations which subsequently (in 1914) led to the realization of his dream.   However this may be, his spirit will have certainly rejoiced over the determination of one Government after another since his death not to relinquish the prize which he so ardently desired, and which he did so much to secure !

One advantage that accrued by Lord Fisher taking up the chairmanship of the Oil Commission was that he was again brought in close touch with the Admiralty, and once more on good terms with Mr. Churchill. He was therefore able to give good advice, and to direct this energetic First Lord in his administration of the Navy.

This was especially valuable when the war-clouds gathered so quickly in August 1914.   Here his advice was of first-class importance.   There is little doubt that it was from the recognition of Lord Fisher's invaluable help that Mr. Churchill insisted on his recall to the Admiralty at the end of October of that year, a decision fraught with the greatest moment to the Navy in the war.

CHAPTER XVII

LORD FISHER'S RETURN TO THE ADMIRALTY, 30TH OCTOBER, 1914

Ainsi, vingt-quatre heures, exactement, avant le combat de Coronel, il semble que l'Angleterre, inspirée par son principal patron, le génie des mers, ait tressailli, ait fait appel, d'instinct, au seul sauveur possible.[1]
FARRÈRE ET CHACK, *Combats et Batailles sur mer.*

Lord Fisher's return—His difficulties—Fatal mistake made by Mr. Churchill—Mr. Churchill as First Lord—His disabilities—Duties of the First Lord—His power at a Board—The War Committee—The qualifications of the members—Fisher's loyalty—The tangle—Fisher's game of chess—The position in the South Pacific—Admiral Cradock's dilemma—Coronel—Fisher's immediate action—His limit of three days—His insistence—Falkland Islands battle—Mr. Churchill's alternative—The fallacies involved—Confidence restored—Latin puns.

LORD FISHER returned to the Admiralty full of confidence and high hope. The account of his time there is sad to write of, and sad to read, for it is a history of a brilliant initial success, and afterwards nothing but disappointment and great schemes thwarted. The whole history of his work is crossed and recrossed by irritating worries. The War Council failed to endorse his conception of the true function of the Navy in war. It was an anæmic body that shunned issues and avoided, whenever it was possible, giving clear-cut decisions. He saw what

[1] Thus, exactly twenty-four hours before the battle of Coronel, England, stricken in nerve, but inspired by her Guardian Angel, the Genie of the seas, appealed, with sure instinct, to the one person who could possibly save her.

RUSH LABEL USED BY LORD FISHER AT THE ADMIRALTY

he considered to be golden opportunities slipping by
for want of the adoption of a cut-and-dried policy.

The office of First Sea Lord had been divorced from
that of Chief of the Naval Staff ; this was unworkable,
as Mr. Churchill had been warned it would be by
Admiral of the Fleet Sir Arthur Wilson ; and, in addition, it was productive of almost daily friction.   Thus
it was that the whole of Lord Fisher's work during
that six and a half months was overshadowed by a
feeling of disquietude, and haunted by the spectre of
the necessity for expostulatory retirement.   Although
this spectre was ever present with him, it neither
abated his strength nor fettered his will ; but his
divergences of opinion with Mr. Churchill, and the
course he was constrained to take, more especially as
regards the Dardanelles campaign, day by day strengthened his conviction that his time at the Admiralty
would be short, and that, once more, he would feel
forced to retire into the cold shades of inactivity.

His advent at the Admiralty was rather like a gust
of wind sweeping into and disturbing the calm atmo-
sphere of that building.   He instituted the " Rush "
label (see reproduction on Plate at p. 160), and with
this came real rush.   Mr. Churchill having monopolized
the red pencils and ink for his minutes, Fisher seized
the green and used that colour exclusively.   He
summoned the heads of the shipbuilding yards, and
personally gave them directions ; he burned the
long-drawn-out correspondence which, for years, had
niggled about patents, and objections to more than
one or two firms building submarine boats ; he threw
the building of those vessels open to all, and at the
same time launched a big shipbuilding programme.

Everything began to move.   Inertia disappeared.

II—11

The huge machine creaked and groaned ; but it began to turn out work at an increased rate. He was known, feared, loved, and obeyed ; but the shadow of impending trouble was always with him ; a breach between him and the First Lord was bound, sooner or later, to occur. It started merely as a small rift, immediately after Lord Fisher's advent at the Admiralty, and widened almost daily ; but the chasm was constantly bridged by his loyalty to his chief. Day by day the strain increased, until at last the structure could no longer bear it, and the crash came.

Mr. Churchill has told the tale, with unconscious *naïveté*, in *The World Crisis* ; a story to which any naval officer, who reads between the lines, can supply the lacunæ. The tale, especially towards the end, is told with fairness ; and the view he takes of the causes that led to the climax is candid, and is by no means over-biased in his own favour. There was, however, one point that he has ever failed to grasp, namely, that he was, as First Lord of the Admiralty, an official with whom no First Sea Lord of ability and good health could work for any length of time. From the very first minute that he entered the Admiralty he entirely mistook the functions of his office, and more especially of that office in war-time. His brilliant abilities were, of themselves, sufficient to ensure his failure in that office. His courage, which led him to make important and valuable decisions in civil matters, such as the acquisition of shares in the Anglo-Persian Oil Company, also reacted on his profound belief in his own opinions, and made him venturesome to an extreme in enforcing his views. His keen brain and fertile imagination served to strengthen his belief in his own infallibility. His in-

domitable energy caused him to meddle in innumerable
details that were infinitely better left to the technical
officers who had the practical experience requisite to
deal with them.   His immense range of superficial
knowledge beguiled him into believing that that
knowledge was accurate and profound.   In executive
command in the field he would, in all probability,
have earned undying fame, but, temperamentally, he
was unsuited to fill the post of civilian head of a
highly technical department in war-time.   He himself
confirms this view.   We read in *The World Crisis* :

> Thus ended my administration of the Admiralty.   For thirty-
> four months of preparation and ten months of war I had borne the
> prime responsibility *and had wielded the main executive power*.[1]

It was the way that he " wielded the main executive
power " that led to the numerous mistakes which took
place, and to the trouble that ended his régime.   The
functions of each Sea Lord of the Board of Admiralty
are executive.   That of the First Lord should be
supervisory.   The functions of the First Sea Lord
are clearly defined, and are distinct from those of
the First Lord.   It was by the invasion of this province, replete with problems that lifelong experience
in the Navy alone could handle, that this young
civilian First Lord came to unfortunate grief.

It will be as well here to outline the constitutional
relationship between the First Lord and the First
Sea Lord and the other members of the Board.

Each member of the Board has special duties
assigned to him, and these should be discharged
without interference from any other member.   Certain matters require Board sanction, but it is not

---

[1] Italics not in the original.

necessary for the whole Board to meet. Two Lords and a Secretary constitute a " Board " ; their signatures on papers therefore constitute a Board decision. This arrangement is a simple one, and saves a mass of unimportant matter being brought up at full Board meetings. In fact, the majority of Board decisions are arrived at by papers passing to the members concerned without formal meeting. All papers dealing with the expenditure of money " pass through " the Financial Secretary. Full Boards are summoned only on matters of general importance.

The decision of the First Lord at a Board meeting is final. The remainder of the members of the Board are merely his advisers, and he can, at will, accept or reject their advice. An extreme instance of this occurred when a question arose as to whether the 13·5 gun should be introduced into some of the " Dreadnoughts " which had been already laid down. The gun was, to a great extent, in the experimental stage, and delay in the completion of the ships would have been incurred by the change. A Board meeting was summoned to decide the matter. Every member of the Board voted for the change except the First Lord, Mr. M'Kenna, who was opposed to it. When each member had expressed his view, the First Lord gave the verdict : " The decision of the Board is that the change shall not take place." One member alone, a civilian demurred, saying, " But, First Lord, the whole of the Board except you are in favour of the change ! " The reply was merely the repetition of : " The decision of the Board is that the change shall not take place."

We are not here concerned with the wisdom of the decision, although it is interesting to note that in this case either decision was fully justified ; but what we

are concerned with is the fact that each member of
the Board is empowered to give decisions in the execution of the functions delegated to him, but, at a
Board, the First Lord is supreme.   But his veto should
only be used in matters of policy, not on technical
matters, where his knowledge is necessarily not so
great as that of the Sea Lords.

Take, for instance, the movement of ships.   This is
primarily a technical naval matter outside the com-
petence of the First Lord, and all movements of ships
in peace and war should be *ordered* by the First Sea
Lord alone ;   but since, especially in peace-time,
political considerations may underlie the movements of ships, consultation between the First Lord
and the First Sea Lord must take place.   Should
the First Lord disagree, he cannot cancel such an
order without calling a Board meeting, when his
decision is supreme.   In practice, of course, these
two officials work in agreement, for the First Lord
naturally does not interfere with the movement
of ships unless he has very decided opinions on the
policy of the move, and the First Sea Lord would not
make any change of far-reaching importance without
first informing the First Lord.   The system at present
in vogue is the adaptation, to modern circumstances,
of the procedure of the olden days, when the First
Lord was a professional sailor, and therefore combined
the two offices of First Lord and First Sea Lord.

Mr. Churchill apparently held quite different views
of the functions of the First Lord.   His opinion was
that the First Lord should decide all questions except
those that he might leave to the Naval Lords, and
this resulted in an unfortunate state of affairs, for
none of the Sea Lords knew exactly how he stood.

Mr. Churchill instituted a War Council inside the Admiralty, composed of himself, Admiral Prince Louis of Battenberg, Admiral of the Fleet Sir A. K. Wilson, Rear-Admiral Sturdee (Chief of the Staff), and sometimes Admiral Sir H. Jackson. When Lord Fisher came to the Admiralty he took the place of Prince Louis, and Rear-Admiral Oliver that of Admiral Sturdee, whom he had succeeded as Chief of the Staff. The value of such a Committee was entirely dependent on how its business was conducted, and upon the extent to which attention was paid to the opinions of the individual members ; but, in any case, it should have been presided over by the First Sea Lord, and not by the First Lord. Lord Fisher was the one person at the Admiralty responsible for the movements of all ships and their actions. To this view we find Mr. Churchill subscribed, for he quite properly states that " only the First Sea Lord can order the ships to steam and the guns to fire." [1] Technical matters were the business of experts, and not of an amateur. Mr. Churchill, however, did not merely consult these officers as a Committee, but he also consulted them individually, and used such of their views as coincided with his own to argue with Lord Fisher when in disagreement with him—a procedure which could only result in friction and irritation. However, such was the system, and it is well to examine the qualifications of the other three officers who composed the War Group.

Admiral of the Fleet Sir Arthur Wilson had a far greater experience in the command of our Fleets than any other Admiral in the Navy. He had a great and well-deserved reputation as a naval strategist and tactician. His conduct of grand manœuvres for a

[1] *The World Crisis*, 1915.

number of years had considerably aided the education
of naval officers. Had the war occurred six years earlier, he would certainly have commanded the Grand Fleet. He was looked on by the Navy at large as rather dangerous, in that he was supposed to favour inshore operations in a war with Germany, whereas the great majority of naval officers had, at that time, an ingrained dislike for coastal work on the part of our main Fleets.

Admiral Sir Henry Jackson was a scientific officer who had worked neck and neck with Signor Marconi in the early days of wireless telegraphy, and had been the father of that class of signalling in the Navy. He had a great knowledge of ships and of gunnery and torpedo work, and he was eminently suited to carry out the detailed staff work at the Admiralty necessary for the preliminary consideration of proposed operations. He afterwards succeeded Lord Fisher as First Sea Lord.

Admiral Oliver was a solid, hard-headed, phlegmatic officer of good judgment, who reasoned soundly and accurately, and was of great value in pouring cold water on rash proposals. The country owes to this little-known officer a great debt of gratitude for his work at the Admiralty during the war.

Such was the composition of the Committee. It had in it the elements of a useful Advisory Committee to help the First Sea Lord ; and, as we have already said, should have been presided over by him. The First Lord should have looked for guidance to the First Sea Lord. But the vicious principle introduced by Mr. Churchill when, in 1912, he created a Chief of the Staff independent of the First Sea Lord, a principle which had immediately led to the resignation of

Sir Arthur Wilson as First Sea Lord, was the cause of a good deal of the trouble at the Admiralty.

But this was not all. After the meetings of the Committee, Mr. Churchill frequently, with his own hand, drafted the orders that were necessary to carry out what he believed to be the decisions reached at the meeting. Undoubtedly he often was carried away by the optimism and enthusiasm of his ardent nature. It was impossible to forecast from one day to another where his imagination would lead him. When First Lord of the Admiralty he left his post in London and rushed over to Antwerp, telegraphing from there asking to be put in command of the troops. This was too much for Mr. Asquith, who rather caustically commented " that he could hardly put an ex-cavalry subaltern in command over a Major-General." The proposal, however, did not seem absurd to Mr. Churchill ! We read in his book that a pact was arrived at between him and Lord Fisher that neither would take any important step without consulting the other—a wise understanding ; but it was one which demanded the most scrupulous observance by both parties, not only in letter, but also in the spirit, otherwise friction was certain to ensue.

Lord Fisher's position was therefore one of great difficulty. Owing to ill-health, Prince Louis of Battenberg had not grasped the reins of his office firmly. Mr. Churchill had not been kept in his proper sphere. The result was a subcurrent of friction. It may well be asked, Why did Lord Fisher not put his foot down and insist on a proper organization ? The answer lies in the understanding arrived at on assuming office, that neither would take important action without consulting the other, and in an ingrained feeling of loyalty to

Mr. Churchill. It is impossible to over-estimate the extent to which loyalty swayed Lord Fisher's actions. It was at once one of his strongest and one of his weakest points. His loyalty to Mr. M'Kenna, after leaving the Admiralty in 1910, was almost childlike in its sincerity. He refused even to meet Mr. Churchill on account of the way he had behaved to Mr. M'Kenna in the Cabinet over the battleship programme of 1909 ; and subsequently, when in 1912 he was asked by Mr. Churchill to come to the assistance of the Admiralty, he first wrote to Mr. M'Kenna and obtained his concurrence before he would consent to have any dealings with him. He did the same thing before he accepted the post of First Sea Lord in 1914. So, in turn, it was with Mr. Churchill himself, he never forgot that Mr. Churchill had brought him back to the Admiralty in the teeth of violent opposition ; and he felt himself bound to support him, even, at times, against his better judgment. In a letter he wrote to Mr. Churchill when the latter asked him to withdraw his resignation on 16th May, 1915, we read :

Your splendid stand on my behalf I can never forget when you took your political life in your hands ; and I have worked hard, very hard for you in return—*my utmost*; but here is a question beyond all personal obligations.

This was the key to much that happened in those fateful six months during which Lord Fisher was at the Admiralty. It accounts to a great extent for his toleration of the Dardanelles scheme, and it accounts for his putting up with much that galled him in his work at the Admiralty. Intensely loyal to his subordinates, he was equally loyal to his First Lord ; and this loyalty was vastly strengthened by Mr. Churchill's bold action on his behalf.

On the outbreak of the war he, most naturally, desired ardently to return to the Admiralty. He had forged the weapon on which the safety of the Empire depended. His fiery energy made him believe that he, and he alone, could prevent such disasters as those which, two months later, were strewing the course that the ship of Admiralty was pursuing, under the guidance of its civilian captain.

He noted that the business of the Navy had not progressed well during the first two months of the war. The *Aboukir, Cressy, Hogue, Hawke, Pegasus,* and *Pathfinder* had been sunk. The *Kaiser Wilhelm der Grösse,* a powerful armed merchant-ship, was playing havoc with our trade on the west coast of Africa, and the *Emden* and *Königsberg* were sinking ships in the Indian Ocean.[1] Then, in October, the *Audacious* was sunk by a mine. Admiral von Spee's squadron, consisting of the *Gneisenau* and *Scharnhorst* and two or more smaller cruisers, was closing on the western shore of South America, where our cruiser force was totally inadequate to protect the shipping or to meet the enemy in action. No wonder, then, that Mr. Churchill felt the need of a strong First Sea Lord to straighten out the tangle. Prince Louis of Battenberg then was a sick man, who had not the strength and virility to handle all the various complicated problems. Moreover, his parentage and name strongly mortgaged his prestige with the nation at large, and stayed him in strongly opposing any proposals put forward by others with which he might not be in accord. No more patriotic officer wore His Majesty's uniform, but sinister reports and rumours,

[1] Dispositions to deal with these raids had been made, but so far had borne no fruit.

without the vaguest shadow of truth for a foundation, were passing from mouth to mouth, and Mr. Churchill naturally turned to Lord Fisher, and rightly too, for there was no officer of standing who could compare with him in general naval ability.

It was not without considerable difficulty that Mr. Churchill carried his point. The old prejudices were still strong and had been carefully nurtured by Lord Fisher's detractors. Those who had suffered at his hands for their sins, or had had their susceptibilities bruised, had by no means learned to forgive and forget. Mr. Churchill, however, had made up his mind, and there was no one in England strong enough to withstand him.

We gather from *The World Crisis* that Mr. Churchill looked on Lord Fisher as an old man, but at the same time a genius, whose brain could be used with advantage, but whose will he could mould to his purposes by appeals to his patriotism and by subtle cajolery. Lord Fisher, on the other hand, had been in constant communication with Mr. Churchill for the previous two years, and had given him much valuable advice, both before and also on the outbreak of the war. Without doubt he, too, thought that he was strong enough to manage this young enthusiast, and to carry on the work with him as he had done with previous First Lords. Both proved to be mistaken.

Such, then, were the conditions at the end of October 1914, when these two men of strong views and undoubted genius came, for the first time, to work in close contact. Flint and steel ! Call either of them which you please—it matters not ; for sooner or later there was bound to be a spark, and then some insignificant scrap of tinder would of a certainty lead to a fatal conflagration.

Fisher aptly described the situation in a letter to a friend :

I am working hard. I'm in the position of playing a game of chess very badly begun by ——. I've got rid of the fools, but it's long and arduous to get back to a good position with a consummate good player for an enemy. *But I'm trying.*

Let not him that putteth his armour on boast himself like him that putteth it off.

The first matter of importance with which it was necessary immediately to deal was the danger to Admiral Cradock's squadron. The history of this peculiar muddle is one of the darkest chapters of the war at sea.

Let us put the matter in its most elemental form, so that we can judge of the difficulty with which Lord Fisher was faced.

Admiral von Spee was in the Pacific with two modern armoured cruisers and three or four smaller ships ; his destination was unknown. The force on the East Indian and China Stations was sufficient to deal with him, but that on the south-west coast of South America was hopelessly outclassed. The Admiralty had grave suspicions that von Spee might attack our commerce on that coast and sink our grain and nitrate ships. How did they face the trouble ? It is hardly credible, but the chief action was to send the *Canopus,* an elderly battleship, to chaperon Admiral Cradock's cruisers. Anything more futile could hardly be imagined. What was required at the Admiralty was a little clear thinking, and a determination to face facts. The obvious question that should have been asked, and answered, was, " What is the use of Admiral Cradock's squadron when at sea if tied to the skirts of a thirteen-knot battleship ? "

Any naval officer with fleet experience must have known that thirteen knots was the maximum that the *Canopus* could be expected to steam continuously at sea. Leaky condenser tubes were not uncommon in this class of ship, and any minor defect would still further reduce that paltry speed.

If the Admiralty had at that time ordered a convoy to be instituted, there would have been some excuse for the presence of the *Canopus*, since her speed would have been ample for such a purpose. The cruisers in her company could have driven off any marauders that might have harassed the tail of the convoy, and they in turn would have derived support and protection from the *Canopus*. Such orders would have been plain and unmistakable. But instead of this the order that Admiral Cradock received, and acted on, was to cruise in protection of trade. How was he to protect trade which was on the eve of being attacked by 22-knot ships, when he had orders to cruise in company with, what turned out to be, a 12-knot battleship? The order was one impossible to carry out.

Another point of the greatest importance in considering war problems is the necessity of taking into account the temperament of the Admiral in command. Admiral Cradock was well known to be a most gallant officer, and one who was certain, if faced by two courses of action, to choose that least likely to savour of pusillanimity. The Admiralty never appear to have asked themselves how he would interpret " protection of trade," when a fast enemy squadron was scuttling our merchant vessels, and he and his cruisers were seeking protection under the guns of the *Canopus*.

Let us put ourselves in Admiral Cradock's place.

Let us imagine ourselves cruising up and down the coast of South America in company with the *Canopus*, and let us suppose the *Scharnhorst* and *Gneisenau* are sighted. The slower of the two German ships has a speed of over 22 knots, and the *Canopus* can steam 12 knots. In five minutes they are out of sight. Where are they going ? Why, of course, to scuttle every British merchant ship that they find. Would you as Admiral remain content in such a case to steam along hiding behind the skirts of the *Canopus* ? Of course not. You would act in the only way possible, as Nelson, in similar circumstances, foreshadowed he would act. Nelson, when inferior in strength to the French, told his captains not to be astonished if he did not attack the French fleet immediately he sighted them, for he would first try to catch them at a disadvantage ; but, he added, " he would fight before they left the West Indies, since, if once his fleet got alongside theirs, by the time the action was over they would not trouble England any more that winter."

This, without doubt, is what Admiral Cradock intended ; namely, to fight and damage the German vessels, so that either the *Canopus* could overtake and destroy one or more of them, or they would be lamed, and so prevented from doing further damage to our merchant shipping for some time. That he would lose his ships was a certainty, but the game was one worth playing if he winged the German cruisers and forced the Admiralty to take some decisive action. The Admiralty had put him in a position of which this was the only solution.

If Admiral Sir H. Jackson's proposal to concentrate the East and West Coast Squadrons at the Falklands had been adopted, there would have been no Coronel.

But then he had no official position or responsibility, so his advice was disregarded. If absolutely clear orders had been sent to Admiral Cradock, all would have been well. However great the difficulties may have been which were facing the Admiralty at the time, there was no excuse for the orders that were sent to him not being explicit, and conveying, without possibility of misunderstanding, the course they wished him to adopt.

The facts that emerge are that the Admiralty failed to recognize the gravity of the situation, failed to send a sufficient force from the Mediterranean or Grand Fleet to make the situation safe, and took the puerile course of tacking a battleship on to the Cruiser Squadron of an intrepid Admiral, telling him, it is true, to cruise in company with her, but at the same time ordering him to " search and protect trade." In September the *Defence* had been ordered out from the Mediterranean to reinforce Admiral Cradock, but she was recalled to the Dardanelles. In October she was again sent out westward, but ordered to remain on the east coast of South America. All these points convey to the naval officer, whatever they may convey to the civilian mind, that at the Admiralty throughout this period there lacked a master mind in the management of our world-strategy.

Twenty-four hours before Coronel was fought, Lord Fisher joined the Admiralty. The *Defence* was at once sent to reinforce Cradock. Mr. Churchill protests strongly that this was done at that moment, solely on account of news being received which exactly located von Spee's Squadron ; but there was no adequate reason why the *Defence* should not have been sent earlier. The fact remains that it was Lord Fisher who ordered this necessary reinforcement ; and he would, without doubt, have ordered it even if von Spee's force had not been located with exactitude.

The news of Coronel reached the Admiralty and fell with shattering force on those whose procrastination had brought it about. Lord Fisher at once rose to the occasion, and all the feeble objections which hitherto had been allowed to obtain were swept on one side. The *Inflexible* and *Invincible* were ordered from the Grand Fleet to coal and leave at the earliest date for the Falkland Islands. No delay was allowed. The cruisers arrived at Devonport on the 8th November, and they were ordered to leave on the 11th. Then came protests from the Yard, and a week was demanded to get the ships ready. Lord Fisher, by virtue of his incomparable experience, fixed three days as the necessary time, and was adamant. They were to sail on the 11th. Mr. Churchill prints, in facsimile, a telegram he wrote at Lord Fisher's insistence refusing to permit delay. Being in his handwriting, it might convey the impression—one, we are sure, Mr. Churchill would not like to remain uncontradicted—that the indomitable urgency insisted on was due to him and not to Lord Fisher. Other telegrams passed. The Dockyard wired that all the brick bridges of the *Invincible's* boilers could not be finished by the 11th. The reply was prompt and in true Fisher style : *The whole material* necessary *and all the bricklayers* in Devonport Yard were to sail in the *Invincible* should the bridges not be finished by the time she was due to sail ! The Admiral-Superintendent came to the Admiralty to protest. He saw Lord Fisher, who informed him that *by the time he had returned to his Dockyard the ships would have sailed ! !* Needless to say, the work was finished in time.

It was on occasions such as this that Lord Fisher towered head and shoulders above those around him. We have seen him more than once, when it was almost as much as life was worth to approach him with a plea of impossibility! Let it also not be forgotten that everyone in the Dockyard, from the Admiral Superintendent down, knew Lord Fisher's methods and the reputation he had earned of never being put off with excuses. " Get on or get out " was known to be his motto ; and had the *Invincible* not sailed to date, there would have been several of the chief billets in Devonport Yard vacant within twenty-four hours. The cruisers did sail with workmen on board to finish the electrical firing circuits, but, thanks to Lord Fisher, and Lord Fisher only, they sailed to time.

An interesting sidelight on the art of issuing orders, and how, up to that time, war orders had been issued from the Admiralty, is shed by the following story. After Coronel the Captain of the *Canopus* received a long telegram from the Admiralty giving him precise orders as to where he was to go, and full instructions regarding the steps he was to take in harbour to ensure the safety of his ship. After reading it, he turned to his Second-in-Command, and said, " Fisher wrote that telegram." He had, of course, no previous inkling that Lord Fisher was even likely to return to the Admiralty ; but he recognized the master-hand, so different from the previous anæmic productions.

It is quite unnecessary to deal with the details of the Battle of the Falkland Islands. The enemy was annihilated. The all-big-gun armament of the " Dreadnought cruisers " was fully vindicated. A delay of twenty-four hours in the sailing of the cruisers might have been fatal, one of forty-eight hours would most decidedly have been so. Admiral von Spee, fortunately, did not know that " Britain's club had been seized and was being wielded by a Titan."

After the news of the action reached England, Mr. Churchill wrote to Lord Fisher the following letter :

> MY DEAR,
>
> This was your show and your luck. I should only have sent one *Greyhound* and *Defence*. This would have done the trick.
>
> But it was a great *coup*. Your *flair* was quite true. Let us have some more victories together and confound all our foes abroad —and (don't forget) at home.
>
> I am not quite happy about Zeebrugge, and have held back the letter till to-morrow. I am shy of landings under fire—unless there is no other way.
>
> Yours,
>
> W.

This letter would have been a handsome addition, in facsimile, to *The World Crisis*, and undoubtedly Lord Fisher's literary executors would have lent the original for this purpose.

The crisis of Coronel, and Lord Fisher's subsequent action, show him in his true light. It had been the wont of his detractors to assert that he was a mere builder of ships, a reactionary Admiral without any real strategical or tactical instincts. Falkland has given the lie to these criticisms. The instinct whereby he dispatched a force that would not merely beat but annihilate, and the taking of risks in so doing from which others had shrunk, were indeed worthy of Nelson. So also was his impatience to brook the slightest delay. Experience and thought had given him a sure judgment in these matters.

Let us turn for a moment to Mr. Churchill's letter, where he says, " I should only have sent one *Greyhound* and *Defence*. This would have done the trick."

It would not. The *Defence* only mounted four 9·2-inch and ten 7·5-inch guns, compared to the *Gneisenau's* eight 8·2 and six 5·9. There was no annihilation in such a small difference in armament. One lucky salvo, or even one lucky shell, might have reversed the difference in strength as shown on paper. Further, the essence of Fisher's tactical insight was to send two ships of the *same class and armament*—a point not appreciated by our amateur tactician.

It is not easy to assess the value of the victory of the Falklands. Not only did it free the operations in the Cameroons of danger, but it removed a grave menace to our trade in three oceans. It left our cruisers free to deal with the commerce-destroying enemy ships without the ever-present possibility of being recalled, and concentrated, to meet a powerful squadron ; and, perhaps most of all, it gave renewed confidence to our Fleet and the Fleets of the Allies. A severe defeat at the beginning of a war is not merely a defeat, but a disaster ; and the only possible way of completely restoring confidence is by swift and adequate retribution. This Lord Fisher had effected in a masterly manner. The guns of the Falklands not only wiped out the defeat of Coronel, but heralded victory at sea, for, in truth, their last boom was heard only on the morning of the final surrender of the German Fleet.

"Les coups de canon des Falklands ont résonné sur toutes les terres, sur toutes les mers britanniques. Parmi les détonations sourdes de la mer du Nord, le vieux Fisher les a reconnus. Il ne s'étonne point : il les attendait, lui, lui seul." [1]

[1] "The roar of the guns at the Falklands sounded across all lands and over all the seas. The aged Fisher recognized them from amid the thunder of cannon in the North Sea. He was not surprised ; he was expecting them ; yes, he, and he only."—*Combats et Batailles sur mer.*

POSTSCRIPT

These two lines of Latin verse are worth recording ; the first is by Sir Herbert Warren, the late President of Magdalen College, Oxford—a glorious pun :

MERSERAT · EX · SPE · SPEM, REDIIT : SPES · MERGITUR · EXSPES.

which, being translated, means :

VON SPEE overwhelmed the [Good] Hope, hope returned : *he* is drowned without hope.

He sent this to Professor Godley, who returned it with the following pentameter added :

Hoc tibi Piscator patria debet opus.
(Thy country owes this work to thee, O Fisher !)

CHAPTER XVIII

THE BALTIC PROJECT

A clever military leader will succeed in many cases in choosing defensive positions of such an offensive nature, from a strategic point of view, that the opponent is compelled to attack them.—VON MOLTKE.

Amphibious warfare—Fisher and the Defence Committee—His disagreement with our troops forming part of a Continental Army—His belief in our troops landing in Belgium—The danger to us of the German occupation—Possible starvation of London —Difficulties of Belgian and Dardanelles projects compared— The Pomeranian project—Its effect on the naval situation— The double blow—The Germans adopt Lord Fisher's scheme— The German view of his proposals.

LORD FISHER had always been a great exponent of the advantages of "amphibious warfare," as he characterized joint naval and military operations. The Army did not like these undertakings; in the Navy it was said that the soldiers disliked "getting their feet wet"! Lord Fisher's view was that a country like Britain, with a relatively large and highly trained Navy, but only a small professional Army, could use that Army to the best effect by throwing it, at a critical moment, on the flank or in the rear of the main body of the enemy.

He had always held the opinion that the arrangement arrived at before the war, to land the Expeditionary Force in France so as to form a, comparatively speaking, meagre addition to the French Army, was strategically unsound. He was a strong advocate of keeping the Expeditionary Force ready till the psychological moment, and then throwing it ashore at some

point where it would place the enemy at a disadvantage.

The following account, given by him to a friend
on 18th November, 1909, of what took place at a
meeting of the Committee of Imperial Defence shows
Fisher's views on the subject of the functions of our
Expeditionary Force. Further, it places beyond all
doubt the fact that the question of a landing in the
Baltic had been laid before the Prime Minister, and
that he had taken no action in the matter. It may
also explain, perhaps, the reason for the Prime Minister's not asking Lord Fisher for his opinion at the
War Council on a subsequent memorable occasion,
with which we shall deal later.[1] At all events, when,
in 1909, he did ask Sir John Fisher for his views, he
seems to have got a very full and unvarnished reply.

During the Morocco crisis the French Government was within
an inch of war with Germany, and insisted on 120,000 British
troops being sent to the French frontier. The Cabinet agreed.
At a meeting of the Defence Committee, where the military plans
were set forth by General Nicholson, Fisher remained silent, seated
opposite to Mr. Asquith at the end of a long table. The only
question put to Fisher was "Whether the Navy could guarantee
transport," to which he answered "Yes." Mr. Asquith then
asked him if he had anything to say ; and he replied that he had
nothing to say that anyone present would care to hear. Mr.
Asquith pressed him ; then a scene took place. Fisher told the
Committee that if 120,000 English were sent to France, the Germans would put everything else aside and make any sacrifice to
surround and destroy the British, and that they would succeed.
Continental armies being what they are, Fisher expressed the
view that the British Army should be absolutely restricted to
operations consisting of sudden descents on the coast, the recovery
of Heligoland, and the garrisoning of Antwerp.[2]

He pointed out that there was a stretch of ten miles of hard

[1] See pages 208 and 210.
[2] "_Garrisoning_ of Antwerp" was, of course, a loose expression.

sand on the Pomeranian coast which is only ninety miles from Berlin. Were the British army to seize and entrench that strip, a million Germans would find occupation ; but to dispatch British troops to the front in a Continental war would be an act of suicidal idiocy arising from the distorted view of war produced by Mr. Haldane's speeches, and childish arrangements for training Terriers after war broke out. Fisher followed this up with an impassioned diatribe against the War Office and all its ways, including conceit, waste of money, and ignorance of war. He claimed that the British Army should be administered as an annex to the Navy and that the present follies should be abandoned.

At this period Mr. Asquith said, " I think we had better adjourn." This was done, but for some months onward the Defence Committee never considered, nor did the soldiers propose, any plan for helping France by means of an Expeditionary Force to take part in the main inland fighting.

The War Office, however, never abandoned the idea of fighting as a fractional part of the French Army ; for when the Great War broke out, the military authorities preferred to co-operate on the main front. It is interesting to note that, in pursuance of this plan, at the beginning of the war the British Army was allotted to a sector which the French General Staff did not expect would be of the first-class importance. But owing to the German advance through Alsace proving to be a feint, while the movement through Belgium was the real attack, the British Army found itself taking the brunt of the first battles ; and it was some time before the bulk of the French Army could come into action. Thus the British Army achieved glory, but at the same time came near to annihilation, as Lord Fisher foretold would be the case.

It would be tempting to speculate on what the result might have been had our Expeditionary Force been landed in Belgium in the early days of the war, on the flank of the German advance, as Lord Fisher had argued that it should have been. Nor did his opinion on the subject change, for when he came to the Admiralty at the beginning of November 1914, he did everything in his power to impress upon the Government the necessity for our troops to attack the German force in Belgium. Obviously, this was the proper thing to do ; and Sir John French, who then commanded our Army in France, was much in favour of the proposal ; but the French would not agree. For political reasons they were strongly against any advance by our troops into the northern part of Belgium, and up to 1917 insisted on keeping French and Belgian troops between our Army and the coast. It is curious now to look back on the extent to which the French mistrusted this country. It was not only generally expected by them that we should desire to remain in occupation of Belgium after the war, but the inhabitants of the north coast of France firmly believed that we had no intention of leaving that part of the country after peace was declared. They never could understand that our one burning desire was for our Army to quit the Continent as soon as possible after the war, nor that the occupation of any French territory would be not only a breach of trust, but a hopeless and financially ruinous entanglement.

There is no doubt that an advance in Belgium in early 1915 would have been a great *coup*. The Belgians did not wish it, since it would inevitably have involved burnings and destructions of some of their towns and villages, and would have brought the full effects of war into the heart of a country which, as long as it remained in the occupation of the Germans, was saved much of this suffering and desolation. From the point of view of our Navy the capture of the Belgian coast was all-important. It was solely on account of the ineptitude of the German Navy, arising mainly from the system of triple control that existed at Headquarters, which paralysed all action on the part of that unfortunate Service, that England was not reduced to actual starvation. It was short-sighted and ill-considered strategy to leave Ostend and Zeebrugge in German hands, within seventy miles of the entrance of the Channel. An active enemy would have blocked Calais, Boulogne, and Havre, and have made traffic up the Channel impracticable. This would have brought starvation to London, since it is impossible to feed its seven million inhabitants by rail alone.

The naval forces that were available for the protection of our shipping in the Channel, after the needs of the Grand Fleet had been supplied, were very small. Our forecasts before the war had never included the possibility of the continued occupation of the Belgian coast by Germany ; it would then have seemed impossible that the Germans could be permitted to remain there for three years without any effort being made to dislodge them. But for prodigious luck, this lack of strategical foresight might well have lost us the war. The people of this country have never fully appreciated the danger that we ran. But Lord Fisher was right, as he invariably was in matters connected with the Navy and naval warfare. If the quarter of a million men who were eventually sent to the Dardanelles had been used for a descent on the Belgian coast, and the occupation of Belgium, the war might well have been shortened by a year.

When the factors that should have governed the final choice as to which campaign should have been undertaken, i.e. the Belgian or the Dardanelles, are set out in plain English, it seems incredible that the wrong decision could have been reached. For here are the two schemes. One was to land an Army and take the Belgian coast, which was only sixty miles from the point of embarkation of our troops. This would have driven the nearest German naval base to a distance of 350 miles from the Channel instead of sixty miles. It would have lifted the last shadow of fear of our coasts being invaded, and left us free to concentrate all our vessels in the waters to the north of Holland, keep a minimum of troops in England, and therefore to send increased numbers to reinforce the Army in France. The point of disembarkation would have been so close to this country, and the line of sea-communication with our troops to be guarded would have been so short, that its protection would have been a comparatively easy matter.

The other proposal was to land troops at the Dardanelles, a place some 2,500 miles from England. This entailed the protection of a very long line of sea-communications. Not only was protection involved, but the distance was so great that it necessitated an immense fleet of transport and other vessels to carry, first the troops, and then the constant supplies of food, ammunition, and other necessities for their maintenance and armament.

As regards facility of landing, supply, etc., the Belgian coast project was much the simpler, because Zeebrugge and Ostend were in Belgian hands for several weeks after the war broke out, and even after the German occupation a landing could have been effected with but little difficulty. Strategically, the Belgian coast was more vital to this country than

Constantinople, and, moreover, our military efforts would have been concentrated in one single theatre, and that the decisive theatre, instead of being dissipated between two regions over 2,000 miles apart.

In favour of the Dardanelles scheme was the political advantage that would result if the attempt were successful. That this was considerable is undoubted, especially so far as the Balkan States were concerned. On the other hand, there was the loss in prestige if the attempt proved unsuccessful. The vital point, however, which should have outweighed all political considerations was that the retention by the Germans of the Belgian coast meant, as far as anyone could foresee at the end of 1914, something approximating to starvation to London. It was only by our experiencing an almost impossible piece of good luck that this did not become a reality. The Dardanelles expedition failed, but by some miracle the German Navy was also stricken with paralysis, and we were thereby saved from defeat.

The other project which Lord Fisher favoured was the landing of Russian troops on the Pomeranian coast. It is strange that this project should have been universally condemned without ever having received detailed examination. One of the fascinating consequences of the scheme is that it would have placed Allied troops within 100 miles of Berlin, and, as Lord Fisher hinted, Allied troops of the right class to strike terror into the German population.

There was no insuperable difficulty, from the naval point of view, in landing the troops and in keeping up communication with Riga. That we should have lost a considerable number of ships is certain ; but the ships used would largely have been ships built for the special purpose ; they would have been cheap, and with small crews, and it must not be forgotten that the Germans would also have lost ships. Lord Fisher's view was that the project was a perfectly feasible one, and one likely to put an early ending to the war. He wrote :

> The Baltic project meant victory by land and sea. It was simply history repeating itself. Frederick the Great, for the only time in his life (on hearing that Russians had landed), was frightened, and sent for poison.
>
> Geography has not altered since his time. The Pomeranian coast has not shifted, and a million Russian soldiers could have been landed within eighty-two miles of Berlin.
>
> It is the Russians we want to enter Berlin, not the French or English. The unparalleled Armada of 612 vessels constructed to carry out this decisive act in the decisive theatre of the war was diverted and perverted to the damned Dardanelles.

The military side of the question is one for the General Staff. That there were very grave *prima facie* objections is certain. The difficulty at once met with, namely, that two nationalities were involved, is certainly grave ; more especially as the operation necessitated the transport of troops whose language was completely incomprehensible to most of our officers. There is also a great doubt whether the Russian Army, more especially the officers, were sufficiently adaptable to be associated with a foreign Navy in a joint land-and-sea operation. With our own soldiers these main difficulties would not have existed. But with foreign troops they appear at first sight to be very formidable.

In this respect it is interesting to note that the military objection to the Dardanelles project lay largely in the doubt whether troops could be thrown

ashore in moderate safety ; and, in a memorandum
prepared by the General Staff in 1906, this objection
is clearly expressed. Starting with the fact that, at
that date, the improvements in armaments had been
so revolutionary in character that history and experience afforded no reliable guide, the memorandum
stated that military opinion leant strongly to the view
that no landing could, in modern times, be effected in
the presence of an enemy unless the Navy was able
to guarantee with its guns that the troops and all their
transport would reach the shore unmolested ; and that
they would find, after disembarkation, a sufficiently
extended area free from hostile fire to enable them to
form up for battle on suitable ground.

How far could these primary conditions have been
fulfilled on the Pomeranian coast ? If the same
scheme for landing which was invented and prepared
for the Belgian coast in 1917 had been applied to a
Pomeranian landing, and if the exact spot for landing
had been kept secret, there is little doubt that two
Divisions, with the whole of their impedimenta, could
have been landed in half an hour, and another two
Divisions on the same day. Other troops could have
followed at the rate of two Divisions daily.

What would have happened after the landing ; and
whether, or not, they would have been able to maintain their ground, is a matter on which military
authorities alone can speak. So far as is known, no
record exists that an authoritative verdict was ever
asked for, or given. Most certainly none was ever
asked for by the War Council.

The subsequent protection of the line of communications is a matter with which it is impossible to deal
here ; suffice it to say that it was intimately bound

up with a descent by our ships on the Frisian coast, carried out at the same time, whereby the Elbe would have been threatened. Extensive mining operations of the Sound and Fehmern Belt would, of necessity, have been undertaken ; and the Baltic should have been flooded with submarine boats.

It is impossible to say, now, whether the scheme would have survived the detailed and critical examination essential before such an operation could be justifiably undertaken ; but it is unjust to dismiss the project offhand as impracticable, and with a shrug of the shoulders to say that it was madness on Lord Fisher's part to propose it. Scientific and thorough preparation would certainly have caused many of the objections which have been hastily advanced to fall into insignificance. The German Battle Fleet would have been placed in a difficult situation, for they would have been forced by public opinion to take some action, and this would have had to have been carried out in the Baltic, in the face of a large fleet of submarines and of extensive and unknown minefields.

On the other hand, it is not just to judge the German Fleet entirely by its performances in the war, since it was paralysed by the futile policy of the Emperor, who was no seaman, and who dreaded finding himself without a fleet when the war ended. In the case of invasion, hesitation on the part of the German Headquarters would have been thrown to the winds and we should have come up against the real German Navy.

All that can now be done is to state the main factors that underlay this project of invasion. Its virtues and dangers can be argued backwards and forwards, and the ultimate considered verdict of whether it should have been undertaken may be that it was either too dangerous to be attempted, or that it offered a fair prospect of success. The final verdict is now immaterial ; but, in all fairness, everyone must agree that the conception was a bold one, which, if successful, offered such substantial advantages (advantages that put in the shade any that success at the Dardanelles might have brought about) that it ought to have received, at the time, the most careful and complete consideration. It should certainly not have been shelved, contemptuously, as impossible. It may well be acclaimed in future years as a sign of genius, and not of madness, on Lord Fisher's part.

An alternative to a Baltic landing that, also, was in Lord Fisher's mind, possibly as a concurrent operation, was a landing on the Frisian coast or the coast of Schleswig-Holstein. The Germans were at one time very perturbed at the possibility that this would be attempted, and they feared, above all things, a landing there, or the seizure of some of the Frisian islands just off the coast. The landing on the Pomeranian coast, however, never seems to have entered their heads.

The postscript to this chapter gives an account of the early German naval movements, which shows that Admiral von Pöhl was very averse to allowing even the oldest of the German battleships (ships which were quite useless in a fleet action with our Grand Fleet) to leave the Elbe for operations in the Baltic. The reason for their retention on this side of the Canal was, without doubt, to keep them ready to frustrate any attempted seizure of territory. Here, indeed, was the chance of making a grand *coup* on the eve of a push on the Western Front : a sweep by some of Lord Fisher's 600 ships into the Baltic, with a threat of a landing on the Pomeranian coast, and at the same time an exit of the Grand Fleet and a threat to one of the Frisian islands. Had our older battleships defeated and thrown back the German old vessels, and laid the Frisian islands bare, their High Seas Fleet would have been forced to emerge, and the repercussion would have been felt at a critical moment on the Western Front. But with a War Council composed mainly of politicians, no possible co-ordination of action between the Army and Navy could be expected, so that that great power, possessed by no country but our own, of administering a swift blow at the ribs of our enemy by sea-borne troops was never properly used ; nor was any attempt made to use it except in a place where it was, from the time of its inception, doomed to failure.

The only note that can be found on the subject of the examination of this North Sea and Baltic project is a minute of the War Council Meeting of the 1st December, 1914, which records that Lord Fisher " pointed out the importance of adopting the offensive. The question of seizing an island off the German coast was adjourned." Questions of importance always were being adjourned by the War Council and rarely decided.

This review can suitably be wound up with a typically forceful letter from Fisher to a friend, written in 1918 :

We had a galaxy of science yesterday, and it is extremely useful for these great Giants of Science to meet and hear each other.[1]

But none of it goes to the root of the matter, which is—TO KNOCK OUT THE ENEMY AT HIS EXITS ! But then, of course, you come up against the Control of the War, which has completely lapsed from the Navy and got to be purely military.

[1] This referred to the Inventions Board.

Never was there such criminal folly as the relegation of the Navy into a " Subsidiary Service," as so described by Sir Ivor Philipps, M.P., in the House of Commons quite recently.

Instead of (with the main help of the Fleet) at the very outset of the war having obtained with our Expeditionary Force possession of Antwerp and the Belgian coast, we had instead thereof " the Massacre of Mons," and our Expeditionary Force was actually detrained under the fire of the German Army under General von Kluck.

In a printed memorandum prepared in 1914, it was incontestably proved that the Baltic constituted the decisive theatre of the war, but this Navy plan was condemned and turned down, notwithstanding Mr. Churchill's representation to the War Council at its ninth meeting at 6.30 p.m. on the 28th January, 1915, and we now see the consequences in two-thirds of Russia being under German domination, and Germany with a greater conquest than [was] ever effected by the Roman Empire.

The changes in Eastern Europe are tremendous. Germany now controls dominions greater than the Roman Empire ever possessed at its utmost period of expansion, and Germany now possesses a new direct route to India, viâ Odessa, Trebizond, and Turkestan.

All this terrible calamity directly results from our not going to the Baltic as the decisive theatre of the war when we could so easily have done so.

Frederick the Great indicated the Baltic as Germany's weakest spot, and when the Russian Army landed on the Pomeranian coast ninety miles from Berlin, he was frightened for the first time in his life, and sent for a bottle of poison, but the Russian Empress died, and peace was made.

But all this that I am saying to you is only a tiny bit of the congenital idiocy that has marked the whole conduct of the war. Think of Mr. Lloyd George's most famous speech, made long ago, of FOURTEEN TIMES TOO LATE !

But the marvellous words of England's greatest orator have to be remembered. Mr. Burke said to the House of Commons in one of his great orations :

" I have no faith in any scheme of war in which the execution is divorced from the plan."

In war, " considered rashness is prudence." Prudence in war is a synonym for imbecility.

Yours,

FISHER.

8.3.18.

II—13

But the bitterest pill to Lord Fisher was to read that the Germans were adopting, against Russia, the scheme he had hoped to carry out against them. On 9th September, 1917, he wrote to Mr. Churchill :

> . . . Some terrible headlines in the newspapers have upset me ! Terribly !
>
> " The German fleet to assist the land operations in the Baltic."
>
> " Landing the German Army south of Reval."
>
> We are five times stronger at sea than our enemies, and here is a small fleet, that we could gobble up in a few minutes, playing the great vital sea-part of landing an army in the enemy's rear and probably capturing the Russian capital by sea.
>
> This is " holding the ring " with a vengeance !
>
> I hear a new order of knighthood is on the *tapis*—O.M.G. (Oh ! My God !) Shower it on the Admiralty ! !

POSTSCRIPT [1]

The second volume of the German Naval Staff
History has now made it clear that the German High Command expected us to adopt a very different naval policy from that which we actually followed, and the measure of their fear of invasion is a good, almost the best, argument in favour of such an attempt. By the 4th August, 1914, the Germans had concentrated every heavy ship in their Navy in the North Sea, including, in addition to the Main Battle Fleet, three squadrons of older battleships. With the whole of their striking force concentrated in the North Sea, the Baltic was thus weakly defended. Prince Henry of Prussia, the German Commander-in-Chief in the Baltic, had meagre forces with which to oppose the Russian Fleet, composed of four old battleships, nine cruisers, and a squadron of seven light cruisers. The Russian flotillas were seven times more numerous than the German, and, in addition, it was expected that two Russian super-Dreadnoughts would be ready for sea in the autumn of 1914—an accession of strength which would make the existing inequality overwhelming.

Reports of Russian activity began to come in from the German forces that were watching the Gulf of Finland, and Prince Henry at once asked to be reinforced by the 4th Battle Squadron from the North

[1] This information is taken from an article published in *The Times* on the 27th October, 1921, and thanks are due to the proprietors for their courtesy in allowing it to be made use of.

Sea, and submitted a sound plan of operations. It was obvious that if the Germans wished to retain their control of the Baltic they must reinforce Prince Henry's squadron, but in order to do so it was necessary to weaken the North Sea Force by one squadron of old battleships for a little more than a week. Surely an inconsiderable force and for an insignificant time! But Russian activity had begun just after our first sweep into the Heligoland Bight, and von Pöhl, the Chief of the Naval Staff, considered the risk too great to be taken. To him the position seemed most hazardous. Would he not be playing into British hands by reinforcing the Baltic at the expense of the North Sea at so critical a moment, if only for one week? At last he did give way, and sent the IVth Squadron and a few heavy cruisers through the Kiel Canal, but he entered in his diary that the whole project caused him " grave anxiety."

Prince Henry then began his operations ; but the restrictions that were imposed upon him further reflect the tension at Headquarters. First he was ordered not to take his ships east of Memel ; then he received a telegram direct from the Emperor ordering him not to " expose the squadron under his command to mishaps " ; and after he had put to sea, he received yet another signal commanding him to use the " utmost caution." The operations were only continued a few days, when von Pöhl received a telegram informing him that the British seemed to be on the point of commencing " great undertakings." Unable to bear the anxiety any longer, he at once ordered all detached forces to return immediately to the North Sea. The mere apprehension of coastal operations in the North Sea thus caused the German Headquarter Staff to

recall from the Baltic a squadron of old battleships
that would have been useless in a fleet action and valuable only for coast defence.

Nearly a month later the German Army Staff requested that a combined demonstration should be made off Windau, in order to prevent Russian forces being sent to Galicia. Von Pöhl again consented to reinforce the Baltic, for a short time, but Admirals von Fehncke and von Ingenöhl were strongly opposed. Von Tirpitz did not object to sending reinforcements through the Kiel Canal, but thought that it would be better to *act* in the North Sea rather than to *demonstrate* in the Baltic—von Tirpitz was the only one of the senior German Admirals endowed with sea-instincts. The IVth and Vth Battle Squadrons were therefore placed under Prince Henry's command, transports collected and troops put on board, and by the evening of the 24th September the squadrons were at their points of assembly with the whole combination working smoothly. But between 9 o'clock and midnight Prince Henry received news which caused him great anxiety. At 10 o'clock he was told that the German Consul at Malmö had heard that the British submarines intended to pass the Kattegat (that is, to enter the Baltic) " on that very night." Almost immediately afterwards he received a signal to the effect that the agent of the German Intelligence Officer at Malmö had reported that at 5.30 p.m. the British Fleet had passed through the Great Belt, after clearing the minefields by means of old ships. A few minutes later another telegram arrived, saying that at 9 a.m. British submarines had been sighted off Vingo, steering a southerly course. To Prince Henry it appeared that if the facts alleged were true, and he had no reason to doubt them, his position was little short of desperate. At the time when he received the telegrams, the bulk of the British Fleet would have been debouching from the southern entrances to the Belts ; the forces at Kiel would shortly be overwhelmed, and his own squadrons would then almost certainly be brought to action and destroyed before reinforcements could be sent. He therefore quite properly broke off his operations and ordered every squadron to return to Kiel.

The reluctance of the German Headquarter Staff to detach old battleships from the North Sea shows conclusively that they dreaded and anticipated an attack on their North Sea coasts, and since they feared such an attack, as we now know they did, the inevitable conclusion is that they recognized that it had a good chance of success. It seems, therefore, that Fisher was advocating the operations that Germany most feared. Moreover, the reiterated taunts in the German Press regarding the inactivity of the British Fleet can now be explained ; for evidently the High Authorities in Berlin considered and made it known that we had failed to use our sea superiority in a manner that they believed we could and should have done.

CHAPTER XIX

THE DARDANELLES

The War Council—Lord Fisher's status—How the proceedings were muddled—Lord Fisher's views—Brief account of the operations—Telegram sent by Mr. Churchill—Lord Fisher's interview with Mr. Asquith—His attempted resignation—Lord Fisher's statement for Dardanelles Commission—The Commission blame Lord Fisher—His difficulties—Mr. Walter Roch's report—Further account of the operations—Lord Fisher's memoranda to Mr. Churchill—How ignored—Mr. Churchill's complaints—Where these fail—The War Council—The gambler's plea.

Divided councils, half-hearted measures, grudged resources, makeshift plans, no real control or guidance.

The World Crisis : " The Aftermath."

THUS Mr. Churchill describes, with profound truth, the dealings of the War Council with the Dardanelles problem.

It is entirely outside the scope of this biography to include a detailed history of those operations. All that it is proposed to do is to give as concise an account as possible of Lord Fisher's connection with the inception and early portion of the campaign. Fuller accounts are to be found in the Official History of the War, the Report of the Dardanelles Committee, and Mr. Churchill's book *The World Crisis.*

The first step to be taken, in order to unravel the tangle into which the proceedings fell during the early months of the operations, must be to examine the constitution and functions of the " War Council " and its method of transacting business ; for much of the trouble that arose was due directly to the unbusinesslike way in which this Council dealt with the conduct of the war.

The War Council was a Committee of the Cabinet, composed of Cabinet Ministers and Mr. Arthur Balfour. Lord Kitchener was a member, and he also represented the General Staff at the War Office; much can be said in favour of this arrangement, since he was a professional soldier and could speak with authority on all military matters. Mr. Churchill was also a member, and similarly represented the Admiralty and acted as spokesman for the Navy. This, however, was a bad arrangement, since he was a civilian and had merely a superficial knowledge of technical naval subjects. The proper person to represent the Navy was the First Sea Lord. There was no reason why the First Sea Lord should have been made a *member* of the Council, but he should, at least, have been the spokesman of the Admiralty. Both Lord Fisher and Admiral of the Fleet Sir Arthur Wilson attended the meetings in an advisory capacity only, and sat silent listeners to Mr. Churchill's expositions of naval matters. They were there to answer questions when asked; but neither of them considered that he was entitled to intervene in a discussion unless asked for his opinion. They both considered it unseemly to wrangle with the First Lord before the other members of the War Council.

How this unsatisfactory state of things arose it is not easy to imagine. It, surely, seems obvious that the naval opinion on any subject should have been stated by a responsible naval officer who knew what he was talking about, and not to reach the Council as a *réchauffé* of the views of naval experts expounded by an amateur. The result was that the Council, on several important occasions, mistook the silence of the

two experienced Admirals for agreement with the
proposals then under discussion ; with which proposals they were, as a matter of fact, by no means in
accord.

The Council was equally in error, so it turned out,
in accepting Mr. Churchill's exposition as being the
opinion of the Admiralty, when he was largely express-
ing his own views. It is difficult to imagine a case
that more clearly shows the absurdity of the civilian
head of a technical department considering himself,
and being considered by his colleagues, as being, by
his appointment, *de facto* endowed with technical and
expert knowledge.

Lastly, the Prime Minister, who presided, never
thoroughly probed any of the proposals before the
Committee. In so important a matter as the Dardanelles Campaign no joint report was called for from
the Staffs of the Admiralty and War Office, and the
considered opinions of the two Admiralty experts on
crucial points were not *definitely* asked for. The proceedings seem to have been merely informal discussions that rarely led to clear-cut decisions. In fact,
the minutes of the Committee are, in the early part
of 1915, largely a record of indecisions.

Here we have the prime cause of the Dardanelles
fiasco. If Lord Fisher had, throughout, been entrusted
with the exposition of the naval case at the Council
meetings, the Dardanelles operations would, in all
probability, never have been undertaken except purely
as a political demonstration. But the brief for the
Navy was undertaken by a civilian Minister, endowed
with a gift of a silver tongue and facile persuasion ; a
visionary whose enthusiasm, inborn pluck and determination minimized difficulties and discounted dan-

gers ; an optimist whose imagination dwelt ever on success and belittled the chance of failure, but who, unfortunately, also was without experience in sea matters.

Before commencing the narrative it is well to see what views Lord Fisher held, at this time, of an operation against the Dardanelles. They are clearly set forth in the following letters :

3rd January, 1915.

DEAR WINSTON,

    I've been informed by Hankey that the War Council assembles next Thursday, and I suppose it will be like a game of ninepins ! Everyone will have a plan and one ninepin in falling will knock over its neighbour !

I consider the attack on Turkey holds the field. But *only* if it's immediate.

However, it won't be. Our Aulic Council will adjourn till the following Thursday fortnight. (N.B.—When did we last meet, and what came of it ?)

We shall decide on the futile bombardment of the Dardanelles, which wears out the guns of the *Indefatigable*, which will probably require replacement. What good resulted from last bombardment ? Did it move a single Turk from the Caucasus ? And so the war goes on ! You want *one* man.

This is the Turkey plan :

Appoint Sir William Robertson, the present Quartermaster-General, to command the Expeditionary Force.

Immediately replace all Indians and 75,000 seasoned troops from Sir John French's command with Territorials from England (as you yourself suggest), and embark this Turkish Expeditionary Force ostensibly for the protection of Egypt with all possible *dispatch* at *Marseilles*, and land them at Besika Bay direct, with previous feints, before they arrive, with troops now in Egypt, against Haifa and Alexandretta : the latter to be a real occupation because of its inestimable value as regards the oil-fields of the Garden of Eden, with which by rail it is in direct communication, and we shove out the Germans now established at Alexandretta with an immense Turkish concession. The last act of that arch-enemy of England, Marschall von Bieberstein.

The Greeks to go for Gallipoli, the same time as we go for
Besika, and the Bulgarians for Constantinople, and the Russians
and Serbians and Rumanians for Austria. (All this you said yourself.)

Sturdee forces the Dardanelles with the " Majestic " class and
the " Canopus " class ! God bless him !

But as the great Napoleon said, " *Celerity* " ; without it, " *Failure.*" In the history of the world a Junta has never won.

You want *one* man.

Again on the next day he wrote to Mr. Churchill :

The naval advantages of the possession of Constantinople and
the getting the wheat from the Black Sea are so overwhelming that
I consider Colonel Hankey's plan for Turkish operations vital and
imperative and very pressing.

So much for the general proposition. Now for the
particular operations proposed.

Lord Fisher had been cast in an entirely different
mould from Mr. Churchill. He had spent a lifetime
in working hard and wrestling with the problems of
the Navy. The result of such constant thought is to
endow the mind with an intuition which is almost
prophetic. New problems are looked at through the
lens of deduction from past experience. The analogies
between past and present may not be exact ; but
they are generally sufficiently close to allow correct
inferences to be drawn. Lord Fisher had studied the
Dardanelles problem in 1898, when the Narrows were
rushed by Admiral Hornby. He had visited Gallipoli
when Commander-in-Chief of the Mediterranean and
discussed the defence of the Narrows with the officer
in command. He had been First Sea Lord when a
joint Army and Navy Committee had sat to go thoroughly into the question of a joint naval and military
occupation of the Peninsula, and had concurred in
their adverse report. His general view in 1915 of

operations against the Peninsula and the Narrows may be summed up as follows :

Either hit hard at once by sea and land on the Peninsula and in Syria—or do nothing.

He could not definitely say the Narrows could not be rushed, but he did not believe that this could be done. He objected entirely to naval operations unsupported by the Army ; but consented to those being undertaken for political reasons only, provided they were broken off if not immediately successful. But when the moment for breaking off did arrive, it was seen that operations could not be stopped without loss of political prestige ; he was, therefore, against his will, forced to participate still further.

He always had been a firm believer in joint naval and military operations on the German northern coast, in more or less tideless waters. He did not believe in operations against the high rocky coast of the Peninsula, and the strong adverse current in the Narrows, which made the destruction of the minefields under gunfire practically impossible.

Unfortunately, when pressing his views against the Dardanelles, he almost invariably pressed the alternative attack in the North. The advocates for the Dardanelles operations were therefore always able, in his absence, to suggest that his opposition was not in reality directed against the feasibility of the Dardanelles project, but because he wished the alternative scheme to be carried out. This also was Mr. Asquith's view after his interview on 28th January (which will be referred to later); but the Prime Minister never, at that interview, or at any other time, directly asked Lord Fisher if, apart from the possibility of a Baltic project, he considered the Dardanelles project to be a sound operation. The Prime Minister never seems to have demanded clear-cut views from experts. An impenetrable fog seemed to hang over his interviews and the meetings of the Council. Had he put definite questions to Lord Fisher, he most certainly would have got a direct answer that he considered the undertaking would be a failure.

To sum up : Lord Fisher's view was that joint naval and military operations were only desirable if carried out at the earliest moment, using the troops of our Allies near the spot. This was not, as a matter of fact, possible ; Russia objected strongly to the Greeks going near Constantinople, and the permanent occupation of that place was the only inducement great enough to tempt Greece to join in the war on the side of the Allies.

We are now in a position to survey the early history of the campaign, as conducted by the War Council.

On 31st October, 1914, Turkey declared war, and on the 3rd November the outer forts at the entrance to the Dardanelles were bombarded by our ships for about ten minutes. Any more foolish proceeding cannot well be imagined. The reason put forward was, that it was desirable to test the range of the Turkish guns ! The fact was that Mr. Churchill suffered from a disease, common among those not accustomed to war, which may be called *cacoethes agendi*, that is, the itch to be always doing something. This bombardment at once brought home to the Germans at Constantinople the necessity for bringing the defences of the Dardanelles up to the highest pitch of perfection, and, incidentally, it afforded them three months in which to achieve their object.

On the 25th November the subject of the Dardan-

elles came before the War Council. A possible attack
was discussed ; but Lord Kitchener stated that the
moment for any such offensive had not arrived. It
was therefore decided to postpone any further consideration of the matter ; but in view of future possibilities of operations in the Near East, horse-boats were
sent to Egypt from time to time as opportunity offered.[1]

On the 2nd January, 1915, a most important telegram was received from Petrograd, saying that the
Russian troops were being hard pressed in the Caucasus, and asking for a demonstration to be made
against the Turks, in order to draw off some of the
Turkish troops. This obviously was an appeal that
had to receive full attention. The request of an Ally
for help is a political, and not solely a military matter.
The Dardanelles was the place which presented the
easiest opportunity for such a demonstration. The
question, therefore, at once arose as to what form the
attack should assume. If the pressure in the Caucasus
was to be relieved, something had to be done at once,
and it was, of course, absolutely impossible to send
troops in time to be of any use. Admiral Carden, the
naval Commander-in-Chief on the spot, was asked if
he considered it practicable to force the Dardanelles
with ships only. He replied that the Straits could
not be rushed, but that they might be forced by
extended operations.

On receipt of Admiral Carden's reply, Mr. Churchill
telegraphed :

High Authorities here concur in your opinion. Forward particulars showing what force would be required for extended operations, how you think it could be employed, and what results could
be obtained.

[1] This was a typical War Council decision.

Now, this telegram adumbrates acceptance of extended operations. It is reasonable to expect that it
would have been sent by Lord Fisher as First Sea Lord,
but it was not. Moreover, so far from being sent by
Lord Fisher, he did not even see it before it was sent !
When this subject was inquired into by the Dardanelles Commission, Lord Fisher told them that, had he
seen the telegram, he would most certainly have asked
for it to be altered, as he did not agree with it. Who,
then, were the High Authorities ? Mr. Churchill explained to the Commission that they were himself,
Admiral Oliver, the Chief of the Staff, and Admiral
Jackson ; the latter two having expressed their opinion
verbally to him. In so important a matter the opinion
of all concerned should have been recorded in writing.
Admiral Carden, in the Mediterranean, however,
assumed that Lord Fisher had blessed the scheme ;
for, as he remarked, Lord Fisher was at the Admiralty
and, therefore, naturally he assumed that he was one
of the High Authorities. This is a good example of
the misunderstandings and confusion which resulted
from the vicious practice introduced by Mr. Churchill
into Admiralty procedure in 1912 of having a Chief
of the Staff who was not First Sea Lord. The result
was that " Operation " telegrams and orders were at
times sent out by him without even the knowledge of
the First Sea Lord.

On the 11th January Admiral Carden replied, and
suggested :

(a) The destruction of the defences at the entrance
of the Straits.

(b) Action inside the Straits.

(c) Destruction of the defences of the Narrows.

(d) Sweeping a clear passage through the mine-field.

Lord Fisher does not seem to have been consulted further at this point, nor was Admiral of the Fleet Sir Arthur Wilson.

On the 13th January the matter was brought up before the War Council. Lord Kitchener thought the plan worth trying, and Mr. Churchill spoke strongly in its favour. Lord Fisher, following his usual practice, said nothing, neither did Admiral Wilson. Neither of them was asked for his opinion. The report of the Dardanelles Commission gives the following account of this meeting of the War Council :

> The decision of the War Council on the 13th January, after hearing the views expressed by Lord Kitchener and Mr. Churchill —Lord Fisher, Sir Arthur Wilson, and Sir James Murray remaining silent—was couched in the following terms :
> " The Admiralty should prepare for a naval expedition in February to bombard and take the Gallipoli Peninsula, with Constantinople as its objective."

How they conceived that the Navy was going to bombard and *take* the Gallipoli Peninsula has never been explained.

It is interesting to speculate what the result would have been had Lord Fisher, Sir Arthur Wilson, and Sir James Murray been the spokesmen of their respective Services, and if Mr. Churchill and Lord Kitchener had merely been members of the Committee.

There is no doubt that, after the meeting of the 13th, Lord Fisher began to consider seriously what the effect on our naval resources would be of action by the Fleet alone. Before the next meeting of the War Council on the 28th January he made up his mind that the scheme was unsound. He intimated to the Prime Minister that he did not wish to attend any more Council meetings, which can well be understood in view of his subordinate position when attending, and the way in which the work of the Council was conducted. This led to the meeting (to which we have already referred) being arranged between Mr. Churchill and Lord Fisher, on the 28th January, in the Prime Minister's room. Then, according to Mr. Asquith's account, Lord Fisher based his objections to the Dardanelles scheme rather on the fact that it interfered with his other projects than on the difficulties inherent to the successful carrying out of that scheme. There is no doubt that this was the case. But there is considerable evidence that Mr. Asquith never asked him whether, from the purely naval aspect of the operation, he was in *agreement* with the proposal to rush the Straits. Had he done so, there is very little doubt what Lord Fisher's answer would have been.

The War Council met shortly after this interview. Lord Fisher was in a disturbed state of mind. The Prime Minister, at the conclusion of the interview, had expressed himself in agreement with Mr. Churchill. There had also been trouble between Lord Fisher and Mr. Churchill over the action the former desired to be taken in consequence of the unsatisfactory result of the Battle of the Dogger Bank. Lord Fisher's proposals were undoubtedly premature ; but he appears to have been convinced that, even when the official report of the battle was received at the Admiralty, Mr. Churchill would not take the action that he considered necessary. He therefore attended the meeting with a feeling that he was, in several important matters, being forced to acquiesce in actions prejudicial to the Navy, and that, if the Dardanelles project was

II—14

adhered to, the best thing he could do was to mark his disapproval in a practical manner by resigning.

He had not expected that the Dardanelles question would be discussed at this War Council meeting. When he saw that the members of the Council were in agreement with the proposal that a purely naval attack should be undertaken, he rose from his seat with the intention of going into the room of Mr. Bonham-Carter, the Prime Minister's private secretary, and there writing out his resignation. Lord Kitchener at the same time rose from his seat, and before Lord Fisher could leave the room, had some private conversation with him at the window, apart from the others present. He strongly urged Lord Fisher not to resign, and pointed out to him that he was the *only one present who disagreed with the Dardanelles operation.* An additional inducement for Lord Fisher to reconsider his decision was that stated to the Chairman of the Dardanelles Commission, that there were overwhelming political reasons why the attempt at least should be made. Eventually, according to a note made by Lord Fisher at the time, he " reluctantly gave in to Lord Kitchener's entreaty and resumed his seat." Yet neither the Prime Minister nor any one member of the Council asked him to state his views and objections.

Now, in the face of the words in italics it is difficult to imagine how any member of the Council could have believed that Lord Fisher agreed to the proposals.

The next step was taken by Mr. Churchill, who rightly felt that the incident of Lord Fisher's threatened resignation could not be left without some definite exchange of opinion taking place between

them. The following is his account of what took
place :

Although the War Council had come to a decision in which
I heartily agreed, and no voice had been raised against the naval
plan, I felt that I must come to a clear understanding with the
First Sea Lord. I noticed the incident of his leaving the table,
and Lord Kitchener following him, and I did not know what was
the upshot in his mind. After lunch I asked him to come to my
room, and we had a talk. I strongly urged him to undertake the
operation, and he definitely consented to do so. I state this
positively. We then repaired to the afternoon War Council
meeting, Admiral Oliver, the Chief of the Staff, coming with us,
and I announced finally, on behalf of the Admiralty, and with the
agreement of Lord Fisher, that we had decided to undertake the
task with which the War Council had charged us so urgently.

All this undoubtedly was the case. Mr. Churchill's
silver tongue was ever able to persuade Lord
Fisher. Appeals to patriotism and good comradeship
were always difficult for him to ignore. Without
doubt he then agreed to carry out the operations, *with which the War Council had charged the
Admiralty so urgently,* and which he now looked on
as inevitable ; but this did not mean that he agreed
with them. On reflection, he without doubt balanced
against his resignation the other work he had in hand
at the Admiralty, the urgent shipbuilding programmes
which he alone could ensure being completed to
promised dates, the provision of mines, the mining
operations, and numerous other things. He strongly
disliked the Dardanelles project, and he foresaw the
very severe drain on the naval forces so urgently
required in home waters ; but, on the balance, he
thought it better to let the Dardanelles operation go
on, and if necessary to call a halt later before matters
became too serious. At the moment the safety of the
Empire was not imperilled.

After a study of the papers available it is impossible to avoid the conclusion that the War Council were completely hypnotized by the eloquence of Mr. Balfour and Mr. Churchill. Attention was mainly focussed on the great political advantages that might accrue if the operations were successful. In fact, as is so often the case when individuals are anxious to follow a line of action, they become somewhat impatient of any objections. It is impossible to account for the fact that no member of the Council asked Lord Fisher to state his opinions or objections when he had returned to the table after his talk with Lord Kitchener, except that they did not wish for objections against the scheme to be put forward and pressed home. No one present could have imagined that Lord Fisher agreed with the scheme, else why did he start to leave the room ? If he did not agree with the proposals, surely he should have been asked to state his objections, and those objections should have been recorded in the minutes. No naval officer could have given a definite opinion that the operations would be unsuccessful, since there was no evidence available as to the strength of the forts or the efficiency of the mine-fields ; but what Lord Fisher would undoubtedly have insisted on would have been that the attempt should not be purely naval, and that the Fleet should not undertake isolated action, but must be backed by an army.

To emphasize Lord Fisher's point of view it is well to reproduce the statement that he prepared for the Chairman of the Dardanelles Commission, and which he wished to appear in their report. After the report was published, this paper was found not to have been included. Lord Fisher was extremely angry, and he

always considered that he had been most unfairly
treated by its omission. The following is his statement :

Mr. Churchill and I worked in absolute accord at the Admiralty
until it came to the question of the Dardanelles.

I was absolutely unable to give the Dardanelles proposal any
welcome, for there was the Nelsonic dictum that " any sailor who
attacked a fort was a fool."

My direct personal knowledge of the Dardanelles problem dates
back many years. I had had the great advantage of commanding
a battleship under Admiral Sir Geoffrey Phipps-Hornby when,
during the Russo-Turkish War, that celebrated flag officer took
the Fleet through the Dardanelles.

I had again knowledge of the subject as Commander-in-Chief
of the Mediterranean Fleet for three years during the Boer War,
when for a long period the Fleet under my command lay at Lemnos
off the mouth of the Dardanelles, thus affording me means of
close study of the feasibility of forcing the Straits.

When I became First Sea Lord on 20th October, 1904, there
arrived that very day the news of the Dogger Bank incident with
Russia.

In my official capacity, in view of the possibility of a war with
Russia, I immediately examined the question of the forcing of the
Dardanelles, and I satisfied myself at that time that, even with
military co-operation, the operation was mighty hazardous.

Basing myself on the experience gained over so many years,
when the project was mooted in the present war my opinion was
that the attempt to force the Dardanelles would not succeed.

I was the only member of the War Council who dissented from
the project ; but I did not carry my dissent to the point of resignation because I understood that there were overwhelming political
reasons why the attempt at least should be made.

Moreover, I felt it to be of vital importance that I should personally see the completion of the great shipbuilding programme
which was then under construction, which had been initiated by
me on my advent to the Admiralty, and which included no less
than 612 vessels.

The change in my opinion as to the relative importance of the
probable failure in the Dardanelles began when the ever-increasing
drain upon the Fleet, as the result of the prosecution of the Dar-

danelles undertaking, reached a point at which, in my opinion, it destroyed the possibility of other naval operations which I had in view, and even approached to jeopardizing our naval supremacy in the decisive theatre of the war.

I may be pressed with the question why did I not carry my objections to the point of resignation when the decision was first reached to attack the Dardanelles with naval forces.

In my judgment, it is not the business of the chief technical advisers of the Government to resign because their advice is not accepted, unless they are of opinion that the operation proposed must lead to disastrous results.

The attempt to force the Dardanelles, though a failure, would not have been disastrous so long as the ships employed could be withdrawn at any moment, and only such vessels were engaged, as in the beginning of the operations was in fact the case, as could be spared without detriment to the general service of the Fleet.

I may next be asked whether I made any protest at the War Council when the First Lord proposed the Dardanelles enterprise, or at any later date.

Mr. Churchill knew my opinion. I did not think it would tend towards good relations between the First Lord and myself, nor to the smooth working of the Board of Admiralty, to raise objections in the War Council's discussions. My opinion being known to Mr. Churchill in what I regarded as the proper constitutional way, I preferred thereafter to remain silent.

When the operation was undertaken, my duty from that time onwards was confined to seeing that the Government plan was carried out as successfully as possible with the available means.

I did everything I could to secure its success, and I only resigned when the drain it was making on the resources of the Navy became so great as to jeopardize the major operations of the Fleet.

On the 14th May, 1915, the War Council made it clear to me that the great projects in Northern waters which I had in view in laying down the Armada of new vessels were at an end, and the further drain on our naval resources foreshadowed that evening convinced me that I could no longer countenance the Dardanelles operations, and the next day I resigned.

It seemed to me that I was faced at last by a progressive frustration of my main scheme of naval strategy.

Gradually the crowning work of war construction was being diverted and perverted from its original aim. The monitors, for

instance, planned for the banks and shallows of Northern waters,
were sent off to the Mediterranean, where they had never been
meant to operate.

I felt I was right in remaining in office until this situation, never
contemplated at first by anyone, was accepted by the War Council.
I felt right in resigning on this decision.

My conduct and the interpretation of my responsibility I respect-
fully submit to the judgment of the Committee. Perhaps I may
be allowed to say that as regards the opinion I held I was right.

FISHER.

7th October, 1916.

This plain, straightforward statement clearly puts
Lord Fisher's opinions and the reasons for his " bowing
the knee to Rimmon."

Let us probe the matter still deeper.

The Dardanelles Commission in their report blame
both Lord Fisher and Sir Arthur Wilson for not, on
the two occasions of the 13th and 28th January,
having expressed their dissent from the proposals
without being definitely asked for their opinions.
They report :

We have not the least doubt that the attitude they [Fisher and
Wilson] adopted at the War Council was dictated by a strong
sense of duty. But we have no hesitation in recording our opinion
that it was a mistaken sense of duty. Lord Fisher himself recognized that he " stretched loyalty to an extreme pitch." . . . We
hold, therefore, that although they were not definitely asked to
express their opinions, they should have done so.

The matter, however, cannot be quite so easily
disposed of. We must put ourselves in Lord Fisher's
place. He disliked the whole scheme ; he did not
think it would be successful ; but he had no evidence
to bring in support of his contention. He had no
direct and valid argument to produce which would
prove his assertion. An Evangelist in preaching his

Gospel of Hope can well be carried away with enthusi-asm. An Angel of Darkness spreading gloom and despair can neither feel enthusiasm himself nor arouse it in others. He had heard Mr. Balfour sketching the vast advantages that success would bring, and Mr. Churchill, like the Pied Piper, piping seductive notes of promise of success, and so drawing the confiding Committee after him, with their eyes fixed on the skies and dazzled by the shining light of hope.

On the other hand, Lord Fisher had his eyes fixed on that area of sullen grey water flowing never-ceasingly down at three knots speed against our ships, hiding as with a delusive screen the remorseless rows of the Dardanelles mine-field. Each side of this stream of death he saw forts which were able to fire, day or night, at point-blank range at any vessels trying to force their way up against that never-ceasing tide—forts that no smoke-screen could blind, for no wind can blow both east and west at the same moment. Both Sir Arthur Wilson and he had wrestled with mines and their destruction; it had been part of their daily work as torpedo officers. Could those mine-fields be destroyed? It depended on the efficiency of the individual mine, on mist, and on luck. Neither of them could assert that the mines could not be over-come; but years of experience had made them more than doubtful.

Then the guns. They knew the ships that were expected to force the passage. They knew their armour belts had never been intended to keep out point-blank fire; they knew the havoc to a ship that modern projectiles could bring about by disarranging its steering and incapacitating its engines. Could they survive? Experience again made them more

THE KINGFISHER

II. 216

than doubtful. Luck and thick weather might, however, help, and again Lord Fisher could not say definitely that the thing could not be done.

All the accumulated experience of these two sea-officers gave them intuitive warning against the proposals, though, if pinned down to hard facts, they had nothing definite and conclusive to bring forward in support of their professional instinct. It was thus that the technical experts and the amateurs differed. The vision of the expert is stereoscopic, that of the amateur is apt to be myopic. Experience, without definite concrete evidence, warned the sea-officers that the scheme would not succeed; but uneducated optimism gave unbridled licence to the hopes of the amateurs.

We are now in a position to appreciate Lord Fisher's essential difficulty, and what was in his mind when he said that he did not think it right to have an altercation with his Chief at the Council meeting. Had he had direct evidence on any point of fact about which Mr. Churchill was in error, he would undoubtedly have corrected him. Since, however, the matter was largely one of personal opinion, he did not intervene. If he had advanced his opinion without the facts to back it up, he undoubtedly would have been led into a wrangle, in which the more skilled debater would have gained the day. If he had intervened and stated that he did not consider the operation could be successful, he would naturally have been asked to give his reasons. He could only have detailed the various difficulties that he foresaw, and given his opinion that they would prove fatal. If he had been asked whether he could state positively that the operation would fail, he could only have replied that he could not definitely say so.

Mr. Churchill's account in *The World Crisis* does not correspond with his own evidence before the Commission, and the conclusions that the Commission drew from the evidence of other persons. Mr. Churchill writes :

I am in no way concealing the great and continuous pressure which I put on the old Admiral. This pressure was reinforced by Lord Kitchener's personal influence, by the collective opinion of the War Council, and by the authoritative decision of the Prime Minister. It was a pressure not only of opinion but of arguments, to which he could find no answer. Moreover, there was, in addition, on the technical side a very great weight of support at the Admiralty. "Naval opinion was unanimous," said Lord Fisher afterwards. "Mr. Churchill had them all on his side. I was the only rebel." [1]

The Commission, however, reported :

There can be no doubt that at the two meetings on the 28th January Mr. Churchill strongly advocated the adoption of the Dardanelles enterprise. When Sir Arthur Wilson was asked, " Did the First Lord express an opinion in favour of it ? " he replied, " Yes, very much ; he pressed it very strongly." We think that, considering what Mr. Churchill knew of the opinions entertained by Lord Fisher and Sir Arthur Wilson, and considering also the fact that the other experts at the Admiralty who had been consulted, although they assented to an attack on the outer forts of the Dardanelles and to progressive operations thereafter up the Straits as far as might be found practicable, *had not done so with any great cordiality or enthusiasm,*[2] he ought, instead of urging Lord Fisher, as he seems to have done at the private meeting after luncheon on the 28th January, to give a silent but manifestly reluctant assent to the undertaking, not merely to have invited Lord Fisher and Sir Arthur Wilson to express their views freely to the Council, but further to have insisted on their doing so, in order that the ministerial members might be placed in full possession of all the arguments for and against the enterprise.

[1] Lord Fisher was prone to make exaggerated statements in the latter part of his life.
[2] Italics not in original.

In other words, although the sole reason for Mr. Churchill's addressing the Council was to provide them with the views of the Admiralty, it is evident that he was not sufficiently careful in this matter, but gave his own views rather than those of the experts. He knew that Lord Fisher was not in favour of the scheme. He also stated in his evidence that if Sir Arthur Wilson had been asked to vote he would have voted in the negative. Yet in laying the case for the Admiralty before the War Council, he does not appear to have mentioned, nor given the slightest hint, that this was the case.

Mr. Walter Roch, one of the Commissioners, in his excellent minority report, puts the matter clearly and forcibly. His conclusions are worth quoting :

(1) The facts disclosed in the course of the inquiry show that the War Council concentrated their attention too much on the political ends to be gained by an offensive policy in the East, and gave too little attention to the means by which that policy could be translated into terms of naval and military action.

The War Council never had before them detailed staff estimates of men, munitions, and material, or definite plans showing them what military operations were possible.

The War Council also underestimated without any real investigation the strength of the Turkish opposition.

(2) The War Council rejected without sufficient consideration all previous opinions against a purely naval attack on forts. The problem of forcing the Dardanelles, even by a purely naval attack, required the consideration of the expert engineer and artilleryman as much as that of the expert naval officer, and should therefore have been subjected to a joint naval and military staff for investigation.

(3) Mr. Churchill failed to present fully to the War Council the opinions of his naval advisers, and this failure was due to his own strong personal opinion in favour of a naval attack. Mr. Churchill should also have consulted the Board of Admiralty before such a large and novel departure in naval policy was undertaken.

Thus a campaign that ended in disaster was forced on the country largely by the action of a single man and by the methods described above.

Further comment on this aspect is needless, and we will turn again to the history of the operations.

After the War Council, on 28th January, had approved the proposed operation, Lord Fisher loyally did all in his power to forward the scheme, although he cordially disliked it.

On the 18th February he pointed out that the Dardanelles operation was retaining in the Mediterranean the *Queen Elizabeth, Inflexible, Invincible,* and *Indefatigable,* a flotilla of destroyers, and a destroyer depot-ship, all of which were wanted at home to reinforce the Grand Fleet.

On the 19th February the first important bombardment took place. The results were not decisive, but, at the same time, were fairly satisfactory.

On the 5th March General Birdwood, who had been sent to the Dardanelles to report, telegraphed :

I am very doubtful if the Navy can force the passage unassisted.

On the 6th he telegraphed :

I have already informed you that I consider the Admiral's forecast is too sanguine, and though we may have a better estimate by the 12th, I doubt his ability to force the passage unaided.

On the 19th Lord Kitchener agreed to send the 29th Division.

General Headquarters in France was strongly opposed to the diversion of troops from the main theatre to the Dardanelles. One important member of the Staff put their view caustically, by suggesting that the Admiralty had no need to worry about the provision of transports, as the Germans would be only too happy to supply all the transports that were necessary to take our troops away from the main front to a subsidiary theatre.

On the 16th March, Admiral Carden was invalided and Admiral de Robeck was appointed to the command. On the 18th the attack was made. The *Irresistible, Ocean,* and *Bouvet* were sunk, and nearly all the crew of the latter were lost. Three days afterwards the Admiral reported that it was necessary to reconsider the plan of attack.

On the 19th Sir Ian Hamilton, who had arrived to command the troops, telegraphed :

From what I saw of the extraordinarily gallant attack made yesterday, I am being most reluctantly driven to the conclusion that the Dardanelles are less likely to be forced by battleships than at one time seemed probable, and if the Army is to participate, its operations will not assume the subsidiary form anticipated.

On the 27th March, Lord Fisher was becoming alarmed at the drain on our resources, coupled with the small progress at the Dardanelles. He wrote to Mr. Churchill a memorandum, of which the following paragraphs form the material portion :

With reference to a private and personal telegram sent this forenoon by the First Lord to Vice-Admiral de Robeck, stating that an official telegram would be sent him from the Admiralty approving his proposed action as conveyed in his private telegram to the First Lord, my decided opinion is that before any such action the Admiralty should have before them the report to the War Office of Sir Ian Hamilton, as to his proposed future action, together with the remarks thereon of the War Office as to the likelihood of the proposed military operations in co-operation with the Fleet being so favourable as to justify the very considerable naval losses that may ensue.

It must be added that the battle-cruiser *Inflexible* has been badly damaged at the Dardanelles, necessitating her being convoyed to Malta for repair, and that the *Queen Elizabeth* is dependent on one engine, so is a cause of anxiety until repaired. And we have lost two battleships, and the battleships *Lord Nelson* and *Agamemnon* are requiring repair. We have sixteen battleships now at the Dardanelles.

The list of ships appended showed that there were at the Dardanelles no fewer than fifteen battleships, including the *Queen Elizabeth*, the very latest of our large ships mounting 15-inch guns, the *Inflexible*, a " Dreadnought " cruiser, six light cruisers (two others had been sunk), twenty-four destroyers, ten submarines, three monitors, two gunboats, fifty-two minesweepers, seven fleet-sweepers, one aeroplane carrier, the *Ark Royal*, five torpedo-boats, six ocean tugs, three salvage steamers, and five other fleet auxiliaries. In addition, there were numerous transports, store and ammunition ships, colliers, water-ships, etc. These were all British ships.

There is little reason to wonder that Lord Fisher was becoming seriously alarmed.

He sent the above memorandum next day to Mr. Churchill, together with the following comment. He had heard the rumour that something big was brewing after the 28th March :

If the Germans decide (as well they may)—influenced largely, no doubt, by our having so large a force away from the decisive theatre —on some big thing at home, there is (you must admit) much cause for anxiety, especially with the German and Austrian submarine menace to the yet unlanded troops and our Dardanelles Fleet. What is Ian Hamilton's report as to probable success ? Admiral de Robeck does not look forward to disabling the Turkish guns. Such justifiable losses, for so great a political prize as Constantinople, might possibly at the same time jeopardize our desired large margin

of superiority over the German Navy in the decisive theatre—
observing that the dispatch of submarines and destroyers from
England to-day to the Dardanelles, together with those detained
there on passage home, is a serious diminution of our required force
in home waters ; and that also, in all directions, such as aircraft,
nets, monitors, repair ships, and light cruisers, our home resources
are being heavily drawn upon by the Dardanelles operations, but
perhaps most especially in the amount of ammunition and wear
of the big guns.

He goes on to point out certain signs of increased
German activity in the North Sea, and then continues :

We cannot lessen the strength of Sir John Jellicoe's command,
some of whose much-wanted light cruisers and destroyers we have
reluctantly been compelled to withdraw for other services, so that
his fleet is not so well equipped as could be wished in these respects.
Therefore there should be a very strong assurance of success in the
Dardanelles project to justify the risks we run by this depletion
of our strength in the decisive theatre of the war.

Vice-Admiral de Robeck is very explicit in pointing out that
our bombardment has not disabled more than one of the Turkish
guns, nor will our passage through the Narrows be effective unless
the military operations give us the possession of the whole of the
Gallipoli Peninsula.   Also, he expresses his anxiety as to any further
considerable use of the big guns of the old ships.

We have also to consider the arrival of hostile submarines when
the troops may yet be in the transports and the Fleet not yet in
the Narrows.

Is the capture of the Gallipoli Peninsula going to be a siege ?
We should have the military opinion on this.

Is Ian Hamilton assured of the sufficiency of his force ?

We know Admiral de Robeck to be a brave man, and he talks
assuredly, but his assurance is really based on military co-operation, and especially the demolition of all the guns, thus assuring
him of his safe communication with the sea and safe passage of
his store ships, colliers, and ammunition supplies.

                                                    F.

P.S.—I am not blind to the political necessity of going forward
with the task ; but, before going further forward, let the whole

situation be so fully examined that success is assured while safety in the decisive theatre is not compromised.

It is as well always to remember the small effective superiority of the Grand Fleet over the High Seas Fleet. This was ever present in Lord Fisher's mind, and although Mr. Churchill brushes aside the real facts, it was one of the main reasons of Lord Fisher's dislike of the operations as the Dardanelles demands increased.

On the 1st January, 1915, owing to one ship refitting and two being seriously damaged, the relative strength of the two Fleets had stood : [1]

			"Dreadnoughts."	Pre-"Dreadnoughts."
British	.	.	.	18	8
German	.	.	.	16	16

There was a fighting superiority of two " Dreadnoughts " only, with an inferiority of eight pre- " Dreadnoughts." Besides the above, light cruisers, destroyers, submarines, and mine-sweepers were being diverted from the Grand Fleet and the North Sea.

On the 1st April, however, the situation had improved, for we then had six more " Dreadnoughts " than the Germans ; but our inferiority remained the same in the pre-" Dreadnought " types.

Bearing the January figure in mind, Lord Fisher always had the dread that some accidental collision, or damage by mines, or other hazard of the sea, coupled—as he points out—with a possible wrong deployment, might put our " Dreadnoughts " so nearly equal in numbers to the Germans, that after an action the command of the sea would depend upon the outcome of an action between the pre-" Dreadnoughts."

[1] *The Grand Fleet*, by Admiral of the Fleet Viscount Jellicoe.

He therefore looked on the number of ships of that type that were locked up at the Dardanelles as a potential danger.

Apparently little attention was paid by Mr. Churchill to Lord Fisher's two letters, for on the 31st March the latter again wrote :

With the departure of the last batch of reinforcements of destroyers, submarines, and mine-sweepers for the Dardanelles we have reached a point when the general situation must be carefully reviewed, more especially with regard to the margin of superiority over the German Fleets which we retain in home waters—at *their* selected moment.

In my view, there are many indications, of which the recent cruise of the German Fleet is an example—that under their new Commander-in-Chief we may anticipate a more forward and aggressive policy in the North Sea. And, therefore, we must be prepared for all eventualities.

I consider that we have now descended to the bare minimum of superiority in home waters, and that to dispatch any more fighting ships, of any kind, to the Dardanelles operations would be to court serious losses at home.

We have been fortunate of late in that we have had no submarine losses of moment in the North Sea, but danger is always present, and a turn of the wheel may give the enemy chances of attrition which he will take. We have been very near it at least once lately (the *Neptune* and *Dreadnought*—U.29).

In addition, the position in Holland appears to be far from stable, and the inclusion of Holland amongst the belligerents, whether for or against us, would necessitate extended operations at home, from which we could ill spare even the force at present at the Dardanelles.

Consequently I desire now to state my definite opinion that we must stand or fall by the ships now out in the Mediterranean or on their way there. If the concerted operations about to be undertaken are not successful, and we incur heavy losses either of great or small ships, we cannot afford to send any more from home waters to complete the work—not even if, by sending reinforcements, there is a possibility, even a certainty, that the operations will then be successful and with only further small losses—nor even if more naval force is required to extricate our Army.

Further, if loss be sustained in the North Sea while the Dardanelles operations are still in suspense, or if some new development decreases our margin of safety in the North Sea below the present level, we must be free to recall at once ships from the Mediterranean to make good the deficiency.

I therefore urge that, before the final plunge is taken and the troops landed, the Dardanelles operations should again be carefully examined from this standpoint by the War Council. We should have before us the considered report of Sir Ian Hamilton, with the remarks of the Army Council thereon ; we should reconsider the position in view of the lack of damage hitherto done to the guns in the forts by the previous bombardment ; we should consider the possible arrival of enemy submarines, and, in a word, all the factors which might result in the next operation being indecisive or unsuccessful so as to call for greater naval force.

It is admitted that the advantage, political and moral, of the forcing the Dardanelles and the occupation of Constantinople will be enormous, and such as to warrant great losses. But, in my opinion, no success in this region will render it justifiable to reduce —momentarily even—our superiority in the decisive theatre beyond the minimum which has now been reached. I am prepared to risk the probable heavy losses in the ships and personnel now at the Dardanelles in order to achieve success, but not to decrease further our available forces at home in any class of fighting ship.

Since the original decision to proceed with these operations, I have been anxious that a sufficient force should be provided to enable them to be carried through, and have proposed reinforcements of several types of ships that have actually been sent and concurred in others. *But I consider that the definite limit has now been reached.* In any event, most of the battleships at the Dardanelles are lost to us for a long time, because they will require repairs, refit, and a change of guns when the operations terminate, while for the oldest we shall certainly be short of ammunition.

We can recover from an indecisive or even an unsuccessful result of these operations in the Dardanelles ; we can recover from an abandonment of the operations, should this be necessary ; but we could never recover from a reverse to our main fleets in the decisive theatre at home. *It would be ruin.* Our existence depends on our unchallengeable *naval supremacy.*

I therefore beg you to forward my previous memorandum with its accompanying letter, and this communication also, to the War

Council, in order that immediate deliberation may take place. I attach copies of that letter and memorandum.

This apparently was not done. The urgent demand of the First Sea Lord was shelved, and the War Council did not meet between the 19th March and the 14th May ! It was the bounden duty of any First Lord to bring so strong a technical protest before his colleagues on the War Council. The protests of the First Sea Lord did not coincide with the views of the First Lord : they were therefore apparently treated as of no account ; for if they had been communicated to the War Council, it is inconceivable that a meeting should not have been held to discuss them. It was Mr. Churchill's duty to insist on this being done, and the blame for the Council not meeting must attach to Mr. Churchill, and to him alone.

It was at this period—that is, after the attack of the 18th March—that Mr. Churchill notes, in *The World Crisis*, that—

Henceforward the defences of the Dardanelles were to be rein-forced by an insurmountable mental barrier. A wall of crystal, utterly immovable, began to tower up in the Narrows, and against this wall of inhibition no weapon could be employed. The " No " principle had become established in men's minds, and nothing could ever eradicate it. Never again could I marshal the Admiralty War Group and the War Council in favour of resolute action.

He then goes on to hint that—

Wemyss or Keyes could have broken through the gun defence and mine-fields had they been allowed to do so.

But what were the real facts ? Surely, the position was clearly enunciated in Fisher's memoranda :

(1) That the gun fire of the ships had been totally unable to

destroy the Turkish guns and gun defences.   Only one single gun
had been destroyed by the bombardments.

(2) That a halt had to be called as regards naval reinforcements.
If more ships were lost, they could not be replaced from England.

Admiral de Robeck had been chosen to command
the sea forces at the Dardanelles as he was known to
be an officer who certainly would be more likely to
err on the side of dash than of caution. He had
probed the nature of the defences, and he had come
to the conclusion that another purely naval attack
meant great loss of life and material, and, in the end,
failure. The War Group at the Admiralty also saw
that Mr. Churchill's infatuation with the scheme, on
which his reputation most assuredly hung, was endan-
gering the safety of the Empire.

No unbiased person, looking back now and studying the history of the Dardanelles, can fail to trace
the sequence of events.   Smitten with the fascination
of a great operation which, if successful, promised
such a vast political reward, Mr. Churchill practically
forced the War Council to adopt his proposals, although
he knew that he had neither Lord Fisher's nor Sir
Arthur Wilson's approval. He never consulted the
Board of Admiralty. He constantly, in the face of
Lord Fisher's objections, persuaded and cajoled him
into acquiescing to send out more and more vessels
urgently required at home.   He never presented Lord
Fisher's memoranda to a meeting of the War Council,
nor insisted that they should be considered.   Was it,
then, surprising that in the end the " negative forces,"
as he termed them, having daily grown in strength
from a conviction of the futility of the attempt, should
have " banded themselves together " and called a halt ?

No historian can come to the conclusion that Lord

Fisher looked with favour on the attempt to force the Narrows. He always disliked it, and in the early stages protested against it. Without doubt it would have been better if, at the War Council meetings in January, he had stated his objections and had not waited, in vain, to be asked for his opinion. He would then have placed on record his own belief in the failure of a purely naval operation. Whether this would have altered the policy of the enthusiasts is doubtful, but it would have caused his objections to have been entered on the minutes.

When the War Council had decided in favour of the operations, he loyally did all that was possible to further the scheme until the point was reached when the expedition bid fair to endanger the war in home waters. He then demanded that the whole matter should be reconsidered before the troops were landed and the die thus irretrievably cast. This request received no answer. The Admiralty, therefore, called a halt. The other Sea Lords were called into council, and they unanimously backed him up and disapproved of Mr. Churchill's proposals. Can any reasonable person believe that Mr. Churchill was right and that all the Sea Lords, the War Group, and the Commander-in-Chief on the spot were wrong? Captain Roger Keyes was an extremely plucky officer. His proposal to lead the battleships, with his own in the van, to force a way through the mine-fields showed high courage and a firm belief in the success of the venture ; but the Admiralty were wise in refusing to allow it. Naval Balaclava charges are not war, and fortress guns and mine-fields are cold, inexorable arguments. To gamble against steel and high explosives is not wise. Gallantry is of enormous value to all fighters ;

but it should be tempered by a judicious reckoning-up of chances. It is not sane warfare blindly to charge modern hidden forces of destruction harnessed to the enemy's purpose. There was no evidence at the time to show that there was not a plentiful supply of ammunition for the Turkish guns and that the mine-field had suffered the slightest damage.

The mine-fields of the enemy definitely prevented the forcing of the Narrows. If the stream of the waters of the Dardanelles had run north instead of south, the operations might have been successful, but, as it was, they were doomed to failure so far as human foresight could determine.

The War Council proceedings in the first eight months of the war were honeycombed by indecision, covered over with a veneer of " wait and see." If a man of action, say Lord Fisher (for we know his methods well), had been chairman of this Council, the business would have been conducted much as follows :

When a proposal for operations had been made, he would at once have asked the Chief of the Imperial General Staff and the First Sea Lord, each, how many days they would require to furnish a joint appreciation of the proposals. The reply, we will imagine, was one week. " Very well," Lord Fisher would have said ; " to-day is Monday ; on Tuesday week your report is to be circulated by the secretary to each member ; they will have Tuesday to consider it, and to raise any point on which they are in doubt direct with the Chief of the Staff or the First Sea Lord. On Wednesday week we will again discuss the matter and come to a decision." That would have been a businesslike way of conducting the proceedings.

Both in the " 1915 " and the " Aftermath " volumes

of *The World Crisis* Mr. Churchill maintains that one
more try to force the Narrows would have been
crowned with success.

It is more than likely that, in years to come, some
historians, replete with post-war information, may
argue that Mr. Churchill was right, and Lord Fisher
wrong, and that a further attempt to force the Narrows
would have been crowned with success ; others may
take the reverse view. Neither opinion, however, can
be of any real value ; no reliable conclusion can ever
be drawn as to the outcome of such an operation,
however much light later-day knowledge may throw
on the quantity of war material, such as spare mines
or ammunition, that was available to the Turk in
April 1915.

In order to illuminate the assertion, let us for a
moment imagine that the landing at Suvla Bay had
never been carried out ; then surely the historian of
the future, fully possessed of subsequent information
as to the unreadiness of the Turkish Forces to repel
such an invasion, might well argue that had such a
landing been attempted, it was bound to have been a
phenomenal success, and that the fall of the Peninsula
would inevitably have followed. However, as we
know, the landing did take place, but the human
element stepped in, and what should have been a
certainty ended in failure. Similarly, historians should
remember, when arguing the probability of forcing the
Narrows, that it is impossible to foresee the many
changes and chances of sea warfare, as well as to forecast
how the human element might have affected the result
in one way or the other. The chance of success or
failure must therefore ever remain hidden by the
mists of uncertainty, and be incapable of reasonable

assessment. Mr. Churchill urged one more try. The "fatal once more" is the seductive will-o'-the-wisp of the gambler ; it is the vain hope which is the cause of his ultimate ruin, or if by some good luck his further downfall is arrested by another cast of the dice being forbidden, then he is eternally haunted by the conviction that, had one more chance been afforded him, his lost fortunes would have been retrieved.

Lord Fisher was no gambler. The existence of the Empire was, in his opinion, whatever may have been the opinion of others, too great a stake to be risked in a gamble. He called a halt ; and, by his resignation, dispelled the dreams of the fanatics and brought responsible politicians face to face with realities and the all importance of maintaining our supremacy in the North Sea under all possible conditions.

In conclusion, let us summarise the true causes of the Dardanelles muddle. First and foremost the blame must rest on our peculiarly inefficient war organization, whereby an aged politician, a man endowed with many gifts, but whose main training in life had been that of a "party" man, with a resultant regard for procrastination and expediency, and whose guiding motto was "wait and see," became the Chairman of the War Council, merely because he happened to be the political leader of the party in power at the declaration of war. This chairmanship should without any doubt have been held by an energetic man of business, who was accustomed to probe matters, without fear or favour, down to their basic foundations. That the Prime Minister should have been kept informed of the deliberations of this Council, have attended its meetings when he desired, and have retained power to sanction or veto the proposals arrived at, is, of course, obvious ;

but the conduct of the spade-work, the sifting of facts
from mere *ex-cathedra* opinions, should have been under
the direction of a man selected from the whole manhood
of the country for his sound sense, energy, and genius
in the conduct of business.

A second cause for the muddle was that both Lord
Kitchener and Mr. Churchill were allowed to state
their personal views instead of the Council being placed
in possession of the considered opinions of the Naval
War Staff and the Headquarter Staff at the War
Office. No information on vital matters was asked
from these two authorities, no joint conferences between these two Staffs took place ; but the personal
opinions of individuals were allowed to take the place
of considered Staff appreciations.

Thirdly, views of these two Staffs should have been
laid before the Council by their technical heads,
not by Lord Kitchener and Mr. Churchill. It was
right and proper that these two Ministers should have
been members of the Council, but they were not the
proper persons to lay the Staff reports before the
members, or to answer any questions which arose
therefrom during debate. The various commands,
both ashore and afloat, were daily, hourly, every
minute of the day, brought face to face with the
realities of war. At home there was an inevitable
tendency for our politicians to conduct the war much
the same as if it had been merely the case of annual
manœuvres. War to them, naturally, had not the
same vital reality that it had for those at sea or in the
field. They patched up their party organization to
deal with an entirely new class of problems, to transact
a novel business, and to make decisions quite out of
the ordinary, but which were of fatal moment to the

Empire.   Political shackles bound the organization
of our Government in war, as it had bound its vision
in peace-time.   No organization of the Government
in war-time had ever been thought out beforehand ;
no training of our Prime Ministers or other high officials
in matters with which, in war, they would have to deal
had ever been suggested.   Our Generals and Admirals
had been trained for war from their youth up, whereas
Prime Ministers, on whom the supreme direction of
the war rested, were apparently supposed to be super-
naturally endowed with knowledge of war and war
conditions, and, with no previous training, to be
capable of conducting a world-wide struggle of supreme
importance to the Empire.   The result was muddle and
disaster, and the greatest of our failures was the Dardanelles campaign.

CHAPTER XX

LORD FISHER'S RESIGNATION

Young men in the Conduct, and Mannage of Actions, Embrace more than they can Hold, Stirre more than they can Quiet ; Fly to the End, without Consideration of the Measures and degrees ; Pursue some few principles, which they have chanced upon absurdly.

LORD BACON, *Essays.*

Mr. Churchill's methods of work—Lord Fisher's system—Lord Fisher's programme of new construction—Progress at the Dardanelles—Withdrawal of the *Queen Elizabeth*—Lord Fisher adumbrates his resignation in a letter to Mr. Asquith—Mr. Churchill's arbitrary manner—Memorandum from the Sea Lords—Mr. Churchill demands absolute power over the Navy—The last interview—Captain Crease's warning—Mr. Churchill refuses to pay attention to this warning—Lord Fisher resigns—Correspondence between Lord Fisher and Mr. Churchill—Lord Fisher ordered to remain at his post—Sea Lords informed—Their memorandum—Shortage of high-explosive shell—The crisis—Lord Fisher's action when the High Seas Fleet put to sea—He thinks he will be asked to remain—His unfortunate letter to the Prime Minister—His resignation accepted—Departure for Scotland—Mr. Asquith and Lord Fisher—Mr. Churchill and Lord Fisher—Mr. Churchill and his four First Sea Lords—Constitutional principles governing retirement.

WE have brought the story of Fisher's period of service at the Admiralty up to the end of March 1915. The War Council had definitely authorized the joint naval and military operation at the Dardanelles, and for some six weeks no important difference of opinion regarding the operations appears to have arisen between Mr. Churchill and Lord Fisher. This, however, did not apply to other matters. Mr. Churchill writes in *The World Crisis* :

Lord Fisher's age and the great strain to which he was now to be subjected made it necessary for him to lead a very careful life. He usually retired to rest shortly after eight o'clock, awaking refreshed between four and five, or even earlier. . . . As the afternoon approached the formidable energy of the morning gradually declined, and with the shades of night the old Admiral's giant strength was often visibly exhausted. Still, judged from the point of view of physical and mental vigour alone it was a wonderful effort, and one which filled me, who watched him so closely, with admiration and, I will add, reassurance.

I usually slept an hour later in the morning, being called at eight instead of seven, and I slept again, if possible, for an hour after luncheon. This enabled me to work continuously till one or two in the morning without feeling in any way fatigued. . . . Telegrams came in at the Admiralty at all hours of the day and night, and there was scarcely an hour when an immediate decision could not be given, if necessary, by one or other of us always awake.

This sympathetic description of Lord Fisher's methods pictures accurately the difference in their hours of work. To understand fully how these dissimilarities affected their relations we must, however, carry the matter a little further. Lord Fisher transacted the most important part of his work in solitude in the cold grey of the early morning,

For in the morning cool reflection comes,

while Mr. Churchill did so in the evening, after the refreshment of dinner and congenial company. Under these latter circumstances the affairs of the Navy, and of the war, would naturally appear full of hope and promise, and his congenital optimism would be then at its highest pitch.

But at the same time this optimistic frame of mind was likely to make him more venturesome in his encroachments on the functions of the First Sea Lord ; nor does he appear to have appreciated the fact that the memoranda, which flowed in a continuous nightly stream from his facile pen, would be received and read by Lord Fisher in the cheerless light of the early morning, when realism was apt to dominate optimism. A few specimens of these memoranda are given in Mr. Churchill's book ; from such samples the quantity can hardly be realized, but they could be numbered by dozens. He never seemed to apprehend that his incursions into affairs that should have been left to the First Sea Lord would taint Lord Fisher's early hours with a feeling of irritation and annoyance. The net result was the gradual overstraining of Lord Fisher's patience in a way that helped to precipitate the final conflagration.

One of the many tragedies of the war was that Mr. Churchill was a civilian, and at the Admiralty, instead of having followed a Service career and holding high rank in the Army or the Navy. It is by no means improbable that in this way the country lost a second Marlborough. On the other hand, the Admiralty would have worked smoothly with Mr. M'Kenna and Lord Fisher, as First Lord and First Sea Lord respectively. Mr. M'Kenna, from his intimate knowledge of Lord Fisher, could have restrained the wilder flights of his imagination, while leaving scope for his marvellous capacity for getting the maximum amount of work in the shortest time out of everyone with whom he came into contact. The genius which always inspired Lord Fisher in emergencies would have remained at the service of the country. It is more than probable that, had he been at the Admiralty, the German Fleet would have been sunk in Kiel Harbour in 1918, two days after the mutiny of the German seamen became known ; most certainly the ships they surrendered would never have been sunk by their

crews in Scapa Flow. This and other crises would
have been met by prevision or a master counter-
stroke, as in the case of the Falkland battle.

Lord Fisher's main activity at the Admiralty was
concentrated in the construction of an Armada of
large ships and smaller vessels. He did, for the
matériel of the Navy, what Lord Kitchener did for
the personnel of the Army. He was under no delusion
as to the length of the duration of the war ; and he
was fully determined that its future stages should be
well provided for in respect to ships and vessels of all
classes. The ships he laid down can be divided into
two classes : those for coastal operations in shallow
waters and those for utility for naval operations generally. A complete list is given in the postscript of this
chapter ; so it is only necessary here to review this
Armada briefly.

The ships of general utility comprised two light
cruisers, five flotilla-leaders, fifty-six destroyers, and
sixty-four submarines. These proved to be absolutely
indispensable when the Germans developed the intensive use of submarines ; but for Lord Fisher's
foresight and indomitable energy in impelling rapid
construction there would have been not only a most
lamentable, but a disastrous shortage at the end of
1916.

When Lord Fisher took over the office of First Sea
Lord, one of his first acts was to review the orders
that had been placed for new ships during the past
three months, and especially for submarines. He
found that practically none of the latter had been
ordered, and he was told that there were great difficulties in the way of so doing, owing to the design of
the machinery being the property of one firm. He

was also informed that negotiations were still in
progress on the matter with a view to orders being
given to other shipyards.   He at once sent for the
papers on the subject, and was presented with a bundle
at least a foot thick.   This bundle he promptly put
on the fire in his own room, saying that he would start
afresh in his own way !   He called a conference next
day of everyone concerned, and appointed to his
personal staff a Submarine Officer [1] to superintend and
speed up construction.   Within a week more than
thirty submarines were ordered and started, sixty-
four in all being laid down during the time that he
was First Sea Lord.

The special ships that he ordered included five
battle-cruisers.   These ships have been the subject
of much criticism, but, nevertheless, their conception
was thoroughly sound.   Germany had numerous light
cruisers capable of steaming at a very high speed,
and we had many similar cruisers with practically the
same armament.   Lord Fisher ever aimed at overwhelming superiority, and the light battle-cruiser was
designed to overtake and annihilate the German light
cruisers.   On one historic occasion the opportunity
occurred for them to justify the vision and genius that
had conceived them ; but the human element most
cruelly stepped in and the chance of a minor Falkland
battle was lost.   Had Fisher's great plan of a landing
on the German coast been adopted, these vessels
were to have been the hounds to hunt the German
foxes.

On the list, also, were thirty-seven monitors, shallow
in draught, and of various armaments from 15-inch
down to 6-inch guns ; two coast-defence ships, and

———
[1] Captain S. S. Hall.

numerous other craft and barges, in all totalling 612 vessels.

Most of these vessels found uses other than those for which they were originally intended. The monitors and motor-launches were of great value in the operations on the Belgian coast ; and the mine-sweepers came into being at the critical time when mines threatened the safety of our Channel transport. It is impossible to overestimate the great value of the vessels of this far-sighted programme, coming into service when they were so badly needed.

Two other matters in connexion with construction may perhaps be mentioned. The five battleships of the " Royal Sovereign " class were altered to burn oil fuel and had their armament strengthened, and they were completed in time to take part in the Battle of Jutland. Lastly, twenty-four river gunboats were built for the Mesopotamia campaign and other purposes.

In launching this formidable programme Lord Fisher interviewed personally the heads of shipbuilding firms and the responsible managers. Dates of delivery were fixed, the times of construction being cut down to the minimum, and the firms were made responsible for delivery on the agreed date. Nothing impossible was asked of them, and they were strictly enjoined to inform him personally if any trouble arose, or was likely to arise, whereby the vessels might be delayed. The matter was to be a personal one between him and them ; he impressed on them that they had the right of access to him at any time, but *their dates had to be kept*. The interview ended with an assurance on Lord Fisher's part that if the dates were not kept, he would see that " their wives were made

THE REV. JOHN FISHER
Lord Fisher's Grandfather

widows, their children orphans, and their houses dung-
hills " ! So each one left pleased and contented, with
a smile on his face and thoroughly determined to do
his very best.

Returning now to the events which led up to the
tragedy of Lord Fisher's resignation. The month of
April, as already stated, appears to have been one of absence of friction so far as the Dardanelles was concerned.
The troops were landed on the 25th April ; but, because the previous bombardments had fully warned
the Turks, trenches had been dug and wire entangle-
ments had been erected everywhere possible, and
very little progress was made. The early part of May
brought nothing but disappointment, and the telegrams from the Dardanelles were anything but re-
assuring. On the 12th May there were signs of
renewed tension at the Admiralty. Lord Fisher insisted on the withdrawal of the *Queen Elizabeth* from
the Mediterranean ; he had never been in favour of
this ship being diverted from the Grand Fleet, and
had acquiesced only on account of the want of heavy
gun fire at the Dardanelles. He became seriously
disturbed at evidence he received, indicating that
submarines would shortly be operating against our
ships at the entrance to the Straits, and he insisted
upon her return. Lord Kitchener was informed of
this by Mr. Churchill, and he strongly demurred. It
was proposed that two old battleships, with four 12-inch
guns apiece and two monitors each with 14-inch guns,
should take the place of the *Queen Elizabeth* ; there
was, therefore, little reason for his objection, more
especially since (as the Dardanelles Commission subsequently pointed out) " naval gun support of the military operations had not hitherto proved to be as

II—16

valuable as had been anticipated." Mr. Churchill further invited Lord Kitchener to come to the Admiralty for a consultation.

This interview appears to have been of a stormy nature. Lord Fisher had his back against the wall, and he was no longer prepared to risk the *Queen Elizabeth* at the Dardanelles, nor to keep her away from her proper station in the Grand Fleet. Lord Kitchener looked on her withdrawal as a sign that the Navy was about to desert the Army, though for this view there was no justification. Lord Fisher, in the end, stated flatly that " either the *Queen Elizabeth* left the Dardanelles that afternoon or he left the Admiralty that night." That settled the matter. As usual, Lord Fisher was prophetically in the right : a dummy ship equipped to represent the *Queen Elizabeth* was torpedoed by a submarine within a fortnight of the real ship leaving the Dardanelles. Lord Fisher, in some mysterious way, always seemed able to scent danger in advance, and as long as he was free to act on the dictates of his instincts, disasters were avoided.

It is only fair to Mr. Churchill to state that after Lord Fisher's mind was made up he nobly supported him with the Prime Minister against the protests of Lord Kitchener [1] regarding the recall of the *Queen Elizabeth*.

The War Council met again on the 14th May. For some, now, unaccountable reason there had been no meeting since the 19th March—practically two months. The outlook had by no means improved in the interval. The battle of Neuve Chapelle had been a failure, so far as making any real impression on the German lines was concerned. The British Army had lost about 20,000 men, and badly needed reinforcements ; but

---

[1] *Memories*, page 67.

the Dardanelles had swallowed up the available troops, which were, to all intents and purposes, marooned on a peninsula, and were calling loudly for ammunition and reinforcements. The Fleet had been powerless to force the Narrows, as Fisher had foreseen.

At the meeting of the Committee Lord Kitchener inveighed against the *Queen Elizabeth* being withdrawn at the moment that the Army had been landed and were fighting for their lives with their backs to the sea. Here, according to Mr. Churchill's account, Lord Fisher interjected the remark that he had been against the operations from their start, and that the Prime Minister and Lord Kitchener knew this fact well. Mr. Churchill states that this remark was received with silence. No wonder that silence reigned, since everyone knew Lord Fisher's statement to be true ! The deficiency of shells and other ammunition, as detailed at length by Lord Kitchener, also weighed heavily on the members of the Council, who, as usual, separated without coming to any conclusions.

On the 12th May Lord Fisher had sent to the Prime Minister a copy of a memorandum he had written to Mr. Churchill recapitulating what had occurred at the Dardanelles and the losses that the Allies had sustained. He recalled the fact that he had always been against the operation, and concluded by saying :

For the above reasons, I cannot, under any circumstances, be a party to any order to Admiral de Robeck to make an attempt to pass the Dardanelles until the shores have been effectively occupied. I consider that purely naval action, unsupported by the Army, would merely lead to heavy loss of ships and invaluable men, without reasonable prospect of a success in any way proportionate to the losses, or to the possible further consequences of those losses. I therefore wish it to be clearly understood that I dissociate myself from any such project.

The following covering letter was sent to the Prime Minister with the copy of this memorandum :

MY DEAR PRIME MINISTER,

It will be within your recollection that you saw me and the First Lord of the Admiralty in your private room, prior to a meeting of the War Council [28th January, 1915], to consider my protest against the Dardanelles undertaking when it was first mooted. With extreme reluctance, and largely due to the earnest words spoken to me by Kitchener, I by not resigning (*as I now see I should have done*) remained a most unwilling beholder (and, indeed, a participator) of the gradual draining of our naval resources from the decisive theatre of the war. The absence, especially at this moment, of destroyers, submarines, and mine-sweepers [which are now] at the Dardanelles most materially lessens our power of dealing with the submarine menace in home waters—a menace daily becoming greater, as foreshadowed in the print I submitted to you six months before the war.

I have sent the enclosed memorandum to the First Lord, and I ask for it to be circulated to the War Council.

Mr. Churchill answered the above memorandum ; but his reply in no way satisfied Lord Fisher, especially as he also received a reply from Mr. Asquith which evaded the direct issue :

MY DEAR LORD FISHER,

Since receiving your letter and memorandum of to-day, I have been given to understand that an arrangement has been come to between the First Lord and yourself. I am very glad.

It is a fact that during the day of the 12th May discussions on the subject had taken place between Mr. Churchill and Lord Fisher, and as a result the latter seemed to be more content. But the relief did not last long, as will be seen from the reply sent by Lord Fisher to the Prime Minister the very next day :

MY DEAR PRIME MINISTER,

Thank you for your letter of yesterday, in which you state that you had been given to understand that an arrangement had been come to between the First Lord and myself, and you kindly added that you were very glad.   But I regret to say that within four hours of the pact being concluded the First Lord said to Kitchener " that in the event of the Army's failure, the Fleet would endeavour to force its way through," or words to that effect. However, for the moment, with your kind assurance of no such action being permitted, I remain to do my best to help the Prime Minister in the very biggest task any Prime Minister ever had— not excepting Pitt and his Austerlitz !   Still, I desire to convey to you that I honestly feel that I cannot remain where I am much longer, as there is an inevitable drain *daily* (*almost hourly*) on the resources in the decisive theatre of the war.   But that is not the worst.   Instead of the whole time of the whole of the Admiralty being concentrated on the daily increasing submarine menace in home waters, we are all diverted to the Dardanelles, and the unceasing activities of the First Lord, both by day and night, are engaged in ceaseless *prodding* of everyone in every department afloat and ashore in the interest of the Dardanelles Fleet, with the result of the huge Armada now there, whose size is sufficiently indicated by their having as many battleships out there as in the German High Seas Fleet !   Therefore this purely private and personal letter, intended for your eye alone and not to be quoted, as there is no use threatening without acting, is to mention to the one person who I feel *ought* to know *that I feel that my time is short.* 13*th May*, 1915.

It might be imagined that, on receipt of this letter, the Prime Minister would have insisted on a general understanding between himself, the First Lord, and Lord Fisher as to Admiralty policy, but he let matters slide.

On the 13th May an important telegram was received from the French Ministry of Marine, stating that they had received information from Admiral Guépratte, who commanded the French men-of-war at the Dardanelles, that energetic action on the part of the Allied Fleet was meditated against the Chanak and Kalessi Forts, a course to which the Ministry did not agree.

Mr. Churchill, as usual, drafted a telegram to Admiral de Robeck which came to Lord Fisher before it was dispatched ; the latter objected to the wording. He was now thoroughly on his guard against any action by the Fleet alone being taken. His proposed wording of the telegram to be sent was :

> You must on no account take decisive action without our permission.

Mr. Churchill replied to Lord Fisher :

> At a moment when the Army may be committed to an attack I cannot agree to send a telegram which might have the effect of paralysing necessary naval action as judged necessary by the responsible Admiral on the spot. *The telegram I have drafted is quite sufficient*; but I have made a small amendment in an attempt to meet your wishes. It is dangerous to delay sending the telegram, and I have therefore directed the secretary to send it in this form.

This was a very arbitrary minute from a First Lord to a First Sea Lord, who, after all, was the man responsible for executive action.

This telegram, together with Lord Fisher's memorandum to the First Lord, was shown to the other Sea Lords, who replied collectively in a memorandum to the First Sea Lord. They agreed with Lord Fisher's views that the Fleet should not be used to force the Narrows, and they also asked that they might be kept informed of any further developments in the situation, so that they might decide on their own individual action.

A minor incident, that had some bearing on subsequent events, was that, just before midnight on the night of 13th-14th May,[1] the Italian Naval Attaché

[1] This date is given in *The World Crisis* as the 14th. This is an error. Mr. Churchill's minute to Lord Fisher on the subject is dated the 14th May, and the telegram was dispatched to Rome by the Foreign Office on the 14th.

came to see Mr. Churchill to press that the arrangements for naval co-operation made the previous week in Paris should be brought into immediate effect. Lord Fisher and Mr. Churchill were in full agreement as to the dispositions involved. The matter being urgent, Mr. Churchill, knowing Lord Fisher's views, telegraphed through the Foreign Office to the Minister of Marine in Rome :

> The battleships *Queen, London, Implacable, Prince of Wales,* and the light cruisers *Amethyst, Sapphire, Dublin,* and *Dartmouth* will be concentrated under Rear-Admiral Thursby at Malta at dawn on the 26th. If absolutely necessary the light cruisers may proceed three days in advance.
> Pray communicate with us.
> *First Sea Lord to see after action.*

Mr. Churchill has attributed Lord Fisher's resignation mainly to the fact that this telegram was sent without his formal concurrence, although he had previously concurred in principle. The telegram had nothing to do with Lord Fisher's resignation ; for he had no knowledge that it had been sent until after he had actually resigned. But when he did see it, the unusual and unfortunate marking in a telegram of this nature, " *First Sea Lord to see after action,*" hardened his resolve to have no further relations with Mr. Churchill. It must be appreciated that the telegram would pass through the hands of several of the Admiralty staff, and the marking could only be read by them as a distinct snub to the First Sea Lord.

On the 14th May we find Mr. Churchill writing to the Prime Minister :

> I must ask you to take note of Fisher's statement to-day that " he was against the Dardanelles, and had been all along," or words to that effect. The First Sea Lord has agreed in writing to

every executive telegram on which the operations have been conducted, and had they been immediately successful the credit
would have been his. But I make no complaint of that.

Mr. Churchill's statement is correct, but so also was
Lord Fisher's. Mr. Churchill knew perfectly well that
Lord Fisher was, and always had been, against the
whole operation, and that it was only at his insistent
request, and under pressure, that Lord Fisher had
reluctantly consented to aid the operation in every
way that he could. In his *World Crisis* he himself
says: " I am in no way concealing the great and continuous pressure which I put upon the old Admiral."

Mr. Churchill had now to reap the harvest of tares
he had sown, by acting against the advice of his professional advisers and, with obstinate optimism, forcing on an operation that, in their opinion, would not
be successful ; and he had only himself to blame.
His naval advisers had said, in essence : " We do not
advise the scheme ; we believe it will not be successful,
and we consider our strength could be used to greater
effect elsewhere, but we cannot definitely say that the
operations must fail." Mr. Churchill, in substance,
had replied : " You cannot say the operations will not
be successful ; you do not consider that their inception
will mortgage the safety of the Empire, and I therefore
beg you not to go against the wishes of the War
Council, but to back up the scheme and try it. If it
fails, haul off ; if it is successful, go on." Lord Fisher,
at the stage then reached, wisely stated in substance :
" The operations have been shown to have failed ;
therefore haul off. I have always been against them,
and you know that I have. I consider any further
depletion of our units in home waters will militate
against the safety of the Empire."

That Lord Fisher would have gained credit had
the operations been successful is probable ; but he
never considered this aspect, for he never had the
slightest belief that they would be a real success.

Mr. Churchill's letter to the Prime Minister continued :

> I am attached to the Old Boy and it is a great pleasure to me
> to work with him. I think he reciprocates these feelings. My
> point is that a moment will arise in these operations when the
> Admiral and General on the spot will wish and require to run a
> risk with the Fleet for a great and decisive effort. If I agree with
> them, I shall sanction it ; and I cannot consent to be paralysed by
> the veto of a friend who, whatever the result, will say, " I was
> always against the Dardanelles."

The First Lord thus in effect wrote to the Prime
Minister to say that he intended to arrogate to himself
the functions of the Sea Lords. He himself has stated
that " no ship could sail or gun fire without the
sanction of the First Sea Lord " ; and, in effect, he
now asked, either that Lord Fisher be dismissed and
a weaker First Sea Lord appointed who would do his
bidding, or that he himself should be given authority
to override the professional views of the Sea Lords.
One must marvel at the assurance of this young politician, who assumed professional naval knowledge
superior to that of picked men whose lives had been
spent in the Navy and in the study of naval problems.
Already, during the ill-fated first few months of his
war administration, disaster had dogged Admiralty
policy, and he had been forced to call in Lord Fisher
to put matters right. Over the Dardanelles he had
brought the Navy into a difficult position by his disregard of the advice of his professional colleagues ;
but he, in spite of this, appealed to the Prime Minister

to relieve him entirely from all professional control, and virtually to dismiss the man who had retrieved the errors of the early part of his administration. If success had followed his previous disregard of the advice of his naval advisers, he might, with some appearance of reason, have asked to be allowed in future to follow his unfettered judgment ; but, instead of success, something approaching disaster had resulted. The letter ends thus :

> But I wish to make it clear to you that a man who says, " I disclaim responsibility for failure," cannot be the final arbiter of the measures which may be found vital to success.
> This requires no answer, and I am quite contented with the course of affairs.

The only comment necessary is that Lord Fisher never disclaimed responsibility for any orders to which he put his signature, nor for any operations in which he had concurred. What he claimed was that he had always been against the operations being commenced. When once they had been begun he accepted responsibility for everything he had ordered to be done.

Obviously the answer the Prime Minister should have given to Mr. Churchill was a sharp injunction to be guided by the views of the First Sea Lord and the Naval Staff. There is no record that any answer was sent by Mr. Asquith ; matters were again allowed to slide.

As already shown, on the 13th May Lord Fisher wrote to the Prime Minister saying that he felt he would shortly have to resign, and Mr. Churchill also wrote the letter quoted above, practically asking to be given a free hand at the Admiralty. Neither was aware of the letter sent by the other.

The meeting of the War Council was held on 14th

May, and about 6.30 the same evening Mr. Churchill went to Lord Fisher's room.   After a long interview he left by the door leading through the room of Lord Fisher's Naval Assistant, saying as he left, " Well, good night, Fisher.   We have settled everything, and you must go home and have a good night's rest.   Things will look brighter in the morning, and we'll pull the thing [i.e. the Dardanelles] through together."

Lord Fisher at once called Captain Crease, his Naval Assistant, into his room, and said he would sign his papers and get away home, remarking at the same time, " You need not pack up just yet "—earlier in the day he had indicated that he might soon be leaving the Admiralty.   He then told him that he had had a satisfactory interview with the First Lord, and had come to a definite and final understanding with him concerning the naval reinforcements that could be sent to the Dardanelles.   He told him generally what these reinforcements were to be, and gave him some minor instructions with regard to the consequent rearrangements.   He repeated that the matter of reinforcements was now settled with the First Lord ; he, however, added quite cheerily, " But I suppose he'll soon be at me again."

During the course of the night four memoranda came to Lord Fisher's office from the First Lord.

No. 1 dealt with the provision of siege artillery, mounting long-range guns ashore, provision of landing-stages and cranes, laying lines of indicator nets watched by drifters, fitting the battleships with trellis-work protection against mines, and the provision of seventy aircraft and some 500-lb. bombs.

No. 2 dealt with a scheme of Commodore Tyrwhitt for submarine and Zeppelin hunting, and made proposals for various arrangements in the Grand Fleet and the North Sea, and also suggested a telegram to Admiral de Robeck about the scheme.

No. 3 proposed an important rearrangement of the Grand Fleet, so as to station cruiser squadrons in the Humber.

No. 4 dealt with reinforcements for the Dardanelles.

It will be seen that Mr. Churchill's activities during the evening and night of the 14th May covered a wide range of subjects, and included a vast amount of detail entirely outside his proper sphere. These memoranda were to be sent on to Lord Fisher, so that he would receive them early in the morning.

Nos. 1, 2, and 3 would probably have been the subject of discussion after Lord Fisher had studied them, but with No. 4 the case was entirely different. The version of this minute given in *The World Crisis* is not complete. The chief and important, in fact vital, point of difference is that, in Mr. Churchill's version, the two final paragraphs are omitted, namely, paragraph 5, which dealt with increased provision for Air Services, and paragraph 6, which proposed to send two more " E " class submarines out to the Dardanelles. The following is an exact copy of the minute received by Lord Fisher :

FIRST SEA LORD,

1. The fifth 15-inch howitzer with fifty rounds of ammunition should go to the Dardanelles with the least possible delay, being sent by special train across France and re-embarked at Marseilles. Let me have a time-table showing by what time it can arrive at the Dardanelles.

The two 9·2 guns will go to the Dardanelles either in two monitors prepared for them or separately for mounting ashore. This will be decided as soon as we hear from Admiral de Robeck.

2. The following nine heavy monitors should go in succession

to the Dardanelles as soon as they are ready : *Admiral Farragut,* *General Grant, Stonewall Jackson, Robert E. Lee, Lord Clive, Prince Rupert, Sir John Moore, General Crauford,* and *Marshal Ney.*

The first six of the 9·2-inch monitors should also go unless the Admiral chooses to have two of their guns for work on shore, in which case the first four only will go.

A time-table should be prepared showing the dates on which they will be dispatched and will arrive. They can calibrate on the Turks. All necessary steps for their seaworthiness on the voyage should be taken.

In the case of the 9·2 monitors it may be found better to send the actual guns out to Malta separately.

It is clear that when this large accession of force reaches the Vice-Admiral he should be able to spare a portion of his battleships for service in home waters, but it may be better to see how the monitors work, and what use they are to him before raising this point.

3. Four of the " Edgars " with special bulge protection against mines and torpedoes are now ready. They carry ten 6-inch guns each and supply the medium armament that the monitors lack. They should be specially useful in supporting the Army at night without risk from torpedo attack. They would also be useful at a later stage in passing a shore torpedo-tube or escorting other ships that were passing.

We have not found any satisfactory use for them here.

It is not necessary to provide crews for them ; working parties which can take them out will be sufficient. The Admiral can man them from his large fleet for any special service that may be required. They should start as soon as possible.

Let me have a report on the manning possibilities as defined above and times by which they can arrive.

It will be for consideration, when these vessels are on the spot, whether a valuable ship like the *Chatham* should not be released for other duties.

4. The Third Sea Lord will make proposals for providing anti-mine protection for a proportion of the battleships employed on the lines proposed at our discussion.

5. The following increased provision will be made for the Air Service.

(D.A.D. will supply on verbal instructions.)

6. During this month five new submarines are delivered, viz.,

S.2, E.18, V.2, V.3, and S.3.   In June the Montreal boats come in. Therefore, in view of the request of the Vice-Admiral, I consider that two more " E." boats should be sent to the Dardanelles.

The following covering letter was attached to this minute :

MY DEAR FISHER,

I send this to you before marking it to others, in order that, if any point arises, we can discuss it.

I hope you will agree.

Yours ever,

W.

Captain Crease [1] gives a vivid description of the events of that fateful night :

I was working in my room at the Admiralty on the night of the 14th May, when towards midnight Masterton Smith [2] came in with the minute (No. 4) and covering letter, and said that the First Lord wished the First Sea Lord to have them in the morning.

Masterton Smith asked me to read them through, and I did so. He was evidently uneasy about the minute and asked me " how I thought the old man would take it."   Knowing well Lord Fisher's frame of mind during the past few days and his letter to the Prime Minister of the day before, and reading that submarines were now included in the proposed reinforcements, in addition to various other ships and materials that Lord Fisher had not mentioned a few hours earlier, I had no hesitation about my reply.   I said at once that I had no doubt whatever Lord Fisher would resign instantly if he received the minute ; for these new proposals, coming at that moment, would be the last straw.

Masterton Smith, who also was very familiar with the First Sea Lord and his ways, said he did not think Lord Fisher would go so far as that ; but I repeated that I felt quite certain that he would.   After some discussion Masterton Smith said he would tell the First Lord my opinion before definitely handing me the minute to pass on.   After some delay—I believe Masterton Smith first spoke to de Bartolomé [3] on the subject before going to Mr.

[1] Captain T. E. Crease, Naval Assistant to Lord Fisher.

[2] The First Lord's private secretary, now Sir J. E. Masterton Smith, K.C.B.

[3] Captain C. de Bartolomé, the First Lord's Naval Secretary.

Churchill—he came back with the dispatch-box and said it must be sent on, for the First Lord was certain that Lord Fisher would not object to the proposals; but the First Lord had also added *that, in any case, it was necessary that they should be made.* I repeated my warning as to the consequences, and then arranged for the dispatch-box to be delivered early in the morning to Lord Fisher.

If Mr. Churchill had been wise he would have kept back the minute, and have discussed the matter next morning; but either, in his optimism, he did not care whether Lord Fisher resigned or not (which is somewhat foreshadowed by his remark that, " in any case, it was necessary that they should be made "), or he had confidence that he could bend " the old Admiral " to his purpose ; whichever of these two may have been the case, he sent on his minute.

Lord Fisher opened the dispatch-box in the early morning and saw at once that the First Lord had already departed from the agreement of the previous evening ; and in his opinion had twice in two days gone beyond his pledges. He felt that it was impossible to work with him any longer, and at once wrote, and sent off before breakfast, a letter to the Prime Minister resigning his office of First Sea Lord.

Lord Fisher did not go to the Admiralty building, but sent for his Naval Assistant, who took him his various documents, including the telegram Mr. Churchill had sent to Rome. The letter of resignation had already been dispatched. Lord Fisher read the telegram to Rome and commented on the " marking," quoting it as further evidence of the impossibility of working with the First Lord.

The following is the letter sent by Lord Fisher to the Prime Minister :

My DEAR PRIME MINISTER,
As I find it increasingly difficult to adjust myself to the increasing policy of the First Lord in regard to the Dardanelles, I have been reluctantly compelled to inform him this day that I am unable to remain as his colleague, and I am leaving at once for Scotland, so as not to be embarrassed, or embarrass you, by any explanations with anyone.

Your admiring Master at Balliol said " Never explain," but I am sure you will understand my position.

Yours truly,
FISHER.

I enclose a copy of my letter of resignation to the First Lord.

This is the letter to the First Lord :

FIRST LORD,
After further anxious reflection, I have come to the regretted conclusion I am unable to remain any longer as your colleague. It is undesirable, in the public interests, to go into details—Jowett said ' Never explain "—but I find it increasingly difficult to adjust myself to the increasingly daily requirements of the Dardanelles to meet your views. As you truly said yesterday, I am in the position of continually vetoing your proposals.

This is not fair to you, besides being extremely distasteful to me. I am off to Scotland at once, so as to avoid all questionings.

Yours truly,
FISHER.

Mr. Churchill replied at once to Lord Fisher's letter of resignation. The most important paragraph is one in which he tried to induce him to reconsider his resignation :

In order to bring you back to the Admiralty I took my political life in my hands—as you well know. You then promised to stand by me and see me through. If you now go at this bad moment and therefore let loose on me the spite and malice of those who are

your enemies even more than they are mine, it will be a melancholy
ending to our six months of successful war and administration.
The discussions that will arise will strike a cruel blow at the fortunes of the Army now struggling on the Gallipoli Peninsula and
cannot fail to invest with an air of disaster a mighty enterprise
which with patience can, and will, certainly be carried to success.

Many of the anxieties of the winter are past. The harbours are
protected, the great flow of new construction is arriving. We are
far stronger at home than we have ever been, and the great reinforcement is now at hand.

I hope you will come and see me to-morrow afternoon. I have
a proposition to make to you, with the assent of the Prime Minister,
which may remove some of the anxieties and difficulties which
you feel about the measures necessary to support the Army at the
Dardanelles.

Though I stand at my post until relieved, it will be a very great
grief to me to part from you ; and our rupture will be profoundly
injurious to every public interest.

These arguments are admirable ; but why did he
bring matters to this pitch ? Mr. Churchill had added
strain after strain to the chain that bound Lord Fisher
to him until, at last, it had snapped. A chain broken
by stress is not easy to mend, for all the links have
been stretched and are weakened ; and, at the best,
a sound repair is doubtful, and such a chain is liable
to break again at any moment under even a feeble load.

Lord Fisher's mind was fully made up, though it
required all his determination to stand out against so
eloquent an appeal to his loyalty. He replied :

The Prime Minister put the case in a nutshell when he stated to
me yesterday afternoon the actual fact that I had been dead against
the Dardanelles operation from the beginning ! How could I be
otherwise when previously as First Sea Lord I had been responsible
for the Defence Committee Memorandum stating the forcing of
the Dardanelles to be impossible ? You *must* remember my extreme
reluctance in the Prime Minister's room in January to accept his
decision in regard to the Dardanelles, and at the War Council held

II—17

immediately afterwards I stated, in reply to a question by the Chancellor of the Exchequer, that the Prime Minister knew my views, and I left the matter to him to explain.

Ever since (as, I fear, to your great annoyance) I have been, as you truly said the other day, in the unpleasant position of being antagonistic to your proposals, until the series of fresh naval arrangements for the Dardanelles you sent me yesterday morning convinced me that the time had arrived for me to take a final decision, there being much more in those proposals than had occurred to me the previous evening when you suggested some of them.

YOU ARE BENT ON FORCING THE DARDANELLES AND NOTHING WILL TURN YOU FROM IT—NOTHING. I know you so well. I could give you no better proof of my desire to stand by you than my having remained by you in this Dardanelles business up to the last moment against the strongest conviction of my life, as stated in the Dardanelles Defence Committee Memorandum.

YOU WILL REMAIN and I SHALL GO—it is better so. Your splendid stand on my behalf I can never forget when you took your political life in your hands, and I have really worked very hard for you in return—*my utmost* ; but here is a question beyond all personal obligations. I assure you it is only painful to have further conversations. I have told the Prime Minister I will not remain. I have absolutely decided to stick to that decision. Nothing will turn me from it. You say with much feeling that *it will be a very great grief to you to part from me*—I am certain that you know in your heart no one has ever been more faithful to you than I have since I joined you last October. *I have worked my very hardest.*

To this Mr. Churchill replied in a long letter :

I am touched by the kindness of your letter. Our friendship has been a long one. I remember how, in 1908, you tried to bring me to the Admiralty as First Lord. When I eventually came in 1911 I proposed to the Prime Minister that you should return to your old position, and only the difficulties that your enemies were likely to make at that time prevented the accomplishment of my first wish. As it was, I followed your guidance in the important decisions which have given us the 15-inch gun and Jellicoe to-day.

He goes on to offer to meet Lord Fisher's views in

every way as regards the reinforcements for the Dardanelles. Nothing could have been more completely in accord with Lord Fisher's views had it not come too late. The chain had snapped, and the ends could not again be brought together. He closes the letter with another eloquent appeal, similar to those which hitherto had been effective and had caused Lord Fisher more than once to acquiesce, though disagreeing :

There ought to be no reproaches between us, and you, my friend, must at this moment in your long career so act that no one can say you were unmindful of the public interests and of the lives of the soldiers and sailors.

In any case, whatever you may decide, I claim, in the name of friendship and in the name of duty, a personal interview—if only for the purpose of settling what explanation is to be offered to Parliament.

Lord Fisher replied on the same day :

As usual, your letter is most persuasive, but I really have considered everything and I have definitely told the Prime Minister that I leave to-morrow (Monday).

Please don't wish to see me. I could say nothing, as I have determined not to. *I know I am doing right.*

Soon after the Prime Minister received Lord Fisher's letter on the morning of the 15th May, he telephoned to the Admiralty that he wished to see the First Sea Lord. Lord Fisher was not at the Admiralty, nor at his official house adjoining the Admiralty, and there is little doubt he spent the morning in Westminster Abbey, where he frequently attended Matins and also repaired when his mind was agitated or disturbed.

Lord Fisher was determined to see nobody, for he feared that if he discussed the matter with any of the persuasive politicians, appeals to his loyalty and patriotism might shake his resolve to resign, and cause him to act against his considered convictions. His own inclination was to go to Scotland, so as to put some hundreds of miles between himself and the eloquence of friendly emissaries. There was no *arrière-pensée* of any sort. It never occurred to him that there would be any difficulty in immediately appointing his successor.

His intention of going to Scotland was, however, frustrated by a letter which came from the Prime Minister during the morning of the 15th May :

> LORD FISHER,
> In the King's name I order you to remain at your post.

In the afternoon Lord Fisher visited the Prime Minister. No record seems to have been left of what took place at this interview ; but on his return he spoke no more for several days of leaving London. He did not go to the Admiralty building, and still refused to deal with any of the routine work attaching to the office of First Sea Lord. All the important telegrams, papers, etc., were taken or sent to his house, that was in communication by a passage with the actual Admiralty building. From there he kept a watchful eye on the progress of the war. He sent the following cryptic telegram to Sir John Jellicoe, probably on account of a previous arrangement that Sir John should wire to him personally if he were in doubt about any orders, or if he disagreed with any instructions that he might receive from the Admiralty :

> From Lord Fisher. Personal and private. Prevented by pressing business from answering your letters.

Another thing he did was to send a message to the Chief of the Staff, directing him to make certain that the *Queen Elizabeth* had received proper instructions about the safe course to steer on her way home, so as to avoid submarines.   He did not, however, inform the other Sea Lords of the situation.   In the evening his Naval Assistant took him the routine papers of the day ; but he would not deal with them.   It was pointed out to him that since none of the other Sea Lords knew of his resignation, business would come to a standstill, and he then, for the first time, agreed to their being informed.

On the early morning of the 16th he wrote this characteristic letter to his Naval Assistant :

DEAR CREASE,
      Make three copies of the enclosed letter to Winston, and then give the original to Masterton and beg him to telegraph to Winston not to come up to see me—it is so painful—and *my decision is irrevocable*.   Ask the Second Sea Lord to do my work, and the C.O.S. to see the Second Sea Lord instead of me.
      I will send for all my gear out of my room to-morrow (Monday) morning—pictures, boxes, etc.
      We shall take rooms at an hotel on Tuesday—the Ritz, I think, as the manager is my devoted friend—I got him the billet—£4,000 a year and all found for his family living at the hotel.
      I was a d——d fool not to take it myself ! ! !   Can't you see me in the restaurant in a white waistcoat and frock-coat ! ! !
      Show the Sea Lords copy of my letter to Winston, also to Hopwood.[1]
      Impress on Masterton the utter futility of my seeing Winston.

As a result of this letter the other Sea Lords were informed of Lord Fisher's resignation and were shown the correspondence.   On the same day they forwarded a joint memorandum to the First Lord and First Sea Lord.   They stated that they believed that the Dardanelles operations most certainly jeopardized

------

[1] Sir Francis Hopwood, Additional Civil Lord.

the crushing superiority of the Grand Fleet, which was essential to the successful prosecution of the war. They further expressed their dissatisfaction at the present method of directing the distribution of the Fleet, and the conduct of the war, " by which orders for controlling movements and supplies appear to be largely taken out of the hands of the First Sea Lord." They also considered that, in order to prevent a national disaster, Lord Fisher's resignation must be averted, and concluded by saying :

> Whatever differences of opinion or defects in procedure may have arisen or become apparent should be capable of adjustment by mutual discussion and concession, and we therefore venture to urge you both to consider whether the national interests do not demand that you should follow the advice we have tendered.

It is difficult to understand what was in the minds of the Sea Lords when they could condemn the system by which control of the movements of ships had been taken out of the hands of the First Sea Lord and could state that they considered that the Dardanelles operations jeopardized the crushing superiority of the Grand Fleet, and yet could suggest that these two matters might be adjusted by *mutual* discussion.

Fisher replied :

> MY DEAR FRIENDS,
>   I am obliged by your memorandum. If you knew as much as I did I am sure you would not wish me to remain—but my motto is " NEVER EXPLAIN " (and always has been).

Throughout this crisis, Lord Fisher, as might have been expected, acted with scrupulous correctness towards the First Lord and his naval colleagues. He did not inform the other Sea Lords of his resignation until twenty-four hours after he had sent it in to the First Lord, and then only because of the extreme inconvenience that was being caused by routine and other papers being held up awaiting the signature of the First Sea Lord or someone acting for him. Had Lord Fisher made the slightest overture to the other Sea Lords, there is little doubt they would have felt it their duty to resign also, seeing that they fully concurred in the stand that he was making on the subject of the Dardanelles. Whether or not they should have resigned when they did learn the position was a matter for them, and them only, to decide ; but, in either event, it was essentially an occasion on which they should have expressed their own convictions clearly and forcibly, and have insisted that in future the procedure that they complained of should terminate, and not temporize by talking of " mutual agreement." Lord Fisher did not hide his opinion of the action that they eventually did take, for later the same day he wrote to Captain Crease :

> I hope the Sea Lords clearly understand my undoubtedly correct reason for not entangling them, but *I grieve they allowed themselves* to be made use of to send me advice which I did not require, and it was exceedingly bad advice ; and they and Sir A. K. Wilson will clearly see this when the Day of Judgment comes along and all chicanery is exposed.
> Was it likely that I did not know all the circumstances ?

It is evident that he considered that the other Naval Members had failed in loyalty to a colleague, and he was much hurt at their action.

Mr. M'Kenna visited him to try to prevail on him to withdraw his resignation, and also went into the country to discuss the matter with Mr. Asquith. The 16th May was Sunday, and Mr. Asquith was out of

London.   Mr. M'Kenna told Lord Fisher that he was
satisfied, after talking with the Prime Minister, that
his resignation was not effective until formally accepted. But Lord Fisher was obdurate. The disagreement about the Dardanelles campaign was not
the sole reason for his retirement. Behind this was
the deep personal irritation caused by Mr. Churchill's
methods of conducting business, his constant bombardment of minutes and memoranda on every possible
subject, replete with details which had far better have
been left to the proper officers ; the manner of sending
orders and telegrams from the Admiralty that should
have come from Lord Fisher himself ; the consultation
with others on matters entirely within the province
of the First Sea Lord, and other similar personal
matters. It was the cumulative effect of all these
that caused Fisher to resign at this moment, and to
adhere to his decision. He felt that any patched-up
agreement would be unsatisfactory, and also knew
from previous experience that it would not be lasting.

Lord Fisher's resignation was not the only trouble
with which the Cabinet were at the moment faced.
The shortage of shell at the front had become severely
felt, and a considerable agitation was brewing that
threatened the existence of the Liberal Government.
The shortage of high-explosive shell was not the fault
of the Government, but, in reality, was due to two
causes which have apparently not hitherto been clearly
stated, but which are given in a postscript at the end
of this chapter.

Lord Fisher's resignation fell like a thunderbolt just
before a debate on this ammunition shortage was to
take place in the House of Commons. Mr. Asquith
eventually bent before the storm and decided to invite

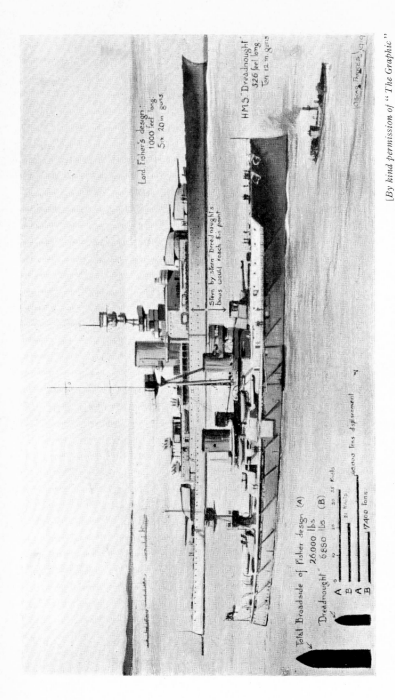

Lord Fisher's design.
1000 feet long.
5 x 20 in guns.

H.M.S. "Dreadnought"
526 feet long.
Ten 12 in guns.

Stem by stem Dreadnoughts
bows could reach this point

Total Broadside of Fisher design (A) 26000 lbs.
"Dreadnought" (B) 6880 lbs.

A 0   10   20   30   35 Knots
B 21 Knots
A 90000 tons displacement
B 17400 tons.

[By kind permission of "The Graphic"

LORD FISHER'S PROPOSED SHIP, H.M.S. INCOMPARABLE, SHOWN ALONGSIDE H.M.S. DREADNOUGHT

the Unionist leaders to enter the Government. At this moment Mr. Churchill visited him with the proposal for Admiral of the Fleet Sir A. K. Wilson to take Lord Fisher's place as First Sea Lord. He was, however, too late, for Mr. Asquith informed him that many changes were about to take place in the Government and that he would probably leave the Admiralty.

He returned to the Admiralty in a disconsolate frame of mind, to hear that the German High Seas Fleet had put to sea. His position then became a peculiar one. Lord Fisher had resigned, Sir Arthur Wilson was no longer to be the First Sea Lord elect ; unless Lord Fisher came out from his seclusion he (Mr. Churchill) would be in sole charge at the Admiralty, for the Second Sea Lord could not well step in until Lord Fisher left the building, and Sir Arthur Wilson had no official status. There was no doubt that if the High Seas Fleet remained out, and were beaten, Mr. Churchill would once more come in on the top of a wave of public enthusiasm, and be installed in an unassailable position amid the plaudits of the nation. If, however, no battle were fought, then political ruin, temporary or permanent, stared him in the face. In the end the fates were unkind to him : the High Seas Fleet returned, after a short cruise, to its base, and he left the Admiralty.

Lord Fisher meanwhile paced his room in the house adjoining the Admiralty. He, also, heard that the German Fleet was at sea, but he was firmly convinced that they were merely out to test whether we had occult means of reading their cipher signals. He remained in touch with the news that was coming in, but refused, in spite of the request of the First Lord, to pass through the passage which led to the Admiralty building.

From the naval point of view, he was still First Sea Lord. His resignation had not been accepted, and the new Board had not been " read in." [1] So long as he was First Sea Lord it was his business to attend to the duties of that office. He did not do so, and in not so doing was in the wrong. Let us see why he kept away.

In the first place, he was determined to keep away from Mr. Churchill, as he feared his persuasive powers. He had given in so often to the blandishments and argument of that silver tongue, that he feared that he would do so once more if they came together. It had been a most terrible wrench to resign ; he had voluntarily given up everything to do with the war, a war for which he had spent his life in preparing the Navy, and in which it had been his highest hope to participate, either in command of the Fleet or at Whitehall. His most cherished dream had been dissolved by a supreme effort of his will. He knew his intense desire to remain ; but so impressed was he with the conviction that ruin to the Empire would result from the insatiate feeding of the Dardanelles maelstrom with the vessels of the Navy, that he was convinced that the only way he could bring the common sense of the nation to bear on the Government was by persisting in his resignation. He felt, therefore, that he dared not risk some hours in Mr. Churchill's company in the War Room.

In the second place, he knew that Sir Arthur Wilson

[1] A member elect does not become actually a member until the warrant constituting the new Board has been read to all the members assembled.

had been offered and had accepted the post of First
Sea Lord. Without the slightest doubt he valued his own opinion higher than that of Sir Arthur ; but had he been asked to name a substitute, he would instantly have named that Admiral. There was little that the Admiralty could do, on the High Seas Fleet putting to sea, except to issue what might be called "routine orders," recalling detached units and weak patrols to harbour ; and to warn the dockyards and bases to prepare for receiving ships which might be damaged in action. Sir Arthur was as fully competent to send these as Lord Fisher himself. Again, although Lord Fisher had refused to attend in the War Room, he was still under the same roof ; and had any crisis arisen and had his advice been urgently required, he was instantly available, and had any imperative need arisen, there can be no doubt he would have emerged from his seclusion. In the meanwhile the First Lord and his First Sea Lord elect could deal with the situation. The destiny of the Empire lay now in the hands of Sir John Jellicoe, not in those of the Admiralty. Technically, Lord Fisher was wrong in not putting in an appearance ; but he himself was convinced that by not doing so no Imperial interest would be jeopardized ; but if he did meet Mr. Churchill and was cajoled into withdrawing his resignation, he was fully persuaded that the safety of the Empire would once more be in the melting-pot. As already said, the German Fleet returned to their ports.

The succeeding days brought a change so far as Lord Fisher was concerned. The reconstruction of the Government introduced an entirely new factor. He began to see that if, in the newly reconstructed Government, Mr. Churchill left the Admiralty he might still remain as First Sea Lord, provided that the new First Lord was not irrevocably committed, in advance, to the Dardanelles enterprise. Later he was told, by someone who professed to know what was in progress behind the scenes, and in whom he believed, that the Unionist leaders were determined he should remain at the Admiralty, and practically made this a condition of their joining the Government. This is clear from letters he wrote after he reached Scotland.

Eventually, however, the rumour reached him that Mr. Balfour would become First Lord, and that Mr. Churchill would remain in the Cabinet. Desirous as he was of staying at the Admiralty and completing the work he had started, he determined not to do so with the Dardanelles millstone hung round his neck ; for, next to Mr. Churchill, the most ardent advocate on the War Council of the Dardanelles operations had been Mr. Balfour. He accordingly, without consulting anybody, seized his pen and wrote to the Prime Minister. His letter amounted to an ultimatum, and Prime Ministers are not accustomed to submit to such dictation, nor to be told whom they are to exclude from their Cabinets. Had Lord Fisher called on the Prime Minister, he might have placed before him his point of view in a perfectly constitutional manner, but the letter that he wrote finally destroyed any chance of his being retained as First Sea Lord. This is quite clear from the remarks on the letter that Mr. Asquith makes in his book.[1] The copy of the letter as retained by Lord Fisher reads as follows :

If the following six conditions are agreed to, I can guarantee the successful termination of the war, and the total abolition of the submarine menace.

[1] Rt. Hon. H. H. Asquith, *Memories and Reflections*.

I also wish to add that since Lord Ripon wished, in 1885, to make me a Lord of the Admiralty, but at my request made me Director of Naval Ordnance and Torpedoes instead, I have served under nine First Lords and seventeen years at the Admiralty, so I ought to know something about it.

(1) That Mr. Winston Churchill is not in the Cabinet to be always circumventing me. Nor will I serve under Mr. Balfour.

(2) That Sir A. K. Wilson leaves the Admiralty, and the Committee of Imperial Defence, and the War Council, as my time will be occupied in resisting the bombardment of Heligoland and other such wild projects. Also his policy is totally opposed to mine, and he accepted the position of First Sea Lord in succession to me, thereby adopting a policy diametrically opposed to my views.

(3) That there shall be an entire new Board of Admiralty as regards the Sea Lords and the Financial Secretary (who is utterly useless). *New measures demand New Men.*

(4) That I should have complete professional charge of the war at sea, together with the sole disposition of the Fleet and the appointment of all officers of all ranks whatsoever.

(5) That the First Lord of the Admiralty should be absolutely restricted to Policy and Parliamentary Procedure, and should occupy the same position towards me as Mr. Tennant, M.P., does to Lord Kitchener (*and very well he does it*).

(6) That I should have the sole absolute authority for all new construction and all dockyard work of whatever sort whatsoever, and complete control over the whole of the Civil Establishments of the Navy.

[*Initialled*] F.

19.5.15.

P.S.—The 60 per cent. of my time and energy which I have exhausted on nine First Lords *in the past* I wish *in the future* to devote to the successful prosecution of the war. That is the sole reason for these six conditions. These six conditions must be published verbatim, so that the Fleet may know my position.

Attached to the copy of this letter is also a note outlining the various changes that he intended to make at the Admiralty and in the Fleets.

If Lord Fisher had remained quiet, as most of his

friends were urging him to do, he would in all probability
have been asked to remain as First Sea Lord, and he
could then have introduced gradually the changes he
felt necessary. But he was obsessed with the idea
that he could not serve at the Admiralty with Mr.
Balfour, who was already deeply committed to the
Dardanelles campaign; more especially as Mr. Churchill was to be retained in the Cabinet, and would therefore be in a position to support Mr. Balfour in that
matter.

It is not easy to understand how Lord Fisher could
have believed that the above was a proper communication to send to a Prime Minister, and not to have seen
that it was a most injudicious act on his part. But
there is no doubt that he did not view his action in
that light. The strain of the previous few days, and
more especially the wrench of his self-sacrifice, without
doubt helped to warp his judgment.

Almost immediately on hearing of the formation of
a Coalition Government, and being persuaded that he
would be retained as First Sea Lord, his active brain
began to prepare for speedy action. He sent the
following memorandum to Captain Crease, his Naval
Assistant :

Prospective.
 Get all below *cut and dried* ready for instant orders being given.
 Get out all enclosed orders in careful detail in telegrams all
written out for signature.
 Ask Hankey [1] about Army being transported from Dardanelles
to Haifa. Get old scheme for this in the C.I.D. prints for landing
at Haifa.
 Remind me to see Kitchener on " Der Tag."
 I. Arrange for Third Battle Squadron and Tottenham's Squadron
and suitable Destroyer Flotilla from other sources for Humber

   [1] Sir Maurice Hankey, Secretary to the War Council.

with " Sentinel" class also there, and section of submarines and strong section of *good* aeroplanes for some to be always at sea scouting off the Humber to 100 miles' distance (this to be a *standing* order). Get Sueter [1] to arrange for an adequate number of aeroplanes always to be scouting off Humber with new bombs for Zeppelins. *The present ones no use at all.*

II. Also arrange for laying down 3,000 more mines. Get minefields exactly marked on *charts.*

III. All these orders to be written out as telegrams ready for signature on " Der Tag."

Keep secret ; tell no one.

P.S.—All necessary telegrams for ordering home vessels from Dardanelles except sufficient for Army protection.

It was not long before Captain Crease heard that Lord Fisher had written something to the Prime Minister which had led the latter to decide to accept his resignation. He went to Lord Fisher's house to inquire from him about this communication. Lord Fisher produced a copy of his letter at once with the notes attached ; and apparently could see nothing amiss with it. Evidently he fully believed that the Unionists would support him in the new administration, and that their influence would enable him to dictate his own terms.

It is impossible, after reading such papers as are available, more especially the draft he had prepared of the new Board of Admiralty, and the other appointments he proposed to make, to avoid a feeling of relief that Lord Fisher did not remain under the conditions he had defined to the Prime Minister. The Board he proposed was a weak one, and he intended to part with everyone who would attempt to exercise any control over him—he saw himself as an uncontrolled autocrat. Such a position was quite impossible in

[1] Captain Murray Sueter, Head of the Royal Naval Air Force.

war-time for a man of seventy-four years of age;
although ten years earlier he could, in all probability,
have undertaken the work that it entailed with great
advantage to the Navy. At this time, his age and the
strain of the last six months at the Admiralty had
begun to warp his calm and clear judgment, and had
made him more intolerant of opposition. With Mr.
M'Kenna as First Lord to curb his vagaries, and an
Assistant Lord to relieve him of all routine work,
leaving him free to spur on construction, and to deal,
as his genius would dictate, with the various emergencies that arose, it is quite possible that he might
have done a couple of years' more good work for the
country at the Admiralty. But under the arrangements he proposed, confusion and inefficiency were
inevitable. The following letter from Sir John Jellicoe
bears out this view :

H.M.S. *Iron Duke*, 22nd May, 1915.

Your letter reached me a few minutes ago and the messenger is
just leaving. I am dismayed at the prospect ahead. I feel the
question is most serious, and if I can help you in any capacity I
am ready and will put aside all personal feelings. If you go back,
I do beg that you will get round you some people with recent
sea-experience, also who are conversant with modern naval warfare. The whole situation has changed in the last two years, and
no one but those afloat can fully realize the changed conditions
except you yourself. But you can't do everything.

The end came on the 22nd May in a letter from the
Prime Minister :

DEAR LORD FISHER,
    I am commanded by the King to accept your tendered
resignation of the Office of First Sea Lord of the Admiralty.
                              Yours faithfully,
                              [*Signed*] H. H. ASQUITH.

This was an abrupt form of farewell after over sixty years of good service to his country ; but a man who precipitates a Cabinet crisis in war-time cannot expect any great courtesy from those whom he has embarrassed.

A mistake that several times has appeared in print has led to the wide-spread belief that Lord Fisher deserted his post after his resignation and left London and the Admiralty before it had been accepted. This is not true. In his letter of resignation to the Prime Minister on the 15th May he most certainly did write :

> I am leaving at once for Scotland, so as not to be embarrassed or embarrass you by any explanations with anyone.

During the afternoon of the 15th, however, Fisher went to see the Prime Minister, after which there was no further suggestion on his part of leaving London until the 17th, when he wrote again to the Prime Minister telling him that he could not remain longer at the Admiralty with Mr. Churchill. To this the Prime Minister replied :

> In the public interest I trust that you will neither say nor do anything for a day or two.

Lord Fisher remained at his house, and it was not until the permission of the Prime Minister had been assured on the 22nd, through Colonel Sir Maurice Hankey, the Secretary of the War Council, that he left London for Scotland. The formal letter of acceptance of his resignation was sent a few hours later.

Mr. Asquith, in his book *Memories and Reflections*, treats Lord Fisher's resignation in a very just and impartial manner. It must, however, be remembered

II—18

that he knew one side only of the troubles at the Admiralty. He thus sums up the situation :

> Lord Fisher was undoubtedly a man with streaks of genius, but he was afflicted with fits of megalomania in one of which this extraordinary ultimatum must have been composed. I always remained on the best of personal terms with him, but the whole of his conduct at this critical time convinced me that it had become impossible that he should remain responsible for the Admiralty.

One must agree with this lucid comment of Mr. Asquith on the incident, but the use of the words " responsible for the Admiralty " is misleading. Lord Fisher was never a member of the War Council, nor when he attended the meetings could he have been looked upon as the responsible exponent of Naval Policy, for this function was invariably assumed by Mr. Churchill. " If the whole of his conduct at this critical time " refers to Lord Fisher absenting himself from the War Room when the German Fleet came out, Mr. Asquith was in no position to know the whole of the facts, and undoubtedly wrote largely on hearsay reports.

Before publishing his book Mr. Asquith sent the " ultimatum " to Mr. Churchill to read, and the comments made by the latter (which Mr. Asquith also published) do not err on the side of generosity, nor do they do justice to their author :

> The document is new to me, and certainly it has never been made public. I knew, of course, that Fisher had demanded powers similar to Kitchener's, but am surprised—and now I think I may say amused—at the categorical manner in which his requirements were explained. The submarine campaign to which he referred was, of course, the first submarine campaign. It was already thoroughly defeated, and did not appear again as a danger for more than eighteen months, and then in entirely different circumstances.

The document seems to show that Fisher *used the uncertain course of events at the Dardanelles as a means of making a bid for supreme naval power.*[1]

The submarine campaign had not been defeated ; for it was just about this time that German submarines began to lay underwater mines, a new method of warfare that caused enormous damage and was most difficult to counter. Among other severe losses it was responsible, a year later, for the loss of the *Hampshire* and the death of Lord Kitchener. Confirmation that the submarine campaign was not dead can be obtained by referring to Lord Jellicoe's book, *The Grand Fleet*. When he wrote the last few lines it can only be supposed that Mr. Churchill had forgotten the letter he had received from Lord Fisher in reply to the appeal he had made to him to withdraw his resignation :

YOU WILL REMAIN and I SHALL GO—it is better so. . . . I have told the Prime Minister that I will not remain. I have absolutely decided to stick to that decision. Nothing will turn me from it.

When Lord Fisher resigned, he believed that his own resignation would be accepted and that Mr. Churchill would remain on at the Admiralty. There was no question of bargaining, and no attempt to displace the First Lord on account of the " uncertain course of events at the Dardanelles." It was not until the Coalition Government had become a certainty that his mind turned to the possibility of remaining at the Admiralty.

In one of Lord Fisher's letters written some time after his resignation, he says, " Winston is most magnanimous." This magnanimity does not seem to have long survived Lord Fisher's death.

[1] Italics were not in original.

POSTSCRIPT NO. 1

Mr. Churchill and his Four First Sea Lords

We have been obliged to place the blame for Lord Fisher's resignation on the shoulders of Mr. Churchill. But the view commonly held by the man in the street is that two strong temperaments, such as those of Mr. Churchill and Lord Fisher, were sooner or later bound to clash seriously; and that it was this that led Lord Fisher to resign; therefore the blame should be equally apportioned. This, however, is not fair to Lord Fisher, for he worked in absolute agreement with Mr. M'Kenna, who possessed as strong, although not so self-opinionated, a temperament as Mr. Churchill. In fairness, therefore, to Lord Fisher's memory it is necessary to compare the services that he and Mr. Churchill rendered to the Navy, and to see whether or no the latter was able to work in harmony with the other First Sea Lords with whom he was associated.

The services of Lord Fisher have been set forth, and need not be repeated. Further, while at the Admiralty, he had worked, not only in agreement with, but in a way to earn the highest encomiums from, eight other First Lords: Lord George Hamilton, Lord Ripon, Earl Spencer (who named a horse after him), Mr. Goschen, Lord Selborne, Earl Cawdor, Lord Tweedmouth, and Mr. M'Kenna.

The services of Mr. Churchill are not so marked— in fact, they were largely diluted with failure; nor were his associations with his First Sea Lords happy.

276

In 1910, after a few months' experience as a Cabinet Minister, his opposition to the Admiralty programme, with which he was in no way concerned except as the youngest and most junior member of the Cabinet, forced Mr. M'Kenna, the then First Lord, to send in his resignation to the Prime Minister. It was only the strong line taken by Sir Edward Grey that prevented the whole of the Board of Admiralty resigning. If Mr. Churchill had had his way, the safety of the Empire would have been seriously endangered. This was his first encounter with the Admiralty.

It is a matter of history that, in the last one hundred years, and probably for longer still, no First Sea Lord had ever resigned through a difference of opinion with his First Lord. Mr. Churchill created a double record in this respect. Two of his First Sea Lords— Admiral of the Fleet Sir Arthur Wilson and Admiral of the Fleet Lord Fisher—both relinquished their posts owing to differences of opinion with Mr. Churchill on naval matters. This record is all the more remarkable when it is appreciated that these two Admirals of the Fleet were probably the most experienced Sea Lords the country had seen for a century ; whereas Mr. Churchill was the youngest and, politically, the most inexperienced of any First Lord who had held office during that time. It is not unreasonable, therefore, to suggest that Mr. Churchill's unfortunate and undue optimistic belief in his own judgment was not only a great disservice to the country, but was the dominating reason for Lord Fisher's resignation.

Nor were Mr. Churchill's dealings with the third of the four Sea Lords who were associated with him much happier. Admiral Sir Francis Bridgeman was practically dismissed under conditions which Mr.

Bonar Law, in the House of Commons, stigmatized as " brutal." The reason for this dismissal that was given by Mr. Churchill was, that the health of Sir Francis was such as to render him unfit to bear the burden of his office in the event of war ; and yet the fourth of the First Sea Lords, Prince Louis of Battenberg, chosen by Mr. Churchill from among all the senior Admirals, had to be relieved from office within four months of the declaration of war, for reasons which Mr. Churchill might easily have foreseen.

Mr. Churchill was not happy with his First Sea Lords ; or, to be more accurate, they, apparently, were not happy with him. It is necessary to take the above relationships into consideration when Lord Fisher's resignation is weighed in the balance of history and its cause determined.

POSTSCRIPT NO. 2

The question of resignation of a First Sea Lord
requires a few remarks, especially in view of the criticism levelled at Lord Fisher for not having persisted in his desire to resign on 28th January, 1915. The Board of Admiralty occupy a unique position in relation to the Government of the day. The ordinary citizen has a firm and instinctive belief in the honesty of the Naval Members of the Board. He knows that in times past they have, even up to the point of resigning, forced the Government of the day to maintain the Navy at a proper standard of strength. When self-constituted Committees and irresponsible Leagues thunder, in pamphlets and at meetings, that the Navy is below its proper strength, the man in the street feels quite secure in the conviction that the Sea Lords would resign if they believed that our supremacy at sea was being imperilled. The Sea Lords have, by custom, a special mandate from the nation to be their watch-dogs in all matters that concern the efficiency of the Navy.

We have seen how, in Lord Spencer's time, the Board nearly resigned,[1] and how their threatened resignation brought about the strengthening of the Navy. In 1909 they were again prepared to back up Mr. M'Kenna to the point of resignation; and, at other times, the shadow of their resignation has impressed a parsimonious Cabinet with a due sense of

[1] See Vol. I, page 112.

its responsibilities. This responsibility attaches especially to the First Sea Lord, and was fully recognized and keenly felt by Fisher. He knew the value of this final weapon ; but he also appreciated the proper limitations to its use. Mere difference of opinion was not an occasion for such an extreme measure. It was the business of the First Sea Lord to carry out the decisions of the Cabinet, *unless the safety of the country would be thereby endangered*. It would be improper for him to resign solely because he thought that any proposed course of action would not be successful, provided always that its inception did not mortgage national security.

Many persons have asked, " If Lord Fisher did not agree with the Dardanelles campaign, why did he not resign ? " Others, with equal reason, have asked, " If Lord Fisher rose from the Council table on the 28th January, 1915, to resign, why did he not persist in that resignation ? "

The answers to these questions become obvious when the facts are fully considered. The Dardanelles operations, as originally conceived, necessitated only the use of various older ships that could be spared from home waters, and whose loss would not have affected our supremacy at sea. There was therefore no reason why he should embarrass the Government by tendering his resignation, solely because he believed (without, however, having any conclusive evidence to support that belief) that this limited operation would not succeed, and that the ships could be employed with greater effect elsewhere. He recognized, after Lord Kitchener's personal appeal to him, that the War Council had arrived at a definite conclusion, that important political considerations were involved,[1] and that the ships could be withdrawn at any moment as long as the troops were not landed,[2] and he felt that he ought to do everything in his power to further the campaign, *unless and until* it became a menace to the general security.   His own view, at a later date, was that he should have persisted in carrying out his intention to resign, despite Lord Kitchener's entreaty ; but it seems certain that, in all the circumstances, he would not have been justified in resigning at that moment, as the safety of the Empire was not then endangered by the decision taken by the Cabinet.

[1] Lord Fisher's report to the Chairman of the Dardanelles Commission : see above, page 213.

[2] *Memories*, page 59.

POSTSCRIPT NO. 3

Reasons for the Shortage of High-explosive Shell

Experience gained in the Boer War had shown that high-explosive shell was of little use against troops in the open, especially on rocky ground, and the proportion of the shell, both for outfit and reserves, was fixed at one-third high explosive and two-thirds shrapnel, which was the allowance when war was declared. About December 1915 the French invented a fuse which could detonate a high-explosive shell a few inches above the ground, instead of several inches below the ground after impact. This meant that high-explosive shell could be used to cut barbed-wire defences, and at once a cry arose for large quantities of high-explosive shell, the demand for shrapnel falling off correspondingly.

A second reason for the shortage was the advent of motor transport. Before the war, when quick-firing guns were about to be introduced, the main argument against them was that it was useless to have guns that fired so rapidly, since it was impossible to bring ammunition quickly enough to the guns to take full advantage of their quick-firing properties. It was, however, decided that occasions might arise when short bursts of very rapid firing would be useful ; and it was on this plea that they were introduced. When war broke out there was practically no motor transport ; but within a few months lorries arrived in

numbers, and the difficulty of supplying the guns
decreased. At the battle of the Aisne the French fired away half the total of their outfit and reserves of field-gun ammunition. Naturally there soon developed a shortage of ammunition at the front, and a storm arose which threatened the existence of the Government.

POSTSCRIPT NO. 4

BUILDING PROGRAMME

Arranged at the meeting on 3rd November, 1914, four days after Lord Fisher became First Sea Lord.

   5 Battle-cruisers of 33 knots and of light draught.
   2 Light cruisers.
   5 Flotilla leaders.
 56 Destroyers.
 64 Submarines.
 37 Monitors.
 24 Light gunboats.
 19 Whaling steamers.
 24 Submarine destroyers.
 50 Seagoing patrol boats.
200 Motor barges, oil engines.
 90 Smaller barges.
 36 Sloops.
————
612
————

CHAPTER XXI

CLOSING YEARS: 1915—1920

Seest thou a man diligent in his business? he shall
stand before kings; he shall not stand before mean men.

PROVERBS xxii.

Head of the Board of Invention and Research—Neglect by the
Admiralty of the labours of the Board—Speech in the House
of Lords—Cession of Heligoland—Jutland—Reception at the
Mansion House—Advised not to speak in the House of Lords
—Mr. Lambert's comments—Smuts and Botha—Sir John
Jellicoe's arrival at the Admiralty—Lord Fisher's disappointment—Suggestion that he should go to the Admiralty as Controller—Second speech in the House of Lords—Letters—Letters
to the Prime Minister—Neglect of his services when the German
Fleet surrendered—Death of Lady Fisher—Becomes a trustee
of the Hamilton estates—Resides at Ferne and Dungavel—His
illness and death.

AFTER the strain and excitement of the previous
fortnight Lord Fisher remained in Scotland
and rested. Gradually he came to repent his
hasty letter to the Prime Minister. He was still thoroughly opposed to the ruinous policy of depleting our
home forces for the Dardanelles campaign; but his
resignation had stopped that wastage, and he came
to see that he might have approached the Prime
Minister in a more diplomatic manner and have
attained the same end without a rupture.

He was not, however, allowed to rest for long; on
5th July he was appointed Chairman of the newly
formed Board of Invention and Research. This is his
description of the work that was carried out:

My three super-eminent colleagues were very famous men:
(1) Sir J. J. Thomson, President of the Royal Society and now

Master of Trinity. I am told (and I believe it) a man unparalleled in science.

(2) The Hon. Sir Charles Parsons, K.C.B., the inventor of the turbine.

(3) Sir George Beilby, F.R.S., one of the greatest of chemists. The Advisory Panel of other distinguished men was as famous as the Magi. There were also many eminent associates.

I felt extremely diffident in occupying the chair ; however, I put it to them all in the famous couplet of the French author who, in annexing the thoughts of other people, took this couplet as the text of his book :

" I have culled a garland of flowers ;
Mine only is the string that binds them."

I said to them all at our first assemblage : " Gentlemen, you are the flowers ; I am the string."

You would have thought that such a galaxy of talent would have been revered, welcomed, and obeyed ; on the contrary, it was derided, spurned, and ignored.

The " permanent-Expert Limpets " did for us ! All the three First Lords at the Admiralty whom we dealt with in succession were most cordial and most appreciative ; but all three were equally powerless. Just a couple of reasons why at last we said to Sir Eric Geddes :

" Ave, Geddes Imperator !
Morituri te salutant."

(1) The chief object of this magnificent scientific organization being to counter the German submarine menace, we naturally asked for a submarine to be experimented with. The answer was, " one could not be spared."

(2) We asked to be furnished with the details of the destruction of German submarines that had already taken place, which, of course, lay at the root of further investigation. This was denied us !

(3) A " submarine detector " was developed under the auspices of the Central Committee by May 1916. A year was allowed to elapse before it was taken up ; even then its progress was cancelled, because nothing more than a laboratory experiment with a competing invention came to the notice of the " Limpets."

(4) The scientific members of our Association had conceived and

practically demonstrated a most astoundingly simple method of discovering the passage of German submarines. It was termed the " Loop Detection " scheme. It was turned down—and then, two years afterwards, was violently taken up, with astoundingly successful results.

I think I have said enough. And really, after all, what is the good of raking up the past ?

I have had two pieces of advice given to me referring to the trials I had experienced.

One was : " When sinners entice thee, consent thou not ! But take the name and address for future reference."

And the other was : " Fear less—hope more ; eat less—chew more ; whine less—breathe more (deep breathing) ; talk less—say more ; hate less—love more, and all good things are yours."

An ungenerous speech by Mr. Churchill in the House of Commons caused him to deliver the first of the only two speeches made by him in the House of Lords. He was, however, determined to avoid entering into any controversy regarding his resignation, and to leave time to vindicate his action. On the 16th November, 1915, he spoke as follows :

I ask leave of your Lordships to make a statement. Certain references were made to me in a speech delivered yesterday by Mr. Churchill. I have been sixty-one years in the service of my country, and I leave my record in the hands of my countrymen. The Prime Minister said yesterday that Mr. Churchill had said one or two things which he had better not have said, and that he necessarily, and naturally, left unsaid some things which will have to be said. I am content to wait. It is unfitting to make personal explanations affecting national interests when my country is in the midst of a great war.

Early in 1916 he began to have hopes that the wheel of fate might again turn in his direction. On the 7th January he wrote to a friend :

I really can honestly aver that all I have done for the Navy since the 10th of June 1902 (when I became Second Sea Lord) has turned out absolutely right! not even a comma altered! And in the conduct of the war every prediction I have made and every vessel I've built has had a reason and has been right! *And I'm out!*, and *those are in* who have brought on us three dire calamities—the Dardanelles, the Tigris, and Serbia; and will be again for the fourteenth time too late in dealing with a big German naval surprise! A naval " Colenso " is irretrievable, irreparable, fatal!

In one letter Lord Fisher tells of his being stopped by a working man, who said : " My Lord, a little time ago you told us to sleep quiet in our beds. We do, and it's the Navy what's done it." The general population of England always had a firm belief in Lord Fisher. As is often the case, they had a truer insight into the worth of public men than is usually vouchsafed to the narrow-minded politician.

In January 1916 he wrote to Mr. Arnold White :

I hope you got my telegram of grateful thanks for your kind words to me. It is really very sad, when one feels quite at one's maximum, to be locked out as I am. And truly, without being egotistical, I have made no mistake since 1902, when I introduced the new officer and the new sailor, also the new Navy, and scrapped fossils, both in ships and men and officers—hence our incomparable personnel of to-day, and every vessel mine up to the *Queen Eliza-beth* (which is not a success, as she draws too much water, is too slow, and they have reverted in her to a museum of guns).

The new battle-cruisers I laid down (on coming to the Admiralty recently) my successors have delayed. A day of reckoning is coming !

It may be that Jephthah will return !

" And Jephthah said unto the elders of Gilead, Did not ye hate me, and drive me out ? Why are ye come to me when ye are in distress ? And the elders of Gilead said unto Jephthah, Therefore are we turned again to thee now, that thou mayest go with us, and fight, and thou shalt be our head ! "

On the 3rd June, 1916, in a letter to Mr. George

[*Photo : Haines*

ADMIRAL OF THE FLEET LORD FISHER OF KILVERSTONE

Lambert, the following newspaper cutting was enclosed :

The official report of the debate in the German Reichstag on the naval estimates contains the following passage in a speech delivered by the Radical Deputy, Herr Waldstein : " We think with gratitude of the German statesman Caprivi, who, by concluding the agreement whereby Heligoland was handed over to us by the British, transformed that island into the most effective protection for the coast of Germany."

The *Deutscher Rundschau* declares, however, that " it is absurd to praise Caprivi for a matter in which he was merely the instrument. It was William II who foresaw the strategic value of Heligoland, and initiated the negotiations which led to its acquisition by Germany. A quarter of a century ago the Kaiser felt instinctively, and knew by the virtue of his insight, that England was our enemy, and that we must prepare to fight England betimes. It might be said with truth that the Kaiser, despite temporary aberrations, has been a hater of England since his earliest manhood ; all credit to him for that, and such aberrations as were noted from time to time, with regret, were doubtless due to the desirability of concealing from the perfidious English his feelings towards them. That was fighting them with their own weapons."

To this Lord Fisher added a note :

Is there any hope of rubbing into the Tories that their Archangel, Lord Salisbury, gave away Heligoland to the Germans, and the First Sea Lord (Sir Vesey Hamilton) never knew a word about it ? I was with him in the First Sea Lord's room at the Admiralty when he was told of it.

Jutland was fought on the 30th May, 1916, and Lord Fisher, like everyone else, was disappointed that the German Fleet, when it came out, was not completely smashed; but when the facts were known to him, he fully realized that Sir John Jellicoe had done all that was humanly possible.

Throughout this year Lord Fisher chafed increasingly at his enforced inactivity. He thoroughly believed that, if he had been at the Admiralty and if his advice had been accepted, he could have ended the war. To be dissociated entirely from the Navy was to him gall and wormwood. The following is a typical letter of many written about this time :

> I was asked yesterday : Could I end the war ?
> I said : " Yes, by one decisive stroke ! "
> " What's the stroke ? " I was asked.
> I replied : " Never prescribe till you're called in."
> But I said this : " Winston once told me, ' You can see visions ! That's why you should come back.' "
> For instance, even Jellicoe was against me in sending the battle-cruisers to gobble up von Spee at the Falkland Islands ! [1] (All were against me !) Yes ! and all were against me in 1904 when the Navy was turned inside-out—ships, officers, and men. " A new Heaven and a new Earth ! " One hundred and sixty ships put on the scrap-heap because they could neither fight nor run away ! *Vide* Mr. Balfour's speech at Manchester about this " courageous stroke of the pen."
> We want now another courageous stroke ! And the stroke is ready ! It's the British Navy waiting to strike ! And it would end the war !
> This project of mine sounds an impossibility ! but so did von Spee's annihilation ! Pitt said, " I walk on impossibilities." All the old women of both sexes would squirm at it. They equally squirmed when I did away with 19½ million sterling of parasites in ships, officers, and men, between 1904 and 1910 ! They squirmed when, at one big plunge, we introduced the turbine in the *Dreadnought* (the turbine only before having been in a penny steamboat). They squirmed at my introduction of the water-tube boiler, when I put the fire where the water used to be and the water where the fire used to be ! Now 82 per cent. of the horse-power of the whole world is turbine propulsion actuated by water-tube boilers.
> They squirmed when I concentrated 88 per cent. of the British Fleet in the North Sea, and this concentration was only found

[1] Not because Sir John Jellicoe did not consider the ships best suited for the purpose, but because he felt it was risky to detach the *Invincible* from the Grand Fleet.

out by accident; and so published to the ignorant world, by
Admiral Mahan in an article in the *Scientific American*.

And they squirm now when I say at one stroke the war could be ended. It could be.

Perhaps had he been in power much might have been done.

Lord Fisher attended the Lord Mayor's banquet in November 1916. He was far more cheered by the crowd than any other guest. As usual, the English man-in-the-street recognized patriotism and worth. This reception is noted in the following newspaper extract :

Who is the most popular man in English life? If one could judge by the cheers as the chief guests of honour were presented at the Guildhall last night—at the " levée " in the Great Library just preceding dinner—Lord Fisher is undoubtedly entitled to that distinction. Next to him Lord French. Nobody, not even the Allied Ambassadors, got nearly so enthusiastic a greeting as " Jacky "; though Lord French was very warmly welcomed. The cheers for Mr. Asquith and Mr. Balfour were desultory by comparison.

Lord Fisher's description is characteristic :

. . . I had a great surprise. I was quite taken aback! They began cheering and clapping in the corridors outside ! However, the mob is fickle—we know of old. To-day " Hosanna ! "—to-morrow " Crucify ! " However, what I am writing to tell you is that though I was behind in the crowd, Asquith made a " bee-line " for me, and shook me most cordially by the hand, *and held my hand* while he told me how he had enjoyed my Dardanelles evidence, etc. Mrs. Asquith cut me dead.

Just before Mr. Asquith's Government came to an end, although there was no sign of the collapse, Fisher, feeling deeply the success of the German submarine campaign, was anxious to make a speech in the House

of Lords calling attention to the matter.   He deals
with this in the following letter :

Please burn this letter and enclosures.

21st November, 1916.

DEAR LAMBERT,
Please burn all enclosed.   I arranged to make a speech of
seventeen words in the House of Lords, and sent it to Mr. M'Kenna ;
but he intreats me not to do so, as it would have absolutely fatal
effect on our Allies.   I rather fancy he showed my letter to
Asquith.   *Please burn this.*   I heard from Jellicoe last night ;
very pessimistic as to German submarines.

Mr. Lambert commented on this letter :

This letter is important.   If Lord Fisher had not been dissuaded
by Mr. M'Kenna from making that speech, it is more than probable
that Lord Fisher would have been backed by Lord Northcliffe as
First Sea Lord.   The date was just before the fall of the Asquith
Government, and Northcliffe was all-powerful then.

If Mr. Lambert's contention is correct, then it is
well that Lord Fisher patriotically, and greatly against
his inclination, followed Mr. M'Kenna's advice.   He
was quite unfit for the strenuous work of First Sea
Lord unless his activities had been circumscribed,
and he had been allowed only to deal with strategical
matters, and all routine work taken away from him.
Then he would have been invaluable to the country.
But who could have done this ?   Only one person—
Mr. M'Kenna ; and it is doubtful if the latter could
have been persuaded to take office after Mr. Asquith's
resignation.   It seems, looking back, as if, after all,
there is a good deal of truth in the saying, " All is
for the best in this best of all possible worlds " ; or,
to use Lord Fisher's favourite saying, " It was one
more proof that we were the lost tribes of Israel."

Some people looked, or pretended to look, on Fisher as mad. His flights of imagination and his natural exuberance of expression were often taken too seriously. This letter should be a corrective :

MY BELOVED FRIEND,

The full remembrance has now come back to me of the letters you mentioned to me last night as having exemplified to your highly placed friend that I was mad !

It is one more sad case of how the lack of a sense of humour is a real affliction like gout or neurasthenia (I beg you to read Sir John Collier's most marvellous article in *The Times* of 27th November, 1916).

Well, this is what happened :

General Botha made a speech extolling Smuts's generalship in East Africa and wishing he could be employed in France !

I cut it out and said " Why not ? ", and how splendid if old Botha (whom I know well) was made Secretary for War ! For he also did marvellously in German South-west Africa, and I believe Bonar Law splendidly pressed for Botha to be made a Field-Marshal, but Kitchener wouldn't have it ! Wouldn't it have been lovely ? Smuts in France, and Botha at War Office ! And the Germans so puzzled at their stabbing them in the back instead of attacking them as desired in the front ! And walking along the seashore to Antwerp covered by the British Fleet, and landing a million Russians on the Pomeranian Coast (as in the time of Frederick the Great), only 82 miles from Berlin ! And infinitely easier to land a million Russians in Pomerania than half a million of " Allied Mixture " at Salonica ! The Baltic has no terrors for us with our new Satanic measures ! No more d——d silly talk now about " civilized warfare " ! Shall your women be ravished or not ? (and deported as slaves *à la* Belgium), which is the sure fate of England if her Fleet should be wrecked ! You've got to get on quick ! You've removed the sure man of victory from the Sea ! [1] You'd better push on ashore !

Now, where we see a German, there we go ! But isn't it rather a good dodge to go where the Germans don't expect you ? and hit them in the back ? Remember, it's very desirable to get the Russians into Berlin !—not the French or English ! You'd get

---

[1] Sir John Jellicoe.

any terms you liked then for Peace, including every ton of German shipping, which is what England wants as her share !

I believe I sent a " repeat " of my letter about Smuts and Botha ! Very " mad," I admit ! It's the mad things that come off in war ! Napoleonic in Audacity—Cromwellian in Thoroughness—Nelsonic in Execution ! Big Conceptions and Quick Decisions ! Think in Oceans—Shoot at Sight ! HAVE WE HAD ANY OF THESE THINGS ?

I don't want to blow my own trumpet, but sending Admiral von Spee and all his Fleet to the bottom is the one and only case in this war, as Winston Churchill owned up in a lovely letter ! Whatever else he may be, he is, as Rosebery says, " magnanimous " ! [1]

The other letters (" mad ") I sent your friend were to send every German-born man and woman in this country back to Germany. This would increase our food-supply. A German eats twice as much as an Englishman, because he bolts his food ! I wrote this yesterday to the Food Dictator (Lord Devonport). Probably he'll think me " mad " also ! (N.B.—It's very interesting that the Saviour was voted " mad " by His family, and they wanted to lock Him up ! " For they said, He is beside Himself " ! But He never argued, and went straight on and did the Biggest Thing on Earth !)

Well ! I've written you enough !

No matter what may be the cause, I am at present " knocked-out " ! And it's just too silly to fuss about it ! And let us pray the German submarine menace will be quickly dealt with—the blockade made real—that our paucity of mines may be made good —that our strategy may be more imaginative—our Secret Intelligence not German, and our construction policy not folly ! I am not a deserter ! I'm an exile !

12th December, 1916.

Sir John Jellicoe gave up the command of the Grand Fleet and went to the Admiralty to cope with the submarine menace. This was a great blow to Lord Fisher, for he saw that it did away with all chance of his again becoming First Sea Lord. He never acknow-

---

[1] See above, page 275.

ledged that this was so ; but based his regrets on a
second reason, namely, that he considered that Sir
John Jellicoe should never have given up a command
for which he was more suited than any other naval
officer. Moreover, he had no belief in Sir John's
successor, and roundly accused Sir John of having
recommended that Sir David Beatty should succeed
him. This Sir John has consistently denied ; for as a
matter of fact, he had pressed Mr. Balfour to appoint
Sir Charles Madden, who had far greater sea experience
than Sir David, and, moreover, was a naval officer of
real ability.

Age undoubtedly was telling on Lord Fisher ; his
judgment was not what it had been ; he himself felt
as young as ever, but he was not the Fisher of 1904,
or even of 1910.

Let us, however, imagine ourselves in his place.
He remembered his past successes : his phenomenal
career, and his time as First Sea Lord when he had
introduced his reforms, triumphed over objections,
and trampled on all obstructions. He appreciated to
the full that he had returned to the Admiralty when
disaster seemed to be rampant everywhere ; and how,
by half a dozen telegrams and by the exercise of his
indomitable personality, he had turned disaster into
victory. He firmly believed that a great strategic
coup could still be brought off by using the Navy and
Army in conjunction, to threaten the north coast of
Germany and force the enemy to detach a large number of men to deal with the threat. He saw the
whole of the force he had had built for this purpose
being dissipated in secondary operations, instead of
being used on a concentrated attack close to home.
Few more, generally, inaccurate statements have been

made in books on the war than that made by Mr. Churchill in *The Aftermath*, page 447 :

> Generals and Admirals mutter " To break away from first-class war, the sort of war that only comes once in a hundred years, for an amphibious *strategico*-political manœuvre of this kind, is nothing less than unprofessional."

Mr. Churchill knew that the two most important Admirals in the Navy, Lord Fisher and Sir Arthur Wilson, were both in favour of amphibious warfare— strongly in favour of it, but only in favour of it in a place which offered some chance of success. Lord Fisher himself, from the time that he was appointed Commander-in-Chief in the Mediterranean until the day of his death, was the apostle of amphibious warfare; but in the main theatre, not in an ex-centric one two thousand miles off.

A suggestion was made to Sir John Jellicoe after he had left the Grand Fleet and taken up the duties of First Sea Lord, that Lord Fisher should go to the Admiralty as Controller and Third Sea Lord. Sir John consulted those who knew Lord Fisher best, and they were unanimously of opinion that he could not do the work successfully. The Controller in war-time should work for at least ten hours a day, and on occasion even for longer. Lord Fisher was good for five or six only. Moreover, as he had himself said on a previous occasion, he " had been first violin " ; and it was most improbable that he would contentedly shake down into a secondary position without attempting to do the work of the First Sea Lord. Sir John Jellicoe therefore felt obliged to negative the proposal.

On March 21st, 1917, Lord Fisher made his second

speech in the House of Lords, shortly after the publication of the report of the Dardanelles Commission.
He rose from the cross-benches, and said :

> With your Lordships' permission I desire to make a personal
> statement. When our country is in great jeopardy, as now she
> is, it is not the time to tarnish great reputations, to asperse the
> dead, and discover our supposed weaknesses to the enemy ; so I
> shall not discuss the Dardanelles report. I shall await the end
> of the war, when all the truth can be made known.

On 28th March, 1917, before the Russian Revolution,
Lord Fisher wrote to the Prime Minister, Mr. Lloyd
George :

> I desire to call your earnest attention to the four enclosures
> herewith in reference to the imminent danger of the German
> High Sea Fleet convoying a large number of transports and taking
> a German Army into the islands of Riga by sea, and into the
> vicinity of Petrograd, thereby endangering the Russian capital—
> a deadly blow to Russia ; and our Grand Fleet, with its unchal-
> lenged sea supremacy, condemned to be a passive spectator of
> such an appalling catastrophe.

This was quoted by Mr. George Lambert in a speech
in the House of Commons on the 13th December, and
created quite a sensation. More than one Member
began seriously to consider whether Lord Fisher's
prophetic instincts were not of value to the nation
and had not been wasted by his enforced retirement.

The following letter is interesting. It should be
remembered that it is written to a very great friend,
and therefore its egotism is pardonable. His remark
in the postscript that " No war scheme that involves
a year's preparation stands a chance," etc., etc., was

quite true. Mr. Lloyd George, who was then Prime Minister, was searching for a sailor or soldier who would win the war in a year, as eagerly and as futilely as the ancient philosophers sought for the Elixir of Life.

28th July, 1917.

MY DEAR ——,

I have been ruminating, brooding, pondering, cogitating, meditating, and studying all aspects of my present position and your kind exemplification of how I stand as regards those in power who control my fate, and how I stand also with the Public, Parliament, and the Press.

I propose to summarize my position :

I may have to be egotistical ! (I've come to the conclusion it's only a d——d fool or a saint who isn't egotistical, and I don't claim to be either !)

The only real British unalloyed victory of this war is the battle of the Falkland Islands, which was not a victory—it was annihilation !—for von Spee's entire Fleet was sunk, and that Fleet, had it not been destroyed, would assuredly have sunk our British Cape Squadron and Botha's transports, which were *en route* to German South-West Africa, and we should thereby have lost Africa.

This great fact has never been properly realized by the Public or the Press or the Parliament, and yet it was accomplished in the teeth of violent naval opposition at my unforgivable rashness in weakening our Grand Fleet by taking away fast battle-cruisers, etc.

" Rashness in war is Prudence ! "
" Prudence in war is Imbecility ! "

(I think I must have said that when I was about twelve years old, after reading Southey's *Life of Nelson*, still the best history of Nelson.)

The Falklands episode restored the drooping spirits of the British public—rehabilitated the British Admiralty . . . ; and an Armada of 612 vessels were authorized by Mr. Lloyd George (as Chancellor of the Exchequer) which, on 23rd July, 1915, were to have carried out a great amphibious series of operations in northern waters that would have finished the war, as we could have landed with certainty and sure success a million of Russian soldiers on the Pomeranian coast within easy distance of Berlin.

The Dardanelles project smashed this great plan, and the great Armada was perverted and diverted to purposes for which it was unsuited, and we lost the opportunity of recapturing the Belgian coast and Antwerp, for which Sir John French, in *November* 1914, only asked for two more Divisions and the co-operation of the British Fleet advancing on the flank of the British Army. (On 12th June, 1917, that project still held the field.) (I enclose a copy of my letter to the Prime Minister.)

The Dardanelles operations bled us white! The British loaf went up at one bound 10% in price, and our Mercantile Marine got locked up in the Mediterranean not only in supplying our own needs, but also those of our Allies ; and Salonica and Palestine and Mesopotamia all flowed out of the original sin in not sticking to the decisive theatre of the war in northern waters, but more especially in the Baltic.

The printed memorandum I prepared respecting the Baltic and naval policy written in the third month of the war still remains irrefutable and impregnable.

After May 1915 we had two years of ineffable apathy at the Admiralty. The Government enticed Sir John Jellicoe to leave his bounden duty in commanding the Grand Fleet to become First Sea Lord. Sir John Jellicoe persuaded himself he could deal with the submarine menace and left his post in face of the enemy, a position for which he had been sedulously prepared since the year 1905, and three days before the war superseded Admiral Sir G. Callaghan in command of the Grand Fleet.

We are not allowed to know the British official report of the tonnage sunk by the German submarines, but this is the German report :

January 1917	.	.	.	439,000 tons.
February 1917	.	.	.	781,050 ,,
March 1917	.	.	.	661,000 ,,
April 1917	.	.	.	1,091,000 ,,
May 1917	.	.	.	869,000 ,,
June 1917	.	.	over	1,000,000 ,,

So Sir John Jellicoe might as well have stayed with the Grand Fleet ! [1]

[1] It was scarcely fair to judge Sir John Jellicoe's work as early as June 1917.

On 11th July, 1917, I wrote another letter to the Prime Minister (Mr. Lloyd George) (copy enclosed), but it has borne no fruit.

What is it you counsel me? To act as follows: To dispel the malignant lies of my being past work by seeing people of all sorts and explaining to them in the words of the great American specialist:

" The brain of those who grow old wholesomely does not seem to age as does the rest of the human body, not to feel so distinctly as do the *locomotive mechanisms* the exasperating vetoes of time " !
(Dr. Weir Mitchell.)

The " locomotive mechanism " I might illustrate by waltzing at some music-hall ! The First Lord of the Admiralty went to a music-hall—why shouldn't I ? I *now* can dance twelve waltzes without stopping ! (and hum my own waltz music !). I did it only the other day !

But do you think this counsel of yours would persuade the solid phalanx of Retrogrades that curse me for democratizing the Navy in those glorious reforming years in which we got rid of 19½ millions sterling of Parasites, and reduced the age of our admirals and produced men like Commodore Tyrwhitt and got it realized that engines, and not sails, produced the better man ?

No ! the only thing I can do is to await Destiny—you can't hustle Providence ! Rebecca tried to and made a d——d mess of it !

POSTSCRIPT [TO THE LETTER]

Had my recent letter of 12th June, 1917, to the Prime Minister (Mr. Lloyd George) been acted upon at once, the late successful German attack on the Yser would have been forestalled and the disastrous catastrophe that befell us (in the loss of thousands of our brave troops) then would have been avoided. But alas ! this war from the very beginning has been waged on a political basis, and no far-flung strategic scheme has ever been elaborated and pertinaciously adhered to. The principle has been lost sight of that the decisive theatre of the war was in the North and that the Baltic shore was the key of the war now just as much as in the time of Frederick the Great, as so fully set forth in my memorandum on the Baltic written in the first months of the war and so very significantly alluded to by the Dardanelles Commissioners in their recent report. The war, so far as the British are concerned, has been a hand-to-mouth war !

No war scheme that involves a year's preparation stands a chance ! Some new political fad turns up and wrecks it ! And yet it is only by the long and studious preparation of a huge, rapidly, specially built Armada that the Navy can come into the war and finish the war, as set forth in my recent letter to the Prime Minister of 11th July, 1917. New ideas are scoffed at or so emasculated as to be impotent when put into force !

Note what took place about the submarine before the war ! It was so ridiculed or ignored by those in high authority that actually there were fewer British submarines when war broke out on 4th August, 1914, than when I ceased to be First Sea Lord !— in January 1910 ! And even so late as 10th July, 1914 (three weeks before the war broke out), Lord Charles Beresford makes a public speech deriding them (see *The Times* of 11th July, 1914), and all this notwithstanding that the naval manœuvres of the previous autumn had established their terrific possibilities, as summed up in the printed memorandum on submarines which I prepared in February 1914, foretelling absolutely all that the German submarine menace is now accomplishing ! The warning fell on deaf ears ! The drastic mining policy shadowed forth in my memorandum of 1914, while subduing the German submarine menace and rendering feasible the Baltic operation, would automatically have made the blockade so effective that Germany would have been starved out long ere this ! But the submarine menace, though practically scotched in May 1915, was by two years' apathy at the Admiralty permitted to reassert itself in its present prodigious and ferocious intensity ! It is just exasperating that with our really astounding naval supremacy the Admiralty policy should be solely to " hold the ring." And now we have the whole of the American Fleet to help us !

As I said in my printed memorandum (nearly three years ago), so far as the British Navy is concerned the British Army might as well be in Timbuctoo ! And yet never in history was the opportunity so great as in the present war for a great amphibian operation in northern waters, and one so absolutely certain to end the war ! But Politics have guided the war and sent our Expeditionary Force in August 1914 to France and Mons instead of to Antwerp and Victory !

Copy of letter from Lord Fisher to Mr. Lloyd George mentioned above.

HOUSE OF LORDS,
12th June, 1917.

MY DEAR PRIME MINISTER,

In November 1914 Sir John French came especially from France to attend the War Council to consider a proposal put forward by the Admiralty that the British Army should advance along the seashore flanked by the British Fleet. Had this proposal been given effect to, the German submarine menace would have been deprived of much of its strength and many enemy air-raids on our coast would have been far more difficult. The considerations which made me urge this proposal at that time have continuously grown stronger, and to-day I feel it my duty to press upon you the vital necessity of a joint naval and military operation of this kind.

I do not feel justified in arguing the military advantages, which are, however, so obvious as to be patent to the whole world, nor the political advantages of getting into touch with Holland along the Scheldt, but solely from a naval point of view the enterprise is one that ought to be undertaken with all our powers without further delay. The present occasion is peculiarly favourable, as we can call upon the support of the whole American Fleet.

Copy of letter from Lord Fisher to Mr. Lloyd George

36, BERKELEY SQUARE, W.
11th July, 1917.

MY DEAR PRIME MINISTER,

In putting before your urgent notice the two following propositions, I have consulted no one and seen no experts.

It is the emanation of my own brain, and, as the Latin grammar says, I write *currente calamo* !

Owing to two years of departmental apathy and inconceivable strategical, as well as tactical, blunders, we are wrongly raided in the air, and being ruined under water.

I remember a very famous speech of yours where you pointed out that we had been fourteen times too late ! This letter is to persuade you against two more too lates !

(1) The Air.

You want two ideas carried out.

(a) A multitude of bombing aircraft made like Ford cars (so therefore very expeditiously obtained thereby).

(b) The other type of aircraft constantly improving to get better fighting qualities.   The air is going to win the war, owing to the sad and grievous other neglects.

(2) The Water.

Here we have a very simple proposition.   Now that America has joined us, we have a simply overwhelming sea-preponderance !

Are you not going to do anything with this ?   Make the German Fleet fight, and you win the war.

How can you make the German Fleet fight ?   By undertaking on a huge scale with an immense Armada of special rapidly-built craft, an operation that threatens the German Fleet's existence !

That operation, on the basis in my mind, is one absolutely sure of success, because the force employed is so gigantic as to be negligible of fools.

It will take ten months to gestate.

If you sweep away the German Fleet, you sweep away all else and end the war, as then you have the Baltic clear, and a straight run of 82 miles only from the Pomeranian coast to Berlin, and it is the Russian army we want to enter Berlin, not the English or the French.

Lord Fisher saw every day the chance of carrying out his pet project diminish.   He saw the Germans doing against the Russians exactly what he had recommended the Russians should do against the Germans.   He saw, or thought he saw, lethargy at the Admiralty ; he felt sure that he could bring a new spirit into the war, into the Admiralty, into the Navy, and yet he was powerless.   All he could do was to send memoranda to the Prime Minister, and pace up and down his room consumed with despair.   He could not realize that he was old, and that his spirit, however willing, could never make his flesh anything but weak.   True, he worked to get back to the Admiralty, call it intrigued if you like, but it was harmless intrigue done not so much for " Fisher," as to enable his schemes to be carried out and brought to fruition. He and von Tirpitz both were shelved! The two protagonists who had built up their respective Navies and trained them for war, both shelved for men who had nothing like their genius either in peace or in war. The politicians in England and the Kaiser in Germany were responsible for the leashing of these two dogs of war. The struggle at sea would have been a very different thing if these two had been given a free hand, and both the Navies would have had a very different record.

But to return. Lord Fisher had seen every one of his prophecies fulfilled and his instincts verified. Six months before the war he had written a memorandum to the Prime Minister forecasting the German submarine campaign. He had foretold the year of the war, and was only two months wrong in the actual date. He had not only prophesied that Sir John Jellicoe would command the Grand Fleet, but had taken care that this prophecy should be fulfilled. He had, as early as 1905, foreseen the great value of mines in naval warfare, and had taken *money* every year in the Estimates to lay in a stock of them against the day when they would be required. This inconvenient item of expenditure was, after he left the Admiralty, subsequently crowded out of the Navy Estimates. Had Lord Fisher been made First Sea Lord on the outbreak of war, *and kept there,* the submarines would have been denied the English Channel at the end of 1916. The barrage, for which mines were only available in the last two months of 1917, would have been available one year earlier. Wherever he scanned the black horizon he saw failure where his advice and precepts had been disregarded (shades of *Breslau* and

LORD FISHER'S GRANDSON, JOHN THE SECOND

Goeben !), and success where he had been allowed a
free hand.   No wonder, then, that he chafed once
more to hold the reins of office, once more to bring
off a second battle of the Falklands.

All this is very sad.   Age will tell.   It is useless to
dwell any more on what might have been, except in
one particular.

When the surrender of the German Fleet took place,
the German ships were, quite rightly, received by the
Commander-in-Chief of the Grand Fleet in the open
sea.   But it would have been a gracious and a proper
act, on the part of the Admiralty, if Lord Fisher had
been ordered to hoist his flag as Admiral of the Fleet
for that day in Scapa Flow, and there to have received
the ships on their arrival.   For no man living had
done anything like as much to build up our sea-
supremacy, which in the end brought about the surrender of the German ships.

But the Admiralty at that time were poor in spirit
and devoid of imagination ;   thus was lost the opportunity for performing an act of generosity and justice
which would have lived in the history of the Navy.

In July 1918 Lord Fisher sustained an inexpressible
loss in the death of Lady Fisher.   They had been
married for over fifty-two years—happy years.   In no
other person could Lord Fisher have found what she
gave him.   Lady Fisher was universally beloved by
all who came into contact with her, and throughout
her married life was a great support and aid to her
husband in his years of reform, success, and worry.
She had lived to see the wish she had expressed shortly
after her marriage fulfilled :

I shall never rest till I see Jack First Sea Lord of the Admiralty.
Never will I stand in his way, even if it means separation for years.

II—20

Her courage and love were rewarded, for she had seen more than this, she had lived to see him an Admiral of the Fleet and given a Peerage.

After Lady Fisher's death, Lord Fisher resided almost entirely with the Duke of Hamilton's family. Kilverstone Hall belonged to his son, a man of energy who had reorganized the estate and improved the shooting; and, although always most welcome there, Lord Fisher found none of the active work that the management of the Hamilton property provided.

The Duke of Hamilton had known Lord Fisher intimately for many years, having served with him first in 1878. Latterly he had been much dissatisfied with the management of the Hamilton estates, which had been left to him in trust.

He had long desired to have as trustee someone who would have his interest and that of the estates really at heart.

After leaving the Admiralty in May 1915, Lord Fisher stayed with the Duke some six weeks, greatly refreshed by the healthy breezes of the moors, far removed from all the bickerings as to the reasons for his leaving the Admiralty, with the result that his vigour and unyielding youth increased and multiplied. During the visit the Duke asked him to become one of the trustees to the estate.

Being cut off from the public work he would have preferred, he gladly acceded to the request of the Duke to help him in administering the trust. These affairs were complicated by the provisions of the late Duke's will; in fact, it required an Act of Parliament before the management of the estates could be satisfactorily settled. The trust, which had included the island of Arran (the property left to the late Duke's daughter, now the Duchess of Montrose) as well as the Hamilton estates, was, by the act, divided in management, and each of the two sets of estates was given separate trustees.

By this Act of Parliament Lord Fisher became one of the trustees of the Hamilton Trust, other trustees being the Duchess of Hamilton, the Rt. Hon. Reginald M'Kenna, and Mr. Theodore Hamilton Hoste (who was also a lifelong friend, having served with the Duke under Lord Fisher in 1878).

The Duke, who had been a trustee, retired, as his health did not permit him to take an active part in business.

Lord Fisher, as was his wont, threw himself wholeheartedly into this new business. It was a herculean task, but one which suited his love of reform. From ships he turned to palaces and broad acres, and the work was successfully carried through.

Naturally, Lord Fisher became a welcome and constant visitor at both Dungavel and Ferne.

During these last years of his life he wrote certain letters to *The Times*, commonly known as the " Scrap-the-lot Letters." These had all his old fire and were as incisive as ever. He denounced the policy of the Admiralty and Government as far as public expenditure and naval construction were concerned ; but the proposals he made were not at the moment possible. That in fifty years much that he wished may come to pass is probable ; but at the time he wrote, when the country was struggling through the dangerous and difficult time immediately following on demobilization and consequent unemployment, *festina lente* had to be the watchword, and not radical reform.

Just before Christmas 1919 Lord Fisher planned to

take a party of friends to the South of France. The Duke of Hamilton's eldest son had been operated on for appendicitis, and was in need of a change. It was while at Monte Carlo that the first symptoms of fatal illness showed themselves. Acting under the advice of Sir Frederick Treves, he left for England, where he was obliged to undergo three operations. Before the first he wrote with characteristic brevity the following note, which he closed in an envelope : " No mourning, no flowers, and the nearest cemetery." The operations were of no avail ; and on the 10th July, 1920, he passed peacefully away.

On the 13th his body was borne in solemn state to Westminster Abbey. The following portion of a description of this progress is taken from *The Times* of the following day :

It was a sight which none that saw it can ever forget. Only the funeral of King Edward, Lord Fisher's devoted friend, could match it. . . . The slow-pacing foot procession was flanked at every yard, every inch of the long way, by crowds upon crowds of the English public, bareheaded, still, silent, reverently paying their inarticulate homage to the great man, the great child, the ruthless foe, the whole-hearted friend, the dark schemer, the open fighter, the " ruthless, relentless, remorseless " tyrant, the perfect play-fellow, who had spent his huge strength and his genius in their service, and whom they had learned to trust, to love, and to mourn.

Let the schoolmen say what they will—such was the inevitable reflection of all who saw the impressive sight—this man's fame is safe with history.

> Two hands upon the breast,
>   And labour's done,
> Two pale feet crossed in rest ;
>   The race is won.

APPENDIX

APPENDIX

FUNERAL SERVICE AT THE ABBEY

(Reprinted from " The Times " of 14th July, 1920)

THE PEOPLE'S HOMAGE

YESTERDAY morning the mortal remains of Admiral of the Fleet Lord Fisher of Kilverstone, G.C.B., O.M., G.C.V.O., were borne in solemn state to Westminster Abbey, where, in the presence of a vast congregation representing all that is most eminent in our national life, an august ceremonial celebrated the passing of a great spirit from the earthly scene of its stupendous labours.

And yesterday morning the British public showed that it loved and mourned one " Jacky Fisher." There is no surer test of public feeling than the size and the behaviour of the crowd in the streets. Till within the last weeks of his long and bellicose life, Lord Fisher was a stormy petrel, bringing the tempests he rejoiced in. Behind him he had, at first, no one ; behind him, he had, in these later years, the whole solid affection and admiration of the people. And yesterday morning the people, in its silent, stolid, reverent British way, wrote its affection and admiration for " Jacky Fisher " upon the social history of our time.

THE PROCESSION

It was a sight which none that saw it can ever forget. Only the funeral of King Edward, Lord Fisher's devoted friend, could match it. From the west side of St. James's Square, where the coffin, draped with the Union Jack, was placed on the gun-carriage, eastwards along Pall Mall, then westward down the great Mall, under the windows of the Royal lady whom Fisher served with knightly devotion, past the Admiralty and under the triumphal Admiralty Arch, coiling

311

within hail of the column of Fisher's earthly god, Lord Nelson, and close under the statue of the King whose ruin Fisher would proudly have shared because it began with the demand for money for English ships, down the broad pomp of Whitehall, and past the still shrouded cenotaph that honours those who fell in the war which Fisher had lived to prevent, and, failing prevention, to win ; and so through Parliament Square, beneath the towering walls of the sacred building which all English-speaking people are now uniting to save, and up to the great West Door of Westminster Abbey, the slow-pacing foot procession—with Marines, arms reversed, in the van, then the band of the Marines, with proudly wailing wind instruments and the drum beating on our ears like distant guns at sea, and then the bluejackets drawing the gun-carriage, and the famous admirals walking alongside it—was flanked at every yard, every inch of the long way, by crowds upon crowds of the English public, bareheaded, still, silent, reverently paying their inarticulate homage to the great man, the great child, the ruthless foe, the whole-hearted friend, the dark schemer, the open fighter, the " ruthless, relentless, remorseless " tyrant, the perfect playfellow, who had spent his huge strength and his genius in their service, and whom they had learned to trust, to love, and to mourn.

Let the schoolmen say what they will—such was the inevitable reflection of all who saw the impressive sight—this man's fame is safe with history. The people knew him and loved him. His body is buried in peace, but his name liveth for evermore.

IN THE ABBEY

Westminster Abbey took to itself, if only temporarily, one more great Englishman, and rarely can even the Abbey have been the scene of a ceremonial, for all that it was simple, more impressive than the funeral service of Admiral of the Fleet Lord Fisher of Kilverstone.

The time set for the service was half an hour after noon. By 12 o'clock, however, the Nave and those portions of the

ADMIRAL LORD FISHER'S FUNERAL PASSING NELSON'S COLUMN

North and South Transepts which were open to the general public, were already thronged, and the Choir and adjacent reserved spaces were rapidly filling up. The ordering of the congregation and showing to seats was done by Commodores in the Service which the dead Admiral loved so well; and, save when some high officers or representatives of a foreign Power, with breast aglitter with decorations, passed to their seats, the gold braid and epaulettes of the naval uniforms gave the only relief to the sombreness of the scene.

From a position on the south side of the Nave the Royal Marine Band from Chatham played at intervals while the assemblage gathered. For the last ten minutes before the appointed time the organ played, the assistant organist of the Abbey, Mr. Arnold Goldsbrough, improvising, and improvising charmingly. The organ ceased, and after a short interval of almost painful silence from far down by the West Door rose the silvery voices of the Abbey choir in Croft's beautiful setting of " I am the resurrection and the life " (St. John xi. 25, 26), followed by " I know that my Redeemer liveth " (Job xix. 25–27), and that again by " We brought nothing into this world, and it is certain we can carry nothing out " (1 Tim. vi. 7).

Scene in the Nave

With infinite slowness to this music the procession moved up the length of the Nave to the choir, the choristers, white surplices over scarlet, in front, then the canons and other dignitaries of the Abbey and the Dean. Behind the Dean was the crimson cushion on which the dead man's Orders and Decorations were displayed, a glittering mass of stars and ribbon, and then the coffin, draped in the Union Jack and crowned with the Admiral's hat and sword, borne by eight bluejackets. The only floral tributes which accompanied the coffin into the Abbey were a large laurel wreath with an anchor in blue cornflowers, sent by the Admiralty, and a cross by members of the family. Immediately behind the coffin walked, as honorary pall-bearers, eight admirals: Admiral of the Fleet Viscount Jellicoe, Admiral of the Fleet Sir H. B.

Jackson, [Admiral Sir Herbert King-Hall,] Admiral Sir Cecil Thursby, Admiral Sir R. F. H. Henderson, Admiral Sir F. C. B. Bridgeman, Admiral Sir R. H. S. Bacon, and Admiral Sir A. G. H. W. Moore.

To right and left the white-robed choristers and canons in their coloured hoods parted to their seats ; the Dean passed on to the chancel, and then, at last, beneath the lantern, between the bowed heads of the congregation, Jacky Fisher came to rest upon the catafalque but a few paces from his own favourite seat ; for, whenever England's work kept him in London, he was one of the Abbey's most constant attendants.

Here, at least, all criticism is stilled, all calumny silent. Now we know him for what he was and would fain tell him that the Empire knows its debt to him. Here, too, it was impossible not to imagine that the other great ones, whose monuments stood around, were witnesses and conscious of what passed. If so, we can be sure that they approved and welcomed him gladly to their fellowship, these others who also lived for England and by whom England lives.

A Simple Service

The service which followed was simple, familiar (as Fisher himself would have loved it), and beautifully rendered : the Ninetieth Psalm, " Lord, Thou hast been my refuge," followed by the Lesson (read with characteristic clearness by the Dean) from 1 Cor. xv., which tells us that " since by man came death, by man came also the resurrection of the dead " ; and then Sullivan's lovely anthem, " Yea, though I walk through the valley of the shadow of death," most tenderly sung.

Then came the hymn " For all the Saints who from their labours rest " ; then prayers from the Burial Service by the Precentor, and, before the Benediction by the Dean, the hymn " Now the labourer's task is o'er " :

> Father, in Thy gracious keeping
> Leave we now Thy servant sleeping.

Always moving, however sung by even the smallest band of mourners, here, in the old Abbey, beside the flag-draped coffin, the pathos of the lingering cadence of that last farewell, as sung by the Abbey Choir, was almost heart-breaking.

The Blessing said, silence fell for a while until, from where the band was stationed in the Nave, swelled up the roll and throbbing of the drums, so full of sorrow and of triumph, in the " Dead March " from *Saul*. Silence once more ; and then, ringing clear from beyond the altar, soaring up into the arches and vaulting of the roof, came from the hidden bugles of the Marine band, the notes (the agony and the proud confidence of them !) of the Last Post.

It was the movement of the bluejackets, coming forward to lift the coffin once more, that broke the spell. Then again the procession formed and, to the strains of Chopin's " Funeral March," repassed between bowed heads down the long pathway of the Nave to the West Door ; and so into the sunlight, where the air of the Broad Sanctuary rocked to the clash of the Abbey chimes.

INDEX

324 INDEX

INDEX

325

Post Captain, promoted to, i. 53
Power standard 2½ recommended,
i. 178
Prayer of the unready, i. 166
Press, the, Fisher's dealings with,
i. 53, 137, 180 ; ii. 120
Prince Consort, H.R.H. the, i. 80
Prophecies, ii. 297, 304
Protection of trade practised, ii. 10
Purvis, Commander, wounded,
i. 88

Queen Elizabeth retained at
Dardanelles, ii. 220
— — withdrawal of, ii. 241, 243
Quickness of decision, i. 132

Raglan, Lord, i. 3
Rapid shipbuilding insisted on,
ii. 23
Rashness may be prudence, i. 168
Readiness for war, importance of,
i. 167
Rear-Admiral, promoted to, i. 103
Reciprocating machinery, dis-
advantages of, i. 262
Redesdale, Lord, ii. 154
Redistribution of Fleet, i. 282, 295
— — comparative effect of, i. 298
— of work at Admiralty, 1902,
i. 180, 220 ; ii. 61
Reference, terms of, to Design
Committee, i. 259
Refits of ships regularized, ii. 3, 10
Reforms, Fisher's views regarding
introduction of, i. 280 ; ii. 92
— the five major, i. 282
Reid, Sir Walter, Inspector-
General of Hospitals, i. 42
Religious views held, i. 20, 43
et seq., 54
Renown, Fisher appointed to, as
Commander-in-Chief, North
American Station, i. 144
Repington, Colonel A'Court, ii. 84,
140, 141
Report of Cabinet Committee on
Beresford's allegations, ii. 55
— on inspection of *Warrior*, i. 32
Reprimand, method of administer-
ing, i. 79, 133, 143

Research and Invention Board,
Chairman of, ii. 285
Reserves, Royal Naval and Fleet,
ii. 9, 10
Resignation of Officers, constitu-
tional practice, ii. 280
— attempted at War Council,
ii. 210
— letter of, to Prime Minister,
ii. 256
— proposed 1905, ii. 65
Retirement, 1911, ii. 101, 105
Richards, Admiral Sir Frederick,
i. 106, 112, 114
Ripon, Marquess of, ii. 276
Roberts, Dean Page, i. 231
Roberts, Field-Marshal Earl, ii. 84
Robertson, Field-Marshal Sir
William, ii. 202
Robinson, Captain Charles N., xx
Robinson, Commander George,
i. 46
Robinson, Dean Armitage, i. 232
Robinson, Lady, i. 19
Roche, Mr. Walter, report on
Dardanelles Commission, ii.
219
Rosebery, Earl, ii. 125
Rosyth, criticism of, ii. 155
Royal Academy Banquet, speech
at, i. 200
Royal Marines, genesis of regi-
ment, i. 194
— — and new scheme of Naval
education, i. 195
Royal Oak affair, ix ; ii. 58
Royal Sovereign, accelerated
building, i. 104
Rush label instituted, ii. 161
Russia, advantages of under-
standing with, i. 159 ; ii. 80
— German troops landed in, ii.
194, 297
Russian attack on North Sea
trawlers, ii. 59
— troops, proposed landing of,
ii. 187

St. Lucia, base closed, i. 298
Salisbury, Marquess of, i. 99, 120 ;
ii. 129, 132, 289